M000316264

Unicorn in the Woods

Also by GORDON PITTS:

*The Last Canadian Knight: The Unintended Business
Adventures of Sir Graham Day*

*Fire in the Belly: How Purdy Crawford Rescued Canada
and Changed the Way We Do Business*

Stampede! The Rise of the West and Canada's New Power Elite

The Codfathers: Lessons from the Atlantic Business Elite

Kings of Convergence: The Fight for Control of Canada's Media

In the Blood: Battles to Succeed in Canada's Family Businesses

*Storming the Fortress: How Canadian Business
Can Conquer Europe in 1992*

UNICORN
in the Woods

How East Coast Geeks and Dreamers
Are Changing the Game

GORDON PITTS

GOOSE LANE

Copyright © 2020 by Hog Lake Inc.

All rights reserved. No part of this work may be reproduced or used in any form or by any means, electronic or mechanical, including photocopying, recording, or any retrieval system, without the prior written permission of the publisher or a licence from the Canadian Copyright Licensing Agency (Access Copyright). To contact Access Copyright, visit www.accesscopyright.ca or call 1-800-893-5777.

Edited by Meg Taylor.
Cover and page design by Julie Scriver.
Cover composed with images from Dreamstime (android) and VectorBox (tree).
Printed in Canada.
10 9 8 7 6 5 4 3 2 1

Library and Archives Canada Cataloguing in Publication

Title: Unicorn in the woods : how East Coast geeks and
dreamers are changing the game / Gordon Pitts.
Names: Pitts, Gordon, author.
Identifiers: Canadiana (print) 20200214381 |
Canadiana (ebook) 20200214500 | ISBN 9781773101514
(hardcover) | ISBN 9781773101521 (EPUB) | ISBN 9781773101538 (Kindle)
Subjects: LCSH: High technology industries—New Brunswick—Case studies. |
LCSH: New business enterprises—New Brunswick—Case studies. |
LCSH: New business enterprises—Valuation—New Brunswick—Case studies.
Classification: LCC HC79.H53 P58 2020 | DDC 338.4/76097151—dc23

Goose Lane Editions acknowledges the generous support of the Government of Canada, the Canada Council for the Arts, and the Government of New Brunswick.

Goose Lane Editions
500 Beaverbrook Court, Suite 330
Fredericton, New Brunswick
CANADA E3B 5X4
www.gooselane.com

To Elaine

Contents

Preface

Writing a book of recent history is a journey. Some of the landmarks are already familiar, while others are hidden or even unformed as you start, about to be discovered along the way. But nothing prepared me for the massive unprecedented shock of a global pandemic. I could not have imagined that, by the time I finished writing *Unicorn in the Woods* in spring 2020, it would be a totally different world than when I set out planning the book a few years earlier — that a novel coronavirus would strike, challenging almost everything, including the economic assumptions, and the health, sometimes survival, of institutions, businesses and people who figure in this book.

Yet, in this time of staggering uncertainty, the stories in this book do provide the outline of a way forward. They underline the importance of resilience in the midst of formidable setbacks, a social mission to keep communities alive and cohesive, and the need for imagination to overcome the limitations of geography and economics. The people in this book exemplify, in many cases, the core values of New Brunswick and the Maritimes — values that are desperately needed now.

I cannot predict where we will be a few years from now, or even a few weeks. But I hope the people and stories featured in this book will inspire us to believe that, yes, we can rebuild whatever was lost in the pandemic. This book is about optimism. We need it more than ever.

I did not expect these would be the lessons of my book when on November 3, 2017, I received an email out of the blue from Bob Skillen, vice president for advancement at the University of New Brunswick

(UNB). Bob had an idea he wanted to explore, and he wanted to meet me at Toronto's Royal York Hotel. University President Eddy Campbell came along with him. They had the seed of a concept, to build a book around the spectacular exits of two local companies, Q1 Labs and Radian6 Technologies, six years earlier. I was skeptical at first, but as I read and talked with people, I saw something bigger — a book on how Canadian technology, conceived far from the beaten path of Central Canada or Silicon Valley, gets out into the world.

Bob and Eddy deserve a lot of credit for initiating and encouraging this project, and the current president of UNB, Paul Mazerolle, provided words of support at a key moment. In time, Susanne Alexander and Goose Lane Editions — along with production editor Alan Sheppard and the rest of the team at GLE — would pick up the responsibility for guiding it through to fruition.

So many other people to thank: my friend Morrey Ewing, for his relentless support of the idea and its execution; my "bosses" at McMaster University, Leonard Waverman and Michael Hartmann, for being so flexible in their demands on my energy and time; John DeMont for sharing his own rich authorial experience; Geoff Flood and Scott McCain for early encouraging conversations; Kelly Anderson for crucial advice and contacts; and Jacques Poitras for his own wise perspective as the chronicler of modern New Brunswick. The folks at the Carriage House Inn in Fredericton, Jamie and Natalie, treated me like family. Dave Pyette accompanied me on a rollicking Toronto-to-Fredericton road trip that yielded good fun and great insights. Thanks to Paul and Nancy Mann for welcoming us into their home, and sharing the excitement of an NBA championship game. Among the contributors, David Foord stands out for his outstanding work, including a key article and case-study draft. Sarah Ketcheson is not just a wonderful niece, but a constant friend through my East Coast adventures.

I have to salute the key actors in the Q1 Labs and Radian6 narratives, who took time to tell their stories (and I kept coming back and back): Chris Newton, Brian and Carolyn Flood, Sandy Bird, Dwight Spencer, Marcel LeBrun, Chris Ramsey (a fabulous door opener), David Alston (ditto), Brian Dunphy, Marie Jo Thibault and Daniella DeGrace. First among equals is the redoubtable Gerry Pond, whose spirit is all over this book.

There are many others who were generous in their time and ideas. I may have missed a name or two but here is a list: Mike Ashar, Rob Begg, John Burnham, Aaron Breen, Barry Bisson, Bonin Bough, Brendan Brothers, David Campbell, Jerry Carr, Shawn Carver, Joe Catalfamo, Ian Cavanagh, Felipe Chibante, Mark Dobbin, Bethany Deshpande, Jeff Dougherty, Regis Duffy, Herb Emery, Scott Everett, Roxanne Fairweather, Sophie Forest, Rory Francis, Jane Fritz, Brian Gallant, Barry Gekiere, Ali Ghorbani, Jody Glidden, Nestor Gomez, Ryan Groom, Mike Hirshland, Sonja Hoel, Patrick Hankinson, Brendan Hannigan, Matt Hebb, Krista Jones, Patrick Keefe, Stefan Larson, Karina LeBlanc, Laura Kilcrease, Max Koeune, George Long, Steve Lund, Alex MacBeath, Willis Marti, Nancy and Chris Mathis, Jevon MacDonald, Rich McInnis, Shaun McConnon, Frank McKenna, John McLaughlin, Terry Nikkel, Kevin Perkins, Patty Phillips, John Risley, Doug Robertson, Kim Saunders, David Shipley, Dhirendra Shukla, John Sinclair, Mark Skapinker, Greg Sprague, Bharath Sudarsan, Salim Teja, Kumaran Thillainadarajah, Jay Tumas, Tom Turner, Gavin Uhma and Jeff White. Meg Nair was so helpful in helping me navigate IBM to get the story of its QRadar team. Faisal Kazi, the president of Siemens Canada, lent great perspective.

New Brunswick is fortunate to have an online business journal called *Huddle*, as well as the Saint John newspaper, the *Telegraph-Journal*, and its sister organs. I relied also on *Entrevestor*'s Atlantic Canada coverage. I need to note my reliance on a few books —*Alpha Girls: The Women Upstarts Who Took On Silicon Valley's Male Culture and Made the Deals of a Lifetime,* by Julian Guthrie; *Lord Beaverbrook,* by David Adams Richards; *The Code: Silicon Valley and the Remaking of America,* by Margaret O'Mara.

I have to extend a deep personal thank you to my agent Dean Cooke for hanging in on this project and so many others. It is great to work again with Meg Taylor, my talented, empathetic editor. Jess Shulman was diligent and encouraging in her copy editing. Mike Faulkner and Steve Hamilton performed valuable tech-savvy reading. My family must be tired of my constant chatter about this latest project, but they stayed loyal and supportive, particularly Elaine, who is a rock in such times. She is my first reader/editor and, this time, I relied heavily on her formidable librarian's skills. Also to Katie, Martha, Thomas, Eleanor and Henry, Jayne, Liz, Gayle and Grant and all my nieces and nephews, I love you. And it is love that will carry us through this.

Gordon Pitts
May 2020

Introduction
WHEN BRIAN MET CHRIS

Chris Newton didn't really expect much from the meeting. He would have been content to spend the day coding software in his tiny office along a dark corridor of the University of New Brunswick's computer science building in Fredericton. But officials of the university — who, after all, were his employers — had insisted he go along to a gathering of alumni and potential investors in the hope of turning his little software idea into something commercial, something that might actually be sold.

He didn't think he had a "product," just a way of dealing with the denial-of-service attacks from mischief-makers that were wreaking havoc on the university's ill-prepared computer networks in these early days of the internet and the wired university. Massive quantities of data would slam into the UNB network and shut it down, inciting a chorus of complaints. It created urgent calls for a cybersecurity tool that could give a real-time snapshot of the health and frailties of the system.

And that was what Newton was working on — this program he called Symon (short for System Monitor) — mostly at home at night as he wrote computer code well into the wee small hours.

But on that warm fall day in 2000, wearing shorts, sandals and a T-shirt, the 28-year-old part-time student and full-time UNB employee lugged his laptop up the hillside from his tiny office, through the cluster of UNB's signature red brick buildings, toward the modernist Wu Conference Centre at the top of the hill. Below him lay the sleepy provincial capital with its 19th-century legislature, its sprawling frame mansions and the broad Saint John River as it curled downriver from its source in northern Maine.

A crowd of interested types — some local, some from as far away as Halifax — had gathered in a meeting room, creating the impression of a pilot for the future hit TV show *Dragons' Den*. At his appointed time Newton flipped open his laptop screen and a chart appeared — a colour guide to the maze of computer networks that coursed through the university, where the emails went, where the downloads landed, where the trouble points were flaring up. There was a silence, and then a large dark-haired man moved closer to the front and fixed his attention on the screen, then started peppering Newton with a torrent of questions. What was this? Could it be sold? Who owned it? Can we talk?

Chris Newton was polite — he was the compactly built, baby-faced son of a police chief in the Miramichi, the rugged northeast New Brunswick region of salmon, forests and old mill sites. The only presenter under the age of 40, and the only non-academic, he projected boyish innocence and showed proper respect to people. He found the whole thing both unsettling and intriguing.

Newton finally managed to tear himself away and scrambled back down the hill to his office in the comfortable corridors of the UNB Computing Centre. But the big intensely energetic man would show up later, talking on about forming a company, creating a product and becoming an entrepreneur. Chris Newton didn't know what an entrepreneur was — or a startup or a business model or venture capital (VC). He just liked fixing stuff, figuring things out, solving problems for the people who employed him.

But his relentless pursuer was obsessed with all those entrepreneurial things. With the rangy build of an athlete, Brian Flood towered over Chris Newton. He was more than a decade older and 100 times more experienced in the ways of the world. Flood was like a man possessed, having spent the past four years preparing for this moment, when he could seize the chance for funding a technology breakthrough in his beleaguered home province.

He didn't seem like a natural tech founder. He had been running a sports bar/restaurant down the road in Moncton, and later added another one in his hometown of Saint John — both cities about an hour or two's drive from Fredericton. Then he got hooked on reading about this hot new thing called the internet. He embarked on a personal crash course to learn about this new pot of technology gold that had entranced everyone from tech titans Bill Gates and Steve Jobs to callow kids such as Mark Zuckerberg, still a student at a New England private school but about to burst on the world as a social-networking Harvard undergrad.

Flood was just back from one of his fact-finding expeditions to California's Silicon Valley when he was invited to this showcase event by the sponsors at UNB. He had first met Newton in the "rubber room," a session where the presenters were prepped for the show. Chris Newton seemed like the answer to his dreams — a whiff of game-changing innovation in the middle of his home province. As he chased Newton around the hillside university, he acted like a suddenly smitten suitor pursuing the reluctant target of his affections. He was not going to let this slip away. In the words of one friend, Brian Flood is the "weirdest, wackiest, hardest working, most tenacious son of a bitch."

At one point in the courtship, Flood asked, almost as a throwaway line, what would IBM pay for this? Chris Newton pondered the thought: maybe the computer behemoth might cough up $25 a month for using the software or even as much as $500. Neither of them imagined that, a decade later, IBM would pay $600 million U.S. for Chris's little product and the company that grew out of it. And that by that time, Newton would have already gone on to co-found another company that he and his colleagues would have sold for about $330 million U.S. The bashful kid from the Miramichi would be New Brunswick's billion-dollar man in value creation, putting him in the same rarified air as the Irvings, McCains, Olands, Sobeys and the other established business families whose names were synonymous with wealth, power and achievement on Canada's East Coast.

—

The story of when Chris met Brian is now part of the high-tech folklore of New Brunswick. (Indeed, there is disagreement among those present about the exact location of that first rubber-room encounter — the Wu Centre or another building.) Newton in particular could not have dreamed that it was the genesis of a high-tech industrial cluster, drawing tech giants IBM and Salesforce into the region, with hundreds of highly paid jobs, a couple dozen new millionaires and value generation beyond what they had dreamed — although the idea certainly flashed through Brian Flood's hyperactive mind. And it would stoke the dream, still unrequited, of someday building a billion-dollar startup company — a unicorn — amid the forests and streams of New Brunswick.

Fifteen years ago, I wrote *The Codfathers*, a book that charted the story of the family dynasties in Atlantic Canada built on fish, food and forestry, of beer and blueberries and supermarkets and oil, with only passing mention of the digital innovation lurking in the background, tucked away in university labs and in dusty corners of the legacy companies. Little did I know that, in 2005, the year *The Codfathers* was published, Chris Newton was in the process of co-founding his second massively successful tech company, an under-the-radar phenomenon that would reverberate far beyond New Brunswick.

But this was a different kind of enterprise — built not on brawn but on brains, not on tangible commodities like lobsters or blueberries, but on digital pulses, on networks (both online and personal) and codes. Newton and Flood were emblematic of the new Codfathers, and they would present their own opportunities and challenges for Canada's economically stressed East Coast.

Flood's meeting with Newton set off a cascade of ripples. Their dream would pull in Newton's UNB buddies Sandy Bird and Dwight

Spencer, fellow geeks and dreamers who had watched their friend develop this new technology and were standing by to help. It would engage Gerry Pond, the visionary boss of the local telephone company, who had spent his life building little ventures inside the organization and was about to stride out into a new career as a backer and mentor to young entrepreneurs. Or Pond's young acolyte Marcel LeBrun, who was struggling to build his own startup in the tech upheaval of the early 21st century, and would soon intersect with Newton in a way neither could have predicted.

It would also engage Daniella DeGrace, a young Acadian woman leaving her mark as a go-to company builder, and Marie Jo Thibault, a Québécoise engineer with an appetite for adventure. It would reach into the centre of the Toronto and Montreal tech communities where it would grab the attention and money of pioneering venture capitalists. And it would send waves as far away as Silicon Valley, where a whip-smart young Harvard MBA Sonja Hoel, emerging as a rare female titan of West Coast venture capital, would become a pivotal player in this East Coast Canadian saga. It would help propel the career of an African-American digital wunderkind, named Bonin Bough, in New York City.

This is a story of global connections and yet also a classic blue-collar story set against a canvas of Canadian rural life. The main actors are the children of auto-parts vendors, cops, forestry workers and potato farmers. The tale has its roots in Canada's oldest English-language university, but also features a character whose ancestor fought beside the French general Montcalm at the 1759 Battle of Quebec. Companies are launched with meetings at Tim Hortons coffee shops in Fredericton. Brian Flood supports his tech habit with the proceeds of restaurants based on the bellicose hockey commentator Don Cherry.

But the story has yet to be written on how sustainable that dream has been for New Brunswick, one of the poorest provinces and, along with its Atlantic Canadian neighbours, among the oldest demographically in the country. Was this a mere blip in the narrative of impoverished, aging, old-economy New Brunswick, or the foundation for a knowledge economy in the land of lumber, fish and tidal bores?

The amazing thing is, almost a decade after the big exit deals, how little New Brunswickers know about Chris Newton, Sandy Bird and Dwight Spencer, or even Gerry Pond and Brian Flood. But within the small tech community on the East Coast, they are legends. Within that community, there is intense pressure to fashion an encore. "Where is the next big one?" wonders Gerry Pond, who has mentored, funded and advised a stable of the young companies that might just produce that elusive unicorn.

The story is important because ultimately, in the future, all of the Atlantic region — indeed much of Canada — faces the same challenges as New Brunswick encounters now: challenged resource sectors, aging or declining populations, debt-stressed governments. But does the province, often called the most imperilled economically in Canada, also offer a road map for survival, even prosperity, in the global digital economy?

Is there a place for high-tech innovation and unicorn-like value creation in the "sticks" of North America — Appalachia, northern Ontario, the post-industrial U.S. Midwest, or rust-belt upstate New York? Or must the benefits of digital disruption and artificial intelligence flow only to Palo Alto, New York City, Waterloo or the corner of University and College in downtown Toronto?

This is not a simple story — there are sellouts and firings, illnesses, massive disappointments, comebacks and vindication, and a great deal of still-unfulfilled promise. It is a story of value creation in the modern technological age, but set in Canadian backwoods and backwaters. It starts by tackling the question: Twenty years after Brian met Chris on that hillside campus of UNB, how did it turn out for them and their dreams?

1. Newton's Law

Patty Newton was convinced the serial killer had broken into her house and walked around upstairs as she lay sleeping — knowing all the while that her police-chief husband was away from home. It was 1989 and Allan Legere had murdered five people and was hiding out from authorities in the forests and small towns of the Miramichi in northeast New Brunswick. And where better to hide, Patty reasoned later, than in the backyard of the local police chief, where no one would think of looking?

The Newtons lived in Newcastle, one of the scattering of towns in the heavily forested Miramichi. Like many of her neighbours, as the Legere terror spread, Patty had acquired a pistol, which she hated to have in the house and hoped never to have to use. But her husband, Dan Newton, was often out on patrols all night and it made sense.

This time, however, he had gone to a father-daughter event with their daughter, Peggy, leaving their teenage son Chris with her. During the evening, Dan's parents had dropped by and decided to stay the night. At one point in the night Patty woke up to the dogs barking and heard someone scampering down the back stairs and out the door. "I'll give Chris hell in the morning," she thought to herself and went back to sleep.

The next morning, young Chris Newton insisted he had not been up in the night and had not raced down the stairs. One of the family dogs rushed over to a backyard bush and was barking like mad. Patty called one of the fellows on the police force to come and look in the backyard, and, yes, it was possible the killer had spent the night there — someone had hidden in the bush. Soon police helicopters were hovering over the neighbourhood. The memory sends a chill through her to this day, as Patty sits today at her kitchen table in a village near Moncton.

The Miramichi region produces rivers teeming with salmon, fishing camps of the well-to-do, forests of timber, the haunting novels of David Adams Richards and, for a horrible moment in the late 1980s, one of Canada's most sadistic serial killers. The ordeal had begun when, along with a couple of low-life pals, Legere had beaten a shopkeeper to death. He had been sent to prison, but cunningly escaped from a hospital where he had been sent for an ear infection He went on to kill four more people — a couple of middle-aged sisters, an elderly woman and a priest. Leaving behind a trail of murder, rape and torture, for 201 days he stalked the woods of northern New Brunswick, earning the name the Monster of the Miramichi.

The nightmare dominated the life of the Newton family, with their dining room table becoming the site of regular nightly meetings of police officers, working with Dan on the desperate manhunt, with Chris looking on with interest as the senior cops planned their strategies.

Legere was finally recaptured on November 24, 1989, following a failed carjacking — he picked the wrong car, this one driven by an off-duty policewoman who managed to escape his clutches and alert her colleagues. "You could hear the whole town take a big sigh of relief," says Patty, a warm and witty woman who was later divorced from Dan Newton and remarried.

It was a nightmarish period in what was otherwise a carefree life growing up in the Miramichi for the Newton kids, Peggy and Chris. It was a reminder that the Miramichi was a thinly populated rural region where a murderer could hide for weeks, but it was also, in better times, an idyllic land where a young Chris Newton could grow up in the outdoors, build tree forts, ride bicycles, tinker with gadgets — room to grow into a young man with a sense of the possibilities life had to offer.

The Newton family circa 1980: Chris, Dan, Peggy and Patty
(Courtesy of Patty Phillips)

Some people in New Brunswick's tech industry speculate that the example of his policeman father may explain why Chris became interested in catching bad guys, whether it was malicious forces invading university networks or predators on the internet. Sometimes the solutions he devised ended up being used in other ways than intended, but Chris was always a guy who believed in rooting out bad actors. And Chris idolized his policeman father.

The Newtons lived an itinerant life as Dan followed his career — from Middleton in the Annapolis Valley where Chris was born, to Nackawic, a little riverside community west of Fredericton, and then to his biggest posting, Newcastle, today part of the amalgamated urban-rural city of Miramichi. It was a traditional family — Dan worked hard and Patty was always busy raising the kids, although she would find a welcome diversion in painting, and later she became a skilled computer graphic artist.

Chris Newton grew up with a rambling curiosity about how things worked, and a great visual sense like his mom, with the ability to express complex ideas in pictures and graphics. Early on, he was a fix-it kid. His mother remembers being in the house when she became aware that four-year-old Chris was being very quiet. She went down to the basement rec room to check on him. He had a sports-car pedal car up on blocks, completely taken apart, with the little kid lying on his back with his dad's tools. Cars became a passion for life.

So was technology. When Chris hit his early teens, he got his own home computer, one of the early ones, a Commodore. He was no whiz in school, but the computer opened a vast world of information. Suddenly this book-averse kid was reading computer manuals and looking up arcane information on the just-forming internet.

This was the era of a visionary New Brunswick premier, Frank McKenna, who pushed a bold plan to wire the province, bringing broadband into rural homes. McKenna had practised law in the Miramichi and represented the local riding of Chatham in the legislature. Chris Newton is a product of the Miramichi but also of the McKenna Revolution that transformed New Brunswick from a backwater to a knowledge economy pioneer. Another beneficiary of the McKenna revolution was Jody Glidden, a Miramichi Valley High School mate of Newton, who was able to buy his first computer with the help of a government subsidy introduced at the time.

Glidden later became a founder of multiple high-tech startups. He remembers Newton as a shy kid in school, whom he would never expect to be a technology leader or a businessperson. Chris was your classic quiet classmate from high school, the late bloomer who fades into the background, until 20 years later when his picture appears in the newspaper and you say, "I never dreamed he would be so successful." In Miramichi, in the 1980s, Newton was living the typical boy's life — hockey, air cadets and senior prom. He was the definition of a good kid who could be trusted to go out on teen excursions to the big bad city of Moncton without getting into trouble.

When he graduated from high school, Newton went to UNB, two hours away in Fredericton, where he enrolled in the top-notch computer science program, a leader in Canada. In 1968, UNB had launched the first computer science department in the country. (UNB has a second smaller campus in Saint John.) Newton liked the courses, and he was naturally curious, but not a top student — he struggled in math, particularly calculus, and wonders to this day why anyone needs it. But he loved fixing things, he read deeply in science, and he spent his time visualizing how things worked, how patterns were formed and how information flowed.

His most formative university experience was getting to know another couple of kids with similar backgrounds and inclinations. Sandy Bird hailed from Fredericton where his dad and his family ran an auto-parts shop on the north side of the river, Central Auto Parts, where the sign over the door says, "If you don't see it, please ask." His mother helped run her own family's fuel-distribution business. Sandy was a small guy, compactly built like Chris, engaging and outgoing but with a way of squinting his eyes that suggested a coiled intensity.

There was also Dwight Spencer, slightly older, a big fellow with an open, friendly face who came from a family that worked in forestry in Chipman, an hour northeast of "Freddy" in New Brunswick's interior woods. Chipman is a town dominated by a Shoppers Drug Mart, a couple of supermarkets and a vast J.D. Irving woodlands operation and sawmill. Dwight's father had worked as a contractor for the ubiquitous Irvings.

The guys were all crazy about computers, but they were also passionate gearheads — they loved to get their heads inside a car engine. They had no money, but life was a lot of fun. And to support their studies they all took on tech jobs around the university. Chris and Dwight both worked at the UNB Computing Centre, the heart of the university network; Dwight went to the Harriet Irving Library; Sandy spent time at both, and in the arts faculty. "It became this weird triangle where we are all trading jobs around the university," Dwight recalls. And they tinkered. At one point, the three of them took down the university network. And Sandy and Chris roomed together for a while.

It's a reminder of how often the world's technology advances occurred because someone met someone else in school — what if Microsoft co-founders Paul Allen and Bill Gates had not met at a Seattle high school, or Google's Larry Page had not run into Sergey Brin at Stanford? Chris met Sandy and Dwight and they got along. What is amazing is they kept getting along — and in the laid-back chemistry of New Brunswick, they get along well to this day. Despite disease, heartache and corporate breakups, their friendship remained strong. They still talk often.

These were blue-collar kids, not showered with money or toys. They could use the extra money from a university job while they continued to study. Chris liked that he didn't need to work in some burger-flipping joint but could make income from a job where he was naturally engaged, and would know when new opportunities popped up. All the time, they figured they would eventually graduate — although for Dwight, the object was never graduation but a way to gain independence and not rely on his parents' support. But for all of them graduation would never happen. Life would get in the way.

Chris was hired as a network analyst even though he didn't strictly qualify in terms of education yet — he had no degree. But that job put him on the ground floor of the internet, as it moved from the gee-whiz stage to the serious-business-possibility stage. It was a halcyon age for tech geeks because the challenges were so new and broad. At the same time as the UNB Three were working away, Page and Brin, also in their early 20s, were playing around with the beginning of Google. It was a few years before Mark Zuckerberg would set up a social network at Harvard so that children of the establishment could hook up.

Newton was also fortunate to be a part of UNB and its computer science program, a true community of scholars and innovators. The early pioneers in the computer science faculty and the UNB Computing

Chris Newton with his first car, a sporty Miata (Courtesy of Patty Phillips)

Centre — people like Dana Wasson and Dave Macneil — had created something that had a reputation far beyond the province. Newton took courses from Jane Fritz, who was dedicated to her smart and slightly obsessive students. Macneil and his colleagues in the Computing Centre, Peter Jacobs and Greg Sprague, created an open and comfortable working environment. And there was Ali Ghorbani, a brilliant Iranian-born academic and entrepreneur in his own right, who would later undertake important research for Chris Newton's real-world applications.

Newton was cloistered in a closet-sized office, along a dark corridor with putrid green institutional walls. That was where he would discover one of his lifetime credos: every pain point is an opportunity. It became Newton's Law, circa 1998: great ideas usually come not from dreamy futuristic navel-gazing but from solving a painful problem for somebody. And UNB certainly had a pain point.

It could be narrowed down to one little white laptop computer that was the fragile front-line defence in UNB's flailing efforts to combat cybersecurity breaches. Newton would watch his colleagues in the Computing Centre as they coped with this new phenomenon — delicate networks would buckle under denial-of-service attacks in which hackers would bombard the system with hundreds of millions of data units called packets. It was as if thousands of letters were suddenly dumped into a country-road mailbox with a ten-letter capacity.

As the network shut down under the weight of this inundation, the Computing Centre would be deluged with angry messages from students, teachers, administration. It was very stressful.

Newton recalls that "the guys in the networking group had one tool for when things go wrong, a program called Sniffer, which ran on this little white laptop." Someone would open this special laptop and plug the network cable from the laptop into the network switches — and the laptop would freeze.

There followed a seeming eternity of pulling cables and inserting plugs, waiting until the laptop calmed down and started to respond, while the whole university stewed. "We're talking a big university, a lot of students and very high-speed connections and this laptop had no hope," Newton recalls.

Newton got to thinking: "Wouldn't it be better if we had something that looks at not single packets but at data flows? Instead of looking at millions of individual packets, look at a single data record that says 'this machine sent 400 million packets to this machine and that is one flow.'" He looked around and saw nothing available, so he started coding a solution.

Newton speaks in bursts of gee-whiz enthusiasm — more Richie from *Happy Days* than the nerdy guys from *The Big Bang Theory*. Everyone is "super-busy" or "super-smart," or to sum things up, it was "all that jazz" — all interspersed with the occasional mild profanity. The unfiltered vocabulary masks a sharply inquisitive mind that ranges far afield, and a wry sense of humour, with low-key observations of the passing parade of life.

The Computing Centre was fortunate to have a number of sage operators who recognized his intelligence and didn't feel threatened by the kid down the dark hall. Macneil, a kindly bearded man, started noticing what Newton was doing and gave him $1,800 to buy a server for his office. Jacobs gave him a network tap so he could look at data across the university.

"You would never get away with that today," Newton marvels. "I never even thought that everybody's emails were going across in front of my eyes. I didn't even think to look at them. Today, I'd think 'Holy shit, I could have got in a lot of trouble even if I accidentally recorded stuff.'"

Macneil, who split his duties among teaching, research and administration, was spending a lot of time with the young student-employee, checking in with him every morning, after Chris had spent the night writing code. Newton found Macneil's interest both scary and thrilling. "He made me nervous because every morning at eight-thirty, he came in my office with a fresh cup of coffee and asked 'what did you do last night?' I would show him the stuff. Then he'd come and get me at coffee and lunch break and we would talk through it.

"It was just weird. I'm super-young and Dave was the head of the department and widely respected worldwide. He'd go to conferences on how to introduce high-speed internet and he was spending time with little old me in the coffee room. A big part of what was driving me to come up with cool stuff was Dave." (Dave Macneil died in late 2018, just as I was beginning research on this book, a huge loss to New Brunswick and computer science worldwide.)

"If that one little pain point hadn't existed, I would never have thought of this flow thing. And then I decided to visualize it and put it on charts and then colour-code it, with blue for good flows and red for bad."

Soon Newton could click on the screen and usher up beautifully coloured charts — all the traffic for the faculty of arts or computer science or the parts of the world they were talking to, or by application – on the web, for example, or in a video stream.

"Everyone seemed amazed when they saw these charts; to me it didn't seem like that grand a thing."

Lots of ideas come out of Canadian university labs, but they rarely catch fire as commercial products or services in a country with only 35 million people and the challenges of geographical remoteness. To meet these challenges, there has to be patient financial capital and a nurturing network of mentors and supporters. At that time, both were horribly underdeveloped generally in New Brunswick, but the mentorship opportunities existed inside UNB and its technology-savvy alumni and faculty. Newton caught a break with a unique confluence of people and agendas, and the support of the university.

As one of the Computing Centre's senior managers through this period, Greg Sprague liked what Chris was doing, as well as the work of his occasional colleagues Sandy Bird and Dwight Spencer. Sprague was trying to get more broadband capacity for the university, and broadband was expensive in those days. He could use the information the trio was collecting in his pleas with the university and governments to beef up the networks. And Newton was also applying his technology to the broader group of 16 Atlantic Canada universities and colleges plugged into what was called the East Coast Network.

Newton came to relish the detective work. At one point, someone posted an online threat against the university, and Newton was able to trace it to a particular chair in a particular computer lab. He spent 18 hours trying to trace a trolling attack on a visiting lecturer, and finally succeeded in linking it to an individual in Australia.

And the world started to notice. In early 2000, there was a conference of university computing centre directors in Central Canada. Newton approached Sprague to ask if he might present the program he had built. Sprague agreed it was worth doing.

So Newton did a presentation and all the computing centre managers from other universities approached him afterward, asking for copies of the software. Sprague had a moment of panic. Before he gave away copies, he should check with UNB to find out who owned the intellectual property, the university or the employee, and what was UNB's share of this? "Can I give it away or should I be selling it, and how much should I charge?"

So he went to John McLaughlin, the vice president of research at that time and later president of the university. McLaughlin was concerned about patents and intellectual property. In Sprague's memory, the vice president said something along the lines of "Look, you've made every mistake that could possibly be made, and now let's fix this mess."

That is where David Foord came in, a lawyer and historian of technology, and recently appointed head of the university's office for technology-transfer. He had worked at British Columbia's Simon Fraser University and had seen the potential for shifting a resources economy into a knowledge economy. In British Columbia, "they had been doing this for ten years before the East Coast had," Foord observes. "They had been developing companies on campus and their economy had been migrating from trees to IT."

Foord wanted to link the university's young innovators with outside investors to build private companies that could develop and market university-hatched technology. Often, universities would take full ownership, with a stream of royalties, for technology conceived in their labs, but at the cost of turning off the researchers who had done the work. There was another way to protect the school's interests and motivate the researchers.

So on that day in fall 2000, Newton stepped into the rubber room with his laptop in his hand, not knowing that this was the day he would meet Brian Flood, and it would change his life, his province and the infant industry of cybersecurity.

2. Life of Brian

In New Brunswick, they remember Brian Flood as a young runner and rower around Saint John and at the University of New Brunswick. He did not have a natural build for a long-distance runner — too big, too muscular — but he was so determined to succeed that he performed beyond expectations. At one point, young Brian wanted to be a world-class rower, and moved to St. Catharines, Ontario, home of the national team, pitched a tent along the river and, without invitation, rowed alongside the elite scullers until he was finally admitted into the group. He was too good for them to keep on ignoring. "Don't put up a wall, or he will run through it," says his old business associate Gerry Pond.

Where did it come from, this obsessiveness? Overachievement is a family trait. Brian is the son of a top radiologist in Saint John, but he also carried the enterprise gene, handed down from one of his ancestors, a tradesman from Ireland who came to Canada in the 1830s. And Brian's cousin Geoff Flood is another prominent Atlantic business leader. Geoff ran T4G, a Toronto-based data services firm with extensive operations in the Maritimes.

Born in 1961, Brian was like many a budding entrepreneur of his generation: his first expression of business drive was a boyhood newspaper route. He had 52 papers that he delivered every day. He loved to tote up his weekly journal of accounts and, above all, "I liked to make money, and I wanted to be a businessman."

He went on to do commerce at UNB but really majored in sports. He and his brother Henry won all kinds of trophies in rowing, running and skiing and both were ultimately inducted into the New Brunswick

A young Brian Flood, right,
with his brother Henry in
a rowing competition
(Courtesy of Brian Flood)

Sports Hall of Fame. (Brian is that rare specimen who belongs to both the province's sports and business halls of fame.) Henry, now deceased, was his athlete-hero: "He was a character; he was an animal," Brian says proudly.

He loved the underdog, as reflected in his lifelong celebration of the Paris Crew, the name given to an unlikely team of Saint John rowers who in 1867 became the first international champions produced by the new nation of Canada. They won the world rowing championship at the Paris International Exposition, beating the posh boys from Oxford University and a tough French crew.

Their names were Robert Fulton, George Price, Samuel Hutton and Elijah Ross. Ross was a lighthouse keeper and the rest were fishermen. They rowed without a coxswain and displayed a lack of rowing refinement that dismayed the effete international circles, but they were successful. They inspired Brian and Henry Flood. "From the Paris Crew, Henry and I learned that we could compete with anybody in the world," Brian Flood once told the Saint John *Telegraph-Journal*.

"You can come from this neck of the woods and go against anybody, and we learned in our rowing career that we could take anybody on."

Brian came out of UNB in 1983 with his first Big Idea. How about a history of sports in Saint John — not of the Maritimes or New Brunswick but just the Saint John area? Thus he embarked on the research and writing of the book *Saint John: A Sporting Tradition 1785–1985*. Henry was the publisher, having formed his own company called Neptune.

One high school teacher in Moncton, who reviewed the book for a young readership, wrote at the time, "This is not a scholarly work, though it is adequately researched." She added that "the writing style is colloquial and self-conscious. The photographs are excellent."

No matter for Brian. He may not have been an elegant writer but he was an exhaustive researcher and canny salesman who knew his market. He had heard that to qualify as a Canadian national bestseller, a book had to hit a sales mark of 7,000 copies. He was determined that this little local book would make the grade.

At the back of the book, he ran 2,000 names of Saint John athletes over the years. He reasoned that each name might represent 100 to 150 descendants, many of whom would feel obliged to buy the book and display it on their coffee tables. Surely, each family at Christmas would want to have it as a gift. He sold 6,000 books in the first year, often lugging cases around to business offices, including multiple copies to the mill-owning Irvings and the beer-brewing Olands. It was a roaring success.

Fresh from his blockbuster book, a 25-year-old Flood was bursting with ideas, many coming out of his insatiable reading. He had devoured the business bestseller *In Search of Excellence*, in which a pair of McKinsey consultants outlined the secrets of great companies. At the top of the pantheon of excellent firms was the U.S. multinational Minnesota Mining and Manufacturing, known as 3M, a company that somehow prospered from making a bewilderingly diverse array of products, from pharmaceutical supplies to Post-it Notes. Its Canadian

operations were based in London, Ontario. Brian Flood showed up on
the 3M Canada doorstep one Monday morning in 1986 eager for a job.

He talked his way into four interviews on Monday, two on
Tuesday and two more on Wednesday. In Flood's telling, he went to
the 3M managers and said, "Look, I have three business suits and it's
Wednesday, so do I get the job or not?" He got the job.

His first mission was selling pharmaceutical products in northern
Alberta out of the Edmonton office. He was told the suggested number
of daily sales calls was four to five. He aimed for nine, assuming that
hard work would make his mark. His sales took off.

He came home briefly to marry his university sweetheart, Carolyn
Demers, whom he had met as a teenager at the Saint John rowing club.
Carolyn must have known that marriage to Brian Flood was going to
be an interesting ride. From that moment, they became a partnership
in life and in business. She was Brian's rock but also a gentle brake on
his over-the-top enthusiasm. They spent the first couple of years of
married life in Edmonton — where Carolyn gave birth to the first of
their two daughters — before Brian took over a 3M sales territory in
New Brunswick.

Back in the East, he ran into Don Cherry, the outrageously
flamboyant hockey commentator who, with his partner Rick Scully,
was building a sports bar/restaurant chain based on Cherry's high-
profile brand. Flood knew nothing about the restaurant business but
he yearned to run his own enterprise. Quitting 3M, he took on a new
Don Cherry franchise outlet in Champlain Place mall in Moncton, and
it was a success — clocking among the highest sales in the small chain.

"I had a bunch of managers running it. I was the front man,
the greeter, and it was a lot of fun," he recalls. It indulged his love
of people, of achievers. He got to meet hockey legends like Rocket
Richard, Jean Béliveau, Gordie Howe and Yvan Cournoyer. When
Carolyn wanted to move back to their hometown of Saint John to
be close to their families, they added a Saint John restaurant. But
Carolyn, dividing time between the restaurant and their young family,

found the late nights hard, and neither Carolyn nor Brian was much of a drinker.

By 1996 Brian was off and running on his new magnificent obsession. He started looking at this internet thing and embarked on extensive research. He noted the huge valuations being accorded the early publicly traded cybersecurity firms. He read books on investing and subscribed to investment newsletters. He immersed himself in the methods of value-investment legends Benjamin Graham and Warren Buffett, and their strategies of buying undervalued stocks and holding them until the market recognized their worth.

He read that Graham, the guru of patient value investing, didn't actually make his best returns from a value play — he actually scored big from an insurance stock bought from some guy who just walked in the door. It was all about growth, Flood decided.

He followed stocks such as Check Point Software Technologies, which hit the market with an early internet firewall and whose profits went through the roof. As Flood describes it, "There were huge increases in revenues and low costs of goods, huge gross profits. I was stunned; it was straight money and that was a light-bulb moment." There was big money to be made in protecting computer systems.

Carolyn could see the light in his eyes. Whenever he set his mind on something, he would not be deterred. A warm woman who exhibits an eternally bemused but loving way of dealing with her obsessive husband, she was willing to go along with this next phase. The restaurant business was wearing on her, and she was the one who "kept the home fires burning."

To figure out how to make money from the internet, in 1999 Brian attended the sprawling Comdex technology trade show in Las Vegas, where the digital nobility was gathered. There were sessions with titans Bill Gates of Microsoft, Scott McNealy of Sun Microsystems and John Chambers of Cisco. The futuristic talk left Flood's head swimming with possibilities. But he needed to know more. "I came out of Las Vegas pumped to the nines and decided I would go to California."

"When Brian has his mind made up, there's no dissuading him," says Carolyn, smiling at the memory. She saw it as their *Beverly Hillbillies* moment — Jed Clampett goes to California. But the difference was he had not yet struck the bonanza he felt was his destiny. "Brian was always 100 per cent sure that this was going to work. I would say it took longer than we thought, but Brian never lost the faith," Carolyn says.

Tapping the cash flow from his restaurants, Flood plunged into a personal crash course on how Silicon Valley worked. In April 2000, he rented a one-room apartment with a Murphy bed in a low-slung building with easy access to the watering holes, hotels and conference centres of Silicon Valley. And he went to every possible event, breathing in the Valley lore.

He watched in 2000 as the dot-com bubble peaked and then burst, sucking people out of the Valley, underlining the arbitrary nature of the technology beast. This was not an economy of rooted trees or rocks but was built instead on highly mobile talent. The Valley kept rising and falling in wicked gyrations. But even failure bred success: the waves of startups would always come back stronger than ever, fuelled by the next cohort of starry-eyed dreamers.

According to Alan Greenspan and Adrian Wooldridge in *Capitalism in America: A History*, this fluidity was the Valley ethos at work. The region had "pioneered a flexible form of capitalism." Its east-coast equivalent, the Boston area, "focused on big self-contained empires while Silicon Valley was freewheeling, decentralized and porous as companies formed, split and reformed." More than anywhere else in the United States, "Silicon Valley was a living embodiment of the principle of creative destruction as old companies died and new ones emerged, allowing capital, ideas and people to be reallocated."

As Flood recalls, "I navigated through the Valley — out for 20 days and back for ten days" — just like the young people chasing a dream and working in the Alberta oil sands. He absorbed the lessons of Valley veterans who had been through the cycles. At one software forum, a seasoned startup founder told the story of a young entrepreneur addressing an industry meeting in the seemingly inappropriate garb of shorts and sandals. The venture capitalist was not impressed, but it turned out the young man was a future co-founder of eBay. The lesson: pay attention to young people in shorts and sandals.

It was an image that stayed with Flood. In Silicon Valley, success came in a different package than at 3M or anywhere in the conventional corporate world. Flood toyed for a while with the idea of launching a venture capital fund, but he needed some startup experience to be credible. Then, David Foord at UNB invited him to the rubber-room session back in Fredericton. When Chris Newton arrived in shorts and sandals and flipped open his laptop, Flood knew right away that he had found his big chance.

As the son of a radiologist, he liked the way Newton's charts looked like colour X-rays of the network. "I got it — it's like, if you have trouble with your lungs, take an X-ray. You keep it simple."

For Newton, Flood was like no one else he had met. But he recognized there was a synergy in their skills and personalities. Brian would be the CEO and sales honcho, and Chris the technical guy working away in the lab. Looking back, he sees that "Brian lived for the sale, his passion was to be the businessman and salesman. But if you handed him a computer to program, then he would be dead by the end of the first session — he would be so bored."

And he learned that Flood was thinking bigger than just building a nice company. He wanted to change the province of New Brunswick and its sense of itself.

That became clear soon after their fateful meeting at UNB. Flood took Newton on a trip to California in January 2001. Brian retraced the steps of his personal journey, taking his young acolyte to San Francisco and then to the Silicon Valley epicentre of Palo Alto. He drove Newton to a little house on the side of the road with a simple garage. He explained that this garage was the birthplace of Silicon Valley, the humble workplace where, in the late 1930s, David Packard and Bill Hewlett started to develop the technology that became Hewlett-Packard, one of the early giants of the Valley. Both Hewlett and Packard had gone to nearby Stanford University and obtained seed money from the university's visionary engineering dean and provost Frederick Terman. They occupied a building on the university's land, before bursting out to become a technology juggernaut.

Flood's message was "we can do the same thing in New Brunswick." Newton now understood that Brian was not just about getting rich. He was about turning New Brunswick around, and if he made some money in the process, that was fine too. "Brian embedded in me this idea that you don't have to start out in a huge place. Hewlett and Packard started in a little garage, and it became Silicon Valley. You need only two, three or four of these [successes], and it can become a place like that."

That same day, as they wandered around Stanford University, they saw it was not overpowering in size, about the scale then of UNB. They came upon a funeral procession, but not just any procession: the celebration of life for Bill Hewlett himself, who had just died that week at 87 years old. It seemed like fate — the garage and this tribute to Hewlett in the same day, and the lessons of Silicon Valley swimming around in young Chris Newton's head.

Of course, every region wants to be like Silicon Valley, that magical mix of university research, venture capital, risk-taking innovation and landmark tech companies. The Valley encompasses immigrant dreamers from India, Israel and other faraway places, part of an endless stream of starry-eyed startup founders, but also huge players like HP, now a shadow of its glory days. Today, the stars of the Valley are Apple, Alphabet (the Google parent) and Facebook, three of the five most valuable tech companies in the world. (The other two are Amazon and Microsoft, up the coast in Seattle.)

Americans have created a misconception about the Valley — that it is the product of free enterprise at its best. It was in fact a co-creation of government and capitalism, propelled by the heavy spending of the Washington policy-makers on defence and space in the Cold War era. The Valley's freewheeling types, often libertarians, were in fact creatures of government activism.

As the historian Margaret O'Mara tells it, the Silicon Valley myth left out some key points: these entrepreneurs were not lone cowboys but talented people who drew on the work of other talented people, on networks and established institutions. "From the Bomb to the moon-shot to the internet and beyond, public spending fuelled an explosion of scientific and technical discovery, providing the foundations for generations of startups to come," writes O'Mara in *The Code: Silicon Valley and the Remaking of America*. Silicon Valley, she says, "is neither a big-government story nor a free-market one: it's both."

Whatever its origins, the Valley offered a shining model for other regions, with its mythology of vaulting ambition, of alternating failure and success and incessant risk-taking. Others have tried to mimic the Valley — Boston, Austin, New York — but they lacked that knife-edge culture of creative destruction. And yet the process was always evolving. In time, Silicon Valley — with its stratospheric housing and living costs — by necessity spilled beyond its physical borders. It was a brand, a spirit, an idea, like Wall Street had become in finance or Nashville in country music or Hollywood in movies.

When you spoke of Silicon Valley, you were alluding to not just Apple or Google, but perhaps a little company doing something cutting-edge in Boise, Idaho, or Buffalo, New York, feeding into the Valley ecosystem. The irony is that in creating the mobile technology that allowed people to work in remote places, Silicon Valley had fashioned its own decentralization, but certainly not its demise as a cultural reference point.

The concept of a business ecosystem started in the Valley. It is a biological term for a system of living organisms that inhabit an area. The business world was moving away from the model of big vertically integrated organizations to networks of partners, collaborators and outsourcers. This new business ecosystem was not just a circle of related companies but of constantly shifting relationships of suppliers, vendors, contractors — from catering firms to law firms to consultants to researchers in universities. The grease that made it work was information, the most valuable commodity of all.

As a remote tech worker, you could survive very nicely from the valley of New Brunswick — the Saint John River Valley — but you were not part of an ecosystem. You would often lack the kind of casual serendipitous interaction with like-minded geeks — over coffee or a kids' sports game — that generates linkages and new ideas. It seemed unlikely you could build a significant company in a region that even struggled to keep its direct air links with major U.S. centres. Face-to-face communication was still important for making judgments on investments, joint ventures and six-figure sales transactions.

As former UNB president John McLaughlin points out, New Brunswick had not yet progressed from its mill town culture to a knowledge culture. Like much of Canada, it still had a business model focused on trimming expenses in a mill or factory, not creating value through innovation. Even the geography defied any easy analogy; instead of a valley, New Brunswick offered a triangle of three centres of significant economic activity — Fredericton, Saint John and Moncton — connected by lonely highways. What's more, New Brunswick was still more about french fries than computer chips (although Hewlett and Packard had arrived in Palo Alto not long after it had primarily been a fruit-growing region, best known for its lavish output of prunes).

Replicating that culture and that magical symbiosis of public and private activity seemed like an impossible dream to most sane observers, but for an insane dreamer like Brian Flood, it was just another wall to run through.

3. From Beaver to Pond
A HISTORY

Brian Flood wanted to call his new company Q1 Labs. "Q" was the name of the quirky gadgeteer in the James Bond novels and films, the odd duck who was constantly outfitting the suavely brutal spy with new contraptions — wrist-mounted dart guns, rigged briefcases and jetpacks for a quick escape. Chris Newton seemed to Flood like a kind of Q, a geeky quartermaster in a world of high-stakes computer security.

What's more, Flood was able to make a tenuous connection from James Bond to his beloved New Brunswick. The Bond character was the creation of British journalist and former spy Ian Fleming who churned out the popular series of espionage novels in the 1950s and 1960s. At one point, before James Bond was a blockbuster movie franchise, Fleming was commissioned to recreate his spy stories in a comic strip at the *Daily Express* newspaper in London. He befriended (and later fell out with) the owner of the *Daily Express*, that mercurial son of New Brunswick Max Aitken, who came out of the remote Miramichi region to make a fortune manipulating markets and investments in Halifax and Montreal. Aitken had moved to England to become a press baron and political mover, and briefly was Winston Churchill's brilliantly successful minister of aircraft production in the Second World War.

Aitken had joined the House of Lords as Lord Beaverbrook, named for a New Brunswick salmon stream, although he originally wanted to be titled Lord Miramichi. But he was advised by Rudyard Kipling that it would be too hard for the British public to pronounce.

The character Q was thus inextricably linked to New Brunswick, according to Flood. It was another classic Brian Flood yarn, and his storytelling would be an essential part of the New Brunswick technology story. He could weave a great tale, tying together disparate details that would exhaust a listener — a venture capitalist or a corporate executive, or an author — trying to follow the currents and crosscurrents and feeling that, yes, in the end, NB truly is the centre of the universe. It was always a positive story about New Brunswick, an underappreciated, overlooked part of Canada that would some day, in the not-too-distant future, have its place in the sun.

And what about the "1" in Q1? That was a reflection of Flood's competitive streak. His brother Henry, his rowing and running partner at UNB, always said you had to shoot to be Number One. Brian loved his brother, and he was a ferocious game-player too.

Beaverbrook — often called "the Beaver" by condescending British contemporaries — plays a central part in the Flood narrative, and the Beaver is a typical East Coast story, although not always in a good way. Max Aitken grew up in late 19th-century New Brunswick but left as a young man to make his mark elsewhere. And he wasn't even a New Brunswick native — he was born north of Toronto to a Presbyterian minister and his wife. His father's long-running pastoral charge was the town of Newcastle in the Miramichi.

Max Aitken grew into a gnomish-looking rogue who was a smooth salesman, cutthroat business operator and notorious philanderer whom his wife is said to have once discovered in bed with his long-time mistress. But Beaverbrook was, if nothing else, loyal to his roots. He felt beholden to his province — by the time he died in 1964, he had made huge gifts for UNB scholarships and buildings, as well as a splendid art gallery in Fredericton stuffed with his collection and many other works. The Beaverbrook name is everywhere in the province, including on the street that winds along the foot of the hill in front of UNB's hillside campus and, nearby, the hotel that has served as the meeting place of the province's movers and shakers.

He reflected the complicated ethos of the Atlantic region, the tug of war between ambition and contentment, between going and staying, of new immigrants and old insiders. The New Brunswick story, in particular, is one of waves of people, pushed out of one place and squeezed into another. And the province today, more than any other, is subject to the heartless laws of demographics — once a province of the young, it is now increasingly a country of old men and women.

New Brunswick is also defined by its rivers and their watersheds: the Miramichi with its sinewy tangle of tributaries, with names like the Little Southwest Miramichi, Renous, Dungarvon, Bartholomew and Barnaby, and the Saint John, wide and graceful, with a gauntlet of mills and dams. The early Indigenous Peoples — the Mi'kmaq and the Wəlastəkewiyik — hunted and fished up and down the Miramichi, which flowed into the Gulf of St. Lawrence, and the Saint John as it wound its way from the highlands in Maine down to what is now the Bay of Fundy. Then the Europeans arrived, led first by the French, setting the historical pattern of the region — a story of displacement, often tragic and shameful.

The French settlers pushed aside the original people and built dykes along the marshes, farms along the river valleys and small settlements in the clearings. They became established in the 17th century, taking the name Acadians — a variation on Arcadia, the idyllic name assigned to the wild Atlantic coast of North America by the Italian explorer Verrazzano.

Then in the mid-1700s the British swept into Acadia, and history repeated itself. The conquerors deeply mistrusted the entrenched Acadians who claimed neutrality in the global Anglo-French wars, but refused to swear allegiance to the British Crown. So the British orchestrated the mass expulsion of Acadians from the Maritimes, burning homes and herding families onto ships bound for the southern 13 colonies and elsewhere. Some ended up in New England or as far

away as Louisiana, some in Quebec and France, and others resorted to
hiding in the woods, later to return but displaced from the best lands
along the rivers.

Henry Wadsworth Longfellow commemorated the tragedy in an
epic poem in 1847 (*Evangeline, A Tale of Acadie*), but beyond the myth-
making there was real suffering and a lingering and justifiable anger
that persists even today.

Following the imperial game plan, British settlers, some from New
England, moved in to replace the reduced Acadian population, and
were ultimately joined by thousands of Loyalists fleeing their own
convulsive uprooting in the American Revolution.

Then in the early 19th century, the Scots and Irish joined the influx
in large numbers. Typical of this wave was George Irving, an ambitious
immigrant from Dumfries, Scotland, who in the 1820s found his way
to the Eastern Shore of New Brunswick. Decades later his grandson
James Dergavel Irving (J.D.) became a prosperous mill owner around
the Acadian town of Bouctouche. And J.D. spawned another ambitious
offspring, a 20th-century empire builder named Kenneth Colin Irving,
or just K.C. His sons and grandchildren now tower over the province's
commercial landscape.

But the biggest flow of incomers were the Irish, who even before
the Great Famine of the 1840s were fleeing poverty in their homeland,
as well as searching for opportunity. William Andrew McCain, for
instance, was a relatively well-fixed Scots-Irish immigrant from
Donegal who in the 1820s ventured into the fertile upper Saint John
River Valley around what would be the village of Florenceville — laying
the roots for a 21st-century frozen-food empire.

Irish immigrants flooded into the hitherto Loyalist-dominated
port of Saint John, from where they spread out, some to the U.S.,
some to the upper Saint John River Valley and some staying put in
the city, making it very much an Irish town, and thus subject to the
tumult that spilled over from the sectarian feuds in Ireland. Brian
Flood's ancestor Michael emigrated from County Kildare in 1836, and

got into the building trades around the city of Saint John. By 1850, he and his son had founded what is now reputed to be Canada's oldest construction company, John Flood & Sons.

Thus, the human geography of the 19th-century province took approximate shape: Loyalist-British settlement in the south; Acadians in the north, but with an urban base in Moncton; and the Irish everywhere. These divisions blurred over time, but some politicians still try to make hay over the divides — particularly over the shape of linguistic accommodation in Canada's only officially bilingual province.

The province was always thinly populated but rich in nature's bounty. The Maritime colonies were a vital cog in the 18th- and 19th-century British commercial empire, providing wooden masts for the ships that ruled the seas and all kinds of commodities for the industrial revolution. Later they joined a post-Confederation national economy that tied them to the markets of Central Canada, only to be buffeted by Upper Canadian dalliances with U.S. free trade and the whims of bankers and prime ministers.

In towns like Bathurst, Newcastle, Saint John and Edmundston, labour and capital were marshalled in the herculean task of harvesting and processing trees, fish and ores. That dominant culture was driven by determined individuals, epitomized by giant, red-haired Boss Gibson, the builder of a 19th-century mill town called Marysville across the Saint John River from the capital Fredericton — before he too was undermined by the loss of British Empire and Canadian trade preferences. Boss Gibson, who built one of the largest textile mills in the British Empire, was a vertical integrator who built a railway to carry his raw material and finished products. His company town is now a dormitory community on the north shore of the Saint John River; the 1885 roundhouse for Gibson's railway is a bustling craft brewery.

In the 20th century Boss Gibson gave way to bosses Irving and McCain. Those two families — their triumphs and highly publicized tensions — dominated the narrative of the latter half of the 20th century and the early decades of the 21st. The Irvings have their roots in forestry and paper mills while branching out into home building stores, construction, ship-building, real estate, food and paper products, newspapers and a giant refinery in Saint John, their commercial base. Indeed, the outsize importance of that refinery and the Irving family is captured in one statistic: more than half of the annual exports of the province consist of refined petroleum products from that one refinery, the largest in Canada. Meanwhile, the McCain hegemony was built on agriculture and food processing along the upper Saint John and branded french fries and frozen food sold around the world.

But with thinning resources, shifting global trade and the technology advances of the 20th century, the Maritimes settled into a long decline relative to the rest of Canada. There were cheaper and more bountiful places to obtain the commodities that were the region's mainstays. A fishing crisis hobbled the whole Atlantic region. Good jobs for tradesmen and labourers got thin on the ground.

Thus began the exodus of young men and women to Ontario and the Canadian West. Many were young professionals, but also tradespeople who joined Canada's booming energy economy. At the height of oil sands fever, I would run into large numbers of young New Brunswickers on their monthly rotations of 20 days out, 10 days back home — bivouacked in dormitories and hotels and making six-figure incomes in the oil sands instead of living in their parents' basements and getting by in menial jobs.

Indeed, over the years, it became a truism that the adventurous left home, while the less ambitious stayed. The Canadian political scientist Hugh Thorburn wrote in a 1961 article, "Those who 'kick against the pricks' are encouraged to leave, while those who accommodate themselves to things as they are choose to remain."

The pattern was that you moved away for the job, to Toronto, Calgary or Boston, but you would come home in retirement. Sir

Graham Day, the Nova Scotian who became a powerhouse executive in Margaret Thatcher's Britain, would say that Maritimers are like salmon, they swim home to die. But it means they do not live in the region for their most productive years.

Meanwhile, the population in New Brunswick was aging, spawning a demographic crisis that, in a cruel paradox, made for severe shortages of skilled talent in the south, while hard-pressed mill towns in the Northeast were shedding jobs. There have been years in which the population has declined on an absolute basis. The answer is to boost immigration, and there are some creative efforts, but they have yet to stem the crisis. Indeed, New Brunswick, with a history of invasions from outsiders, now needs another convulsive invasion if it is to meet the cherished goal of policy-makers — a million people in 2040, up from 780,000 in 2020.

A national sport has thus developed — shaming New Brunswick, as the lowest in the Canadian pecking order. It has become known not as flyover country, like parts of the U.S. interior, but drive-through country, a place that vacationers motor through to get somewhere else. They might stop at an Irving gas station to fill up, or spend a night at a Best Western or Rodd Motor Inn but for nothing more. Except, perhaps, for a quick visit to the majestic Hopewell Rocks on the Bay of Fundy, their prime destination lies elsewhere.

In Atlantic Canada, Newfoundland and Labrador can boast of the comic talents of Rick Mercer, Mary Walsh and CODCO and the heart-warming *Come from Away* musical; Prince Edward Island is known for Anne of Green Gables and a bucolic charm; Nova Scotia has ruggedly beautiful Cape Breton and the grand history of Halifax, major port and government centre. New Brunswick is famous for failure.

The dagger to the heart of New Brunswickers was Martin Patriquin's March 2016 article in *Maclean's* magazine with the headline "Can anything save New Brunswick?" followed by the subhead "The province's economy is in free fall, it has more deaths than births and an ugly language war to rival Quebec's." The article continued, "Wood, metals and fish used to be New Brunswick's economic staples; now, more and more, it is old age." The message: New Brunswick is Canada's West Virginia — overlooked, aging, backward.

According to Patriquin, about half of New Brunswick's population lived in rural areas, more than double the number in neighbouring Quebec. He said it all meant "fewer higher-paying jobs and more reliance on an extraction economy and the federal government. Federal cash transfers make up about 36 per cent of the province's budget, the second-highest percentage in the country, behind Prince Edward Island."

Other articles pointed to the zero-sum game played by the province's regions and particularly its three largest cities, all between 100,000 and 140,000 in census-area population and an hour or two apart. Saint John is an old industrial town with two big Irving operations on opposite ends. Fredericton — known as "Freddy" — is university and government, quaintly prosperous and often resented for it. Moncton projects an image of growth as the province's francophone hub, logistics entrepot and geographical centre of the Maritimes. A suburb, Dieppe, propelled by inflows of Acadians from the Northeast, is one of Atlantic Canada's most dynamic communities, tripling its population to 25,000–30,000 people in a quarter century. Moncton often sees itself as more the regional rival to Halifax than to its New Brunswick neighbours.

If a government were to advance one of these regions, or one of the major interest groups, it would have to balance the books somehow by advancing the others, leading to costly duplication and lack of economic development focus. Compare this with Nova Scotia where Halifax is the clear power centre, or Ontario where Toronto is undeniably the financial and tech focus.

New Brunswickers own up to a lot of this critique. The province's political sage Donald Savoie, from Université de Moncton, put it most succinctly in 2018 in the *Globe and Mail*: "The province has a sharp linguistic divide with some politicians exploiting it for partisan political purposes; a pronounced north-south economic divide; a declining population; a ballooning provincial debt, which now stands at $14.5 billion; some of Canada's highest tax rates; too much infrastructure; and not enough people."

Too often, the search for solutions has led to crushing disappointment — consider the Bricklin sports-car fiasco in the 1970s, the seemingly shattered dream of a new pipeline, or the failed notion of selling NB Power to Quebec's utility. When these ideas went up in smoke, the mood reverted to defeatism or anger. Often this anger finds easy targets — the Irvings for being too smothering; Quebec for being obdurate about pipelines across its territory; the federal government for being so mercurial.

Yet, amid the negativity, there are shoots of positive thinking. For one thing, the sense of isolation, of being alone in a hostile world, has bred a kind of scrappy inventiveness. New Brunswickers pride themselves on resilience in the face of an economic bad hand. They see themselves as more entrepreneurial than people in more favoured areas. The image is of a down-to-earth can-do region, where the answer to a business challenge is often a quick local phone call or a chat on Main Street.

Covid-19, of course, dramatically altered the economic reality for all countries and regions. But from the perspective of recent history, New Brunswick's problems have been more about distressed pockets than province-wide crisis. Contrary to the *Maclean's* "save New Brunswick" theme, the province did not need to be saved, argued Herb Emery, an economics professor at UNB and an outsider who pricks the myths of New Brunswick's underperformance. Speaking before the pandemic, he noted that a generally flourishing economy existed along the ribbon of Trans-Canada Highway that ran from Edmundston in the northwest, south to Fredericton and then curled eastward through Moncton and the marshes on the Nova Scotia border. New Brunswick did not suffer from a provincial economic problem, he said — it had a

Northeast problem, encompassing areas of the Miramichi, the Acadian peninsula and the hardscrabble Bathurst area, where there was economic duress from the closing and downsizing of mills and mines.

Then there existed the great paradox of Saint John, once the Maritimes' leading city and now its faded industrial powerhouse. Despite a solid core of Irving and Moosehead-driven industry, and a strong infusion of tech companies, it had some of the worst child poverty in the country, rivalling Toronto but more visible in a much smaller city.

As the 21st century dawned — and Chris Newton tackled UNB's cybersecurity pain — New Brunswick was certainly on no one's list of innovation hotspots. It could not measure up to Vancouver with its direct line to Silicon Valley; the Toronto-Waterloo corridor with thousands of startups and big tech salaries; or Montreal, with footholds in the hot space of artificial intelligence. The Maritimes were nowhere, and New Brunswick was below nowhere.

With its regions of affluent haves and struggling have-nots, New Brunswick has emerged as the microcosm of Canada. The country contains many communities off the beaten path of technology innovation and trying desperately to make the transition from its resource base to the knowledge economy. Across Canada, these struggling areas include old manufacturing centres abandoned by multinational branch plants, or former boom towns of oil, mining and forestry. They are scattered through much of the Maritimes and Newfoundland and Labrador, rural Quebec and Ontario, and now big parts of Western Canada. They comprise communities like Peterborough, Thunder Bay, Prince George, Port Alberni, even Fort Mac itself, whose boomtown horizon is quickly narrowing. The sour spirit of decline pervades beautiful places where there is often no work, or only poor-paying jobs for those who haven't already left. It is death in paradise.

More broadly this is the story of coal-dependent Appalachia and the industrial wastelands of northeastern France; of eastern Germany, parts of southern Italy, and the old mining and manufacturing regions of England, all of which have become breeding grounds for political populism, which can be empowering but is also laced with a corrosively narrow tribal defensiveness, prone to ethnic hatred and racism. While the information economy brings untold wealth to San Francisco, Toronto, Cambridge (England or Massachusetts), and Austin, Texas, what is it doing for Wheeling, West Virginia, Nottingham, in England's Midlands, or Campbellton, New Brunswick?

Given the odds, how could a sparsely populated, historically resource-dependent province like New Brunswick break into the information economy? Here was a remote community in a remote region, with about the same population as Mississauga, the Toronto bedroom community — but without the immigrant population and its dynamism from being cheek-to-jowl with Toronto. It has fewer than 800,000 people spread across 75,000 square kilometres — about a third of the population of Atlantic Canada, comprising the Maritime provinces of Nova Scotia, New Brunswick and Prince Edward Island, plus Newfoundland and Labrador.

These were the hard truths that faced a young lawyer named Frank McKenna, when in 1987 he became the premier of New Brunswick. Like most incoming premiers, he did an inventory of what was working in the province and what was not. It was easy to pick out the weaknesses and hard to find the strengths. A towering weakness was the fact that the province was relying primarily on natural resources, and those resources were either diminishing, as in the case of mining, or mechanizing, as in the case of forestry, fishing and others. McKenna observed that one mill that used to employ two thousand people, could run with 650 people by the 1990s. And instead of some guys in the woods with chainsaws, modern forwarders and harvesters provided industrial-scale cutting and clearing.

"My view was that this trend was going to overwhelm us," McKenna says, 32 years later, now deputy chair of Toronto-Dominion Bank. "So we had to find new opportunities." McKenna travelled the world to try to attract major manufacturers, but the region was constrained by the small labour pool and distance from markets.

When McKenna turned to the strengths of the province, he fastened on the local phone company, New Brunswick Telephone, known widely as NBTel. "I had not appreciated this as an ordinary citizen, but when I became premier, I very quickly appreciated that we had a jewel, an absolute jewel." Perhaps he was not so surprised at another strength — the University of New Brunswick, where he had graduated from law school. UNB had a fine tradition as a research university and an engineering training ground, as well as a growing reputation as a generator of computer science talent.

So McKenna began to rely on NBTel and UNB, combined with a nimble and talented public service, to build a different kind of economy and a different image for New Brunswick. His ten years in office took on the theme of knitting the province through highways — improved physical thoroughfares and information highways with digital fibre-optic networks stretching into small communities, and using remote connectivity for services like issuing government licences. He brought better jobs in the short term and laid the foundations of a knowledge economy into the future. "We set out to become a digital world leader," McKenna recalls.

NBTel certainly helped as a leader in implementing a fully digital telephone system. It was the first Canadian phone company to offer internet service, the first Canadian telecom company to offer all customers voice mail... the list of firsts goes on.

NBTel benefited from a number of inspiring leaders, including the last one, Gerry Pond, who as president and CEO partnered up with McKenna to digitize the province. NBTel leaders recognized that faced with a far-flung customer base, and increasing threats to its monopoly, the provincial telecom provider could not succeed based on economies of scale — it had to be an incubator of research and talent. The thinking was: we are small so we have to be innovative in areas

NBTel president Gerry Pond, left, in 1996, launching a new high-speed internet service, with Nortel's Wes Scott (Courtesy of Gerry Pond)

like internet telephony and video technology. NBTel also pioneered the revolutionary idea that customers could choose the time to get their service visits, rather than be at the mercy of the phone company.

Working with NBTel, McKenna latched on to the idea of deploying these networks to establish a lucrative call-centre business for out-of-province companies. These were solid well-paying jobs built on a hard-working labour force with a bilingual aptitude. New Brunswick for one glorious decade climbed out of its woe-is-me rut to become the province everyone wanted to emulate. The recent story is about trying to recapture the magic of the McKenna era, now two decades in the rear-view mirror.

McKenna's collaborator, Gerry Pond, became a mirror of New Brunswick's economic journey over the last 40 years. Born in northern Quebec, he comes from a forestry family with roots in New Brunswick's Miramichi region. He graduated from UNB and, the antithesis of Beaverbrook, he never left. He joined NBTel and carried on the legacy of a customer-first spirit that drove the company for years. But the utility disappeared in the early 21st century, absorbed in the merger of the four Atlantic phone companies, which became Aliant. Now Bell Aliant, it is part of the BCE empire, and a subsidiary of Bell Canada, the much bigger, stodgier telecom carrier from Central Canada.

As company president, Pond had nurtured units inside NBTel, some developed in a research and development (R&D) hothouse called the Living Lab. He would put bright young people in charge of these units, and in some cases set them loose in the world with startups.

One promising technology hatched in NBTel was internet-protocol video, which would allow the transmission of television content over the internet, bypassing cable TV and potentially revolutionizing how consumers could gain access to video in their homes. It was Netflix before Netflix. Pond created a unit to market the technology, called iMagic TV.

But iMagic was too far ahead as a technology, unlucky in its market timing and the victim of corporate plotting in Paris and Central Canada. It was sold off and wound down, dismissed as another one of the disastrous New Brunswick silver bullets — big noise, lots of promises, government money — but in the end, nothing. Looking back now it's clear that analysis was short-sighted. The people who came out of the iMagic experience, sadder but a lot wiser, would be at the heart of an amazing flowering of startup success.

The iMagic veterans, who got their start at NBTel, joined forces with the founders at Q1 Labs — all of them with UNB pedigrees — in a subversive underground movement of innovation in a province of sometimes suffocating conservatism and pessimism. This enterprising band has been determined to break out of the traditional mould of hopelessness that drove out earlier generations of venturesome New Brunswickers. And that was the movement Brian Flood and Chris Newton joined in the rubber room 20 years ago when their different paths collided.

4. Angels and Angles

When Brian Flood entered Chris Newton's life, it gave the younger man a bracing whiff of adventure, but also a tremor of trepidation. He was 28, settled in his university job, newly married to his wife, Tracey, thinking about a family, and in the process of buying a house — and now this guy Brian Flood wanted him to give it all up and launch a company. "I was scared as shit," Newton would say later. "And you're telling me I am leaving a position where I could work for 30 years to join a startup with no money or sales?"

Newton knew how tenacious Flood would be in his counter-argument, that this was a life-changing opportunity. "But I felt I might quit my job and a month later, I might be out of work. Then I'd be losing my house. I thought I'd probably have to say no," he concluded.

After some months, the moment of decision came: his university boss, Greg Sprague, called to say he should make a choice, leave to join the startup or commit to work full-time at UNB. Newton was torn. Then Sprague offered a suggestion — the university was willing to give him an unpaid leave of absence of two years, allowing him to try the new venture. Newton was enthusiastic — what was there to lose? "I would not be getting paid but I knew if things didn't work out, I could just come back to my job."

He now concludes that this was the critical step that got his new venture off the ground. Many people in university or public service come up with great ideas but hesitate to pursue them for fear of failing without any safety net for themselves and their families. This was a way to provide that buffer.

He feels governments in particular should be open to dispensing leaves of absence, more than private-sector companies, which might feel threatened competitively by allowing key personnel to take two years' leave (though it would probably work well for many private companies too). Looking back on UNB's offer, "I don't think I understood at the time how important that would be." He could go out in the world and know he had options if the thing didn't work out.

Newton had to make other decisions. He had poured himself into developing his Symon idea, working on his own, but now it was more than he could handle. Early in the process, he reached out to his friends Sandy Bird and Dwight Spencer; Bird was still working at the university and Dwight at a government technology job. They had been buddies for years and were about to become partners.

It was intense. The old pattern continued: the trio were working at their jobs full-time and heading home at night to work some more. Newton is derisive of entrepreneurs who think they can launch companies working 9-to-5 days. The UNB trio would come home from their jobs around five-thirty, spend time with families and friends, and then get online, working with each other, from eight o'clock or so, till 1:00 a.m. or later.

"We had this chatting system and we could tell when someone fell asleep," Newton recalls. "You could see their keystrokes go in a line — l-l-l-l-l — and you'd think, 'Uh-oh, Dwight has fallen asleep on his keyboard.'"

Newton's message to young entrepreneurs is, "If it doesn't keep you up at night, it is probably not worth doing." A great new idea can't be easy. Anything of value in technology has to be hard, and yet it can't be so hard that it seems impossible.

Even after the company was founded, Dwight and Sandy were toiling away at their old jobs. It was about a year and a half before they quit to go full-time with the new company. There was no longer talk of graduating; they were too busy. In the future they would cover up their lack of degrees by simply saying, "We attended UNB."

The Q1 Five: clockwise from top left, Gerry Pond, Brian Flood, Sandy Bird, Chris Newton and Dwight Spencer (Courtesy of Brian Flood)

All these moves laid the foundations for the new company that Newton, Flood and the university were trying to put together. It was a major step for UNB and for David Foord, the technology-transfer officer who was balancing a delicate issue. How do you structure an agreement that protects the university's interests in intellectual property but also rewards and offers incentives for these young people?

If Newton and his friends had been faculty members, they would have clearly owned the intellectual property. But Symon had been developed while they were employees of UNB, which meant that, strictly speaking, UNB owned the technology. And yet it was developed largely on their own time, while using the university's networks to test and develop the programs.

Foord pushed toward the model he had seen on the West Coast. Instead of demanding royalties, UNB would assign the intellectual property to a new company as part of a founders' deal, and then take equity in the company in return for signing rights.

The university's stake was about 5 per cent, according to various sources, and the rest of the ownership was divided up largely among Brian Flood — the major financial investor with the majority stake — Chris Newton, Sandy Bird and Dwight Spencer. The three young developers collectively held about a third of the ownership, with Newton taking the largest cut of the three. Two other smaller share-holders came from Brian Flood's network: Steve Beatty had been Flood's accountant in his restaurants, and lawyer Linda Fung had been one of Flood's guides through Silicon Valley and did a lot of the legal work around the formation of Q1 Labs. Fung ended her active involvement in the early stages, while Beatty would remain chief financial officer for a period.

The new firm, Q1 Labs, could still use the university network for research and product demonstrations, and the university could develop research papers based on the work. In the dry wording of the university website, "In April 2001, [the office of research services] transferred the UNB-owned technology to Q1 Labs for equity in the company and the right to continue to use the technology for research and educational purposes.... Q1 Labs established R&D facilities in New Brunswick and formed an alliance with UNB whereby seventeen live networks were available for product testing and research."

The deal underlined the role of the university in the early life of Q1 Labs. To call it supportive would be to underplay its importance. There was a lot of trial and error — the university and the founders had never done this type of thing before. Brian Flood may have published a book, sold 3M products or run a restaurant, but he had never launched a startup tech company with a groundbreaking product, young co-founders and a university backer. A UNB professor named Ali Ghorbani, emerging as a research leader in cybersecurity, effectively became part of the Q1 team, though he was not officially employed by the company.

The other critical factor was getting the funding to turn this idea into reality. Flood beat the bushes in New Brunswick and far afield to assemble a group of what's known as angel investors. The term "angels" is not celestial but entirely materialistic — it was originally used to describe the collection of friends, family and theatre groupies who funded the incubation of new Broadway plays. Later it was extended to the people who, from love or loyalty, extend small amounts to get a startup off the ground. "Friends, family and fools," says one tech veteran.

Brian Flood was milking cash flow from his restaurants to fund the high-tech venture and was maxed out on a slew of credit cards, just staying ahead of the banks. Meanwhile, the UNB kids and their families had nothing to give but time and sweat. The most fertile field of funding came from the faculty, alumni and supporters of UNB. This was the critical moment when you needed true believers who were also realistic enough to know the whole project could sink like a stone.

Jane Fritz was the very definition of true believer. She was dean of the faculty of computer science that day when Brian Flood burst into her office with the news that he had found his startup baby, right here under her nose with one of her favourite students, Chris Newton. Soon Flood would be coming back and asking for money.

Fritz was an easy touch. She had an affinity for young men and women with bright ideas. "I love my geeks," she says. "I've taught thousands of geeks, and they're just awesome people. I love what they do." She is a pioneering academic in computer science who had come to Fredericton in 1970. A UNB masters of science grad who got her PhD in England, she had followed her metallurgist-turned-systems-consultant husband back to New Brunswick, where he was helping install the province's first medicare system. She stayed to become a pillar of UNB's outstanding computer science faculty.

She recalls that when she came to Fredericton in 1970, there was one computer in the government and one computer at the university— and NB Power used it as well. "It was the biggest one east of Montreal. And that was it."

She was a difference maker in the province, planting the seeds of a knowledge industry. Then along came Chris Newton and his friends, who, initially as part of their internships, ended up in the Computing Centre. Her recollection is that she and her husband put $15,000 into Newton's company, not a lot but enough to make a difference in the early days of Q1 Labs. It took a long time before they saw any return, but Fritz has since then done other deals for other students. They were not as fruitful, but that is what you do when you truly believe in people.

Meanwhile, UNB officials helped Brian Flood comb through lists of alumni who might contribute, reaching into the Bay Street–Toronto crowd to find graduates with a tolerance for risk. In the end, Flood had $770,000 U.S. of seed money to work with, of which he had contributed about $400,000 of his own. He had recruited a dozen angels, seven of whom had contributed $10,000 U.S. or so, but two contributors came in at $100,000 and another two at $50,000. The angel investors took convertible debentures — essentially securities convertible later into common shares. It all helped, Flood said, and it was fortunate that there wasn't a lot of competition for cash. "We were in a bubble up here, the only game in town."

The missing piece was a beacon of credibility, a corporate chair who had been around the block a few times. That person presented himself one day as Flood was driving around Saint John. The radio news reported that Gerry Pond, the much admired head of the former NBTel — now absorbed by Aliant — was retiring from the phone company. The reality was a bit different. In the merger of the Atlantic phone companies and the increasing consolidation with Bell Canada, Gerry Pond ended up as president of the telecom arm of Aliant, a job he enjoyed. But he also felt uncomfortable with the emerging corporate structure where Bell Canada would dominate. He doesn't spend much time ruminating about old hurts, except to say, "The truth was I was let go." At 57, he was ready to move on. It meant that Pond was available.

On hearing the news report, Flood drove straight to the Aliant headquarters in the Brunswick Square office building, which dominates the skyline in downtown Saint John. He marched in to see Pond, who was packing up boxes, the detritus of 30 years at the company, during which he had transformed the former NBTel into what many considered the most innovative telecom provider in North America.

The two knew each other: they were neighbours in the cozy Saint John suburb of Rothesay. "I want you to be the chair of Q1 Labs," Flood announced, during a conversation that ran to about two hours. Pond agreed he might take on the role, but he needed an office. Flood went away for a couple of hours and came back to say he had secured space in the same building, two storeys below. Pond moved his boxes to the new space. Brian Flood had landed his credibility.

Pond also provided $50,000 of angel funding, but more importantly he linked Q1 Labs up with his extensive network of venturesome New Brunswickers, many of whom had worked with or for him at the phone company or in its spinoffs.

A case in point was Ian Cavanagh, an electrical engineer who came out of Acadia University in Wolfville, Nova Scotia, and TUNS (Technical University of Nova Scotia) in Halifax (now part of Dalhousie University) and joined NBTel. He became a key cog in Gerry Pond's plan to put NBTel into the vanguard of telecom companies, including helping in the iMagic venture. Cavanagh then managed an NBTel joint venture with a U.S. West Coast firm called Genesys Labs. (The successor to that joint venture is still very active on the New Brunswick tech scene.) In time Cavanagh left NBTel to join Genesys Labs full-time, working out of Saint John.

After a stint with Genesys Labs, he moved on, planning on a year's hiatus, when he got a call from a friend at a California startup. He was not eager to get into that Silicon Valley whirlwind. He suffered from what he calls "the Maritime mindset" — that he was not good enough to run with the super-bright grads of MIT and Harvard.

But he joined the startup, and quickly realized Maritimers could play in the big leagues. He learned a lot more going through the dot-com boom and bust, and came home to found his own consulting company. By the time Q1 Labs had emerged, he had sold his company and slipped into semi-retirement, allowing him to pursue his love of fly-fishing.

One day he was invited by his old mentor Gerry Pond to visit him in Brunswick Square. His recollections of that meeting: "I walked in and Brian Flood and Gerry Pond were sitting at a table, and the glint in Gerry's eyes said, 'We've been waiting for you.'" Cavanagh, who likes to spin a yarn, says, "I felt completely set up, but after two to three hours, I became an investor." He adds that he came in with $50,000 U.S., "a lot for me at the time; in hindsight I wish I had put in more."

He knew that he could be consulting to Q1 Labs, and he had something else that was invaluable: he had a network in Silicon Valley. That would be very important to the Q1 saga.

Until that point Q1 had been a male bastion, but as the business got more complex, the founders had to look more widely for talent. Marie Jo Thibault came into their sights. Blessed with a sense of adventure, she had come to UNB from Sherbrooke, Quebec, to improve her English while getting more education. She had an undergraduate degree in electrical engineering, and she enrolled in the university's Technology Management and Entrepreneurship program, known as TME — a diploma course for science, math and engineering types that acted as an incubator of companies and ideas. (It would later add a master's program.) When that course ended, she stayed to manage the TME program and teach a bit.

But after years of academic life, she needed a change, and suddenly she found herself sitting in her UNB office talking about opportunities with Brian Flood and Sandy Bird. She had never met them before, but she sensed this Q1 Labs venture would be exciting. She would be

Marie Jo Thibault, an engineer, was hired as the first full-time Q1 Labs employee, taking the role of Vice President of Operations
(Courtesy of Photography Flewwelling)

the first full-time employee besides the founders. She immediately moved to Saint John and started up the Canadian headquarters of Q1 — actually, the effective headquarters of the entire company. Although for practical reasons the firm was registered in the U.S., all the administration activities were centred in New Brunswick.

It was a revelation for someone who knew entrepreneurship only from the classroom. "It was exciting to watch Brian never giving up, and always kicking down doors," Thibault recalls.

She had the title Vice President of Operations, which sounds grand until you realize there were only eight or nine people in operations at the start, but the numbers quickly grew. Everything was positioned to make Q1 look bigger than it really was to impress prospective customers.

By now, Flood had already embarked on his new challenge of finding what is known as Series A venture capital. It was a race between the ability to sign up customers and the rate Q1 Labs was burning through the seed capital from the angels. Flood was under intense stress, but he kept it from his young partners as they worked to define the product and the approach to customers.

Venture capitalists are professional investors who take money from rich people, institutions and companies — known as limited partners — and put together large pools of capital, and then use those funds to build a portfolio of stakes in startup investments. Not every startup will get off the ground, and fewer than half might even return the capital investment over the five or ten years of the fund. The chances of a so-called home run are incredibly tiny — some may be singles or doubles or loud fly-outs. Everyone dreams of a Google or a Facebook that explodes into a unicorn — a billion-dollar private company that delivers huge returns through an exit event, which may be an initial public offering on the stock market or a sale to a bigger company.

The venture funds do not usually do the earliest-stage, bare-bones angel investing; their first investment round, known as Series A, comes when the company has shown it has a product and sales are starting to build. The Series A venture capitalists, if they are still buying into the idea, often stick around to do the Series B round, which comes later.

The first venture capital firm was the grandly named American Research and Development Corporation, formed in 1946 by a Harvard Business School professor named Georges Doriot, a French-born former U.S. army general who has been called the father of venture capital. In 1957, he put $70,000 into Digital Equipment Corporation, the Boston-area firm that unleashed the minicomputer on the world. That investment harvested an exit sum of $38 million when DEC went public in 1968. Venture capitalists do well on these big exit deals. They make their money from "the carry" — a percentage of the gains made in the fund — or from a management fee based on the fund's assets.

The venture capital industry truly took off in Silicon Valley, along a mundane stretch of thoroughfare called Sand Hill Road, where companies like NEA, Kleiner Perkins and Menlo Ventures set up shop. The industry maintained a strong presence in Boston, funding companies out of Harvard and MIT. It was slower to germinate in

Canada, for understandable reasons — fewer rich people, smaller institutions and a generally risk-averse culture, as well as legislated constraints on public pension funds, potentially the biggest actors in any investment sector.

But by the year 2000, there was a growing cottage industry in places like Toronto, Montreal and Vancouver, although it was still constrained in its ability to write big cheques. And there were no VC firms of any consequence in Atlantic Canada.

Venture capitalism had become an inviting career path for young business graduates like Salim Teja, a graduate of Western University's esteemed Ivey Business School, whose career has alternated between launching new ventures and investing in them. He often warns entrepreneurs that venture capital funding is the most expensive money they will ever raise. "You're going to have to give away 20 to 30 percent of your company every round that you do, so just be prepared for that kind of dilution."

In addition, venture capitalists have a clear business model, he advises. They need to exit within five to ten years, which requires a steep growth trajectory. "If you as an entrepreneur are not comfortable with what that path demands, you shouldn't go after venture capital funding."

He also points out that the venture firms are looking for hyper-growth companies — not high-growth companies, but off-the-charts growth enterprises. A founder who may have been good in the early stages of a company may not be the right leader in the scaling-up stage. The founder has to be prepared to admit new blood with complementary skills — as Q1 Labs would learn.

Teja, who returned to VC investing in 2019 after a stint at Toronto's MaRS innovation hub, has another piece of advice: "The venture capital world often is binary. Because you're going for this breakout success, it either works or it doesn't, and that can be a very emotionally draining experience for an entrepreneur and a team. You have to be prepared for it."

On the Q1 Labs team, Brian Flood was the one who best understood these facts, and he pushed his young colleagues to look beyond New Brunswick for customers. The Q1 founders nailed down some early clients, starting with notable names close to home. Assumption Life in Moncton and the local electrical utility NB Power signed on, as did the provincial government and of course UNB. Next, they managed to sign up an international client, a company in California called Agile Networks.

That was an important breakthrough because it reflected Flood's philosophy. He noted that many Maritime companies target the easier home market exclusively in the early days, but it is a flawed strategy. Those startups end up with no global profile, no entry point into knowledge circles outside their home market and no way of measuring themselves against would-be competitors. If you wanted a winner, you had to target right away the big customers in the biggest market in the world, and that is the United States.

The Q1 Labs team was out there with big clients, such as U.S. government agencies, educational institutions and Fortune 500 corporations. Flood had registered the company in the low-cost, easy-compliance jurisdiction of Delaware, which provided a U.S. provenance that would impress the VCs and customers. He used law firms known for representing U.S. venture capitalists. There was a need to out-American the Americans.

Symon, which had evolved into QVision and later QRadar, turned out to be a very intriguing product, but it was expensive to sell. Back in 2000, software was still a commodity, a product sold to personal computer consumers in shrink-wrapped packages. For business software, it would be a long and intense sales experience. These were the years before software as a service (SaaS), whereby programs could be plucked from the broad internet, known as the cloud. This was "pre-cloud."

Q1 sales teams would fan out over the continent to make their pitch to would-be clients. The visits would lead to product demonstrations and the customers' hardware was usually not up to running the software. Back in the labs in Fredericton, Chris Newton was watching this roll out. "I had to deploy software in people's data centres, but running it on their gear almost never worked; we had to deploy our own specialized hand-picked computers."

More visits ensued, with teams running back and forth. The product might eventually sell for tens or hundreds of thousands of dollars, but the time spent nailing down the sale was long, and there were periods of post-sale handholding. Meanwhile, the cash drain turned into a torrent, before the revenue could be booked.

The result: long sales cycles and huge spending, with teams of people travelling from Fredericton and Saint John. This process also engendered a lumpy sales pattern whereby purchase decisions often came late in the customer's fiscal year. And every sale was a one-time thing — there would be updates but they too involved restarting the process of client visits.

Chris Newton felt there was "friction" in the sales process. It was a great product but a hard sell. That realization precipitated an important shift in the company. Newton was the key architect of the technology but at the time he hated to travel and to be away from his young family. He was a brilliantly curious thinker and researcher but not a natural salesman. And yet it was clear that the Q1 product needed both the straight sales talk that Brian Flood could deliver with a flourish, but also the technical pitch to chief information officers and computing centre directors. It turned out Sandy Bird could excel at standing at a white board and telling the technical story. Like Newton, he was smart on the technical mastery, but he was also good on the explanatory role, comfortable and congenial, and he would travel. So Bird started doing the pitches, while Newton had lots to do back in the lab.

It was a perfect match, but in a sense the Q1 Labs narrative shifted from Chris Newton to Sandy Bird. The remarkable thing is both were comfortable with this shift, and remain comfortable to this day.

According to one early investor, "Chris was the brains, but Sandy was the intersection between the business and the technology. If it wasn't for Sandy Bird, this company would have never ever worked. Sandy could go into a customer and sell them their own shorts."

Dwight Spencer was a marvel at post-sale customer service, helping get the product up to speed in the big contracts. Soon Q1 had people travelling to places like College Station, Texas, the home of Texas A&M University, and meeting officials like Willis Marti, the head of the university's computing centre.

Marti, who has since retired from the university after a stroke, was typical of the tough audience Q1 Labs had to win over. Looking back, Marti thought the sales pitch was a little extreme and felt frustrated that the salesperson did not respond readily to his questions. But he liked the technology and he acquired it, although it never really lived up to all his expectations.

He loved the way the support specialist, Dwight Spencer, could speak to him in a way that the salespeople often couldn't. He communicated to him in the engineering language that broke down barriers among the professionals who would actually have to install and use the Q1 technology. Spencer is a natural people person, radiating good vibes, without the tense go-go drive of the classic sales type. He is the consummate happy warrior, just thrilled to be making a good living doing work he loves.

And yet, some observers say, he had a reputation as a stickler in the kinds of people he hired. In one case, managers interviewed a young recruit when Spencer was out of the office because they feared he would reject the candidate on the basis that his knowledge didn't measure up. The new recruit later became a close friend and a leader in the company.

Despite the high cost of sales, Q1 Labs had that fortuitous blend of startup ingredients — a complementary mix of skills, a novel idea that addressed a serious problem, and loyal friends and family with a few dollars to spare. What was missing was penetration into the dense networks of financiers who could vault the company forward to the next stage of commercial success. That would not be easy when the big pools of VC money lay in bicoastal United States — in Boston and Silicon Valley — while the founders were operating out of small cities perched on Canada's remote Atlantic coast.

5. Hi, I'm from New Brunswick

Tony Van Bommel was in the room on that day in 2000 when Brian met Chris. Like Flood he was entranced with what he saw when Chris Newton opened up his little laptop and showed everyone his colour chart of the flowing rivers of university data networks. The Halifax-based venture capitalist came away thinking, "This is the most interesting thing I've seen in all of Atlantic Canada. This is a hot space; it's a really interesting technology."

Van Bommel had some money to spend. He was new in his job as a venture capital investor for the Business Development Bank of Canada, better known as the BDC, the federal Crown corporation that supports small and growing companies. And Van Bommel knew the region. Born in Ontario, he was trained as a lawyer, and in time moved east with his Maritimer wife so she could be close to her family. He got an MBA at Dalhousie and stayed in the region.

He was recruited by Innovacorp, the Halifax venture capital outfit funded by the Nova Scotia government. He was later seconded to a startup called Ocean Nutrition, built by Halifax businessmen Robert Orr and John Risley, and a pioneer in producing Omega-3 dietary nutrients from fish oil. Then he was headhunted away by BDC. He was eager to make his mark for his new employer when he got an invitation from David Foord to attend the showcase event at UNB.

While Flood was pursuing Chris Newton around UNB, Van Bommel was quietly thinking he needed to do some more work on cybersecurity and, if possible, come back with a proposal. But when he did decide to act, he felt his messages to Q1 Labs were being ignored — and it happened more than once.

Van Bommel thought that may have reflected some sort of classic "New Brunswick first" attitude among the founders, augmented by their resistance to federal government involvement in the new company. Brian Flood admits he may have been playing hard-to-get and, even at that point, was hoping to tap the richer U.S. funds for the first venture capital round. Van Bommel also believes the Q1 gang underestimated how much he was willing to invest. "I wasn't looking at putting $250,000 in. I was looking at doing a significant financing to move it forward."

He concluded that as the new kid on the block, he needed a partner with some local roots. At Innovacorp he had worked with another venture capitalist, George Long, who had recently joined the New Brunswick Investment Management Corp., the firm that managed the money for a number of public pension plans in the province. It had great Maritime provenance, and it was open to the kind of deal Q1 represented.

NBIMC was going through a transition that was typical of public pension plans at that time. In the past, the plans were limited to a basket of very safe investments, including government treasury bills and bonds, but as a result generated relatively low yields. Public pensions were under a lot of pressure because of the aging of the Canadian population — which was even more critical in New Brunswick. Led by the Canada Pension Plan, the country's largest, they were creating separate independent entities that could invest in a broader pool of assets, including startup companies. NBIMC had followed that route.

So Van Bommel tipped off his old colleague that this Q1 Labs thing was interesting, just as Brian Flood was reaching out to the pension fund manager. Long and the president of NBIMC, John Sinclair, invited Flood and Newton to pitch their idea. Flood was known to them — John Sinclair had gone to UNB at the same time, and they had done alpine skiing together. Q1 fit the bill of the pension fund manager's objectives, which included looking for companies that were "pre-commercial." That is, these companies were still in the development stage but showing early sales success. Also, under Premier Bernard Lord the province had stepped up with a $1.5-million loan guarantee.

Sinclair and Long were impressed with the contracts, but they did their due diligence, while Brian Flood was on tenterhooks as the angels' money continued to drain away. But the fund manager finally agreed to join with BDC in providing the funding to keep the Flood-Newton dream alive.

In January 2003, Q1 Labs announced it had received about $3.3 million U.S. (close to $5 million Canadian at that date, with exchange rates heavily favouring the U.S. currency) in this Series A round of venture financing. They split the financing, with NBIMC coming in with a little more than half and the BDC with a little less.

It was a big moment in Brian Flood's money chase. The early angel investment was hope-and-prayer financing to develop a product that was in a raw pre-commercial stage. Van Bommel and NBIMC had provided the next phase of development to build a product aimed at widespread acceptance.

But this Series A financing was not the end. Flood figured he needed about $40 million U.S. in funding, maybe more, if he was going to hit a home run — the venture capital jargon for a huge payday, which might generate ten times the original investment.

At that point in the history of venture capital, that kind of money was hard to find in Canada, but it was attainable south of the border. Over the next six months, Flood led a frenetic cross-continent hunt for the funds that would keep Q1 Labs afloat. As he says, "We roared out of NB with $3.3 million in the bank and $30,000 in sales."

Flood was determined that he would be able to show the venture capitalists that he was landing sales in their own market of the United States. That led to two parallel tracks — approaching the venture capitalists with a compelling pitch and pursuing an aggressive sales effort with high-profile U.S. institutions and companies.

The VC chase was a hard grind, not just because the New Brunswickers were beginners at the game, but also because of Silicon Valley's regional myopia. When the founders of Q1 Labs illustrate the daunting challenges of raising money for companies from Canada's East Coast, they tell the story of when Sandy Bird and Brian Flood gave a geography lesson to the partners at Accel, one of the premier venture capital firms in Silicon Valley.

It all took place in an Accel boardroom in Palo Alto. In the middle of Flood's pitch about the product's virtues, one of the Accel senior partners asked, "Where does this technology come from?" Flood answered without hesitation that it came from "UNB."

"We don't invest in Nebraska," the partner grumbled, assuming "NB" was the abbreviation for the state best known for cornfields and John Deere tractors.

"Not Nebraska, it's New Brunswick," Flood explained patiently.

"Oh, New Jersey," the man replied, recalling that New Brunswick was the name of a New Jersey city. "Shouldn't you be looking for money in New York?"

"No, we're in Canada, just beyond the State of Maine," Flood answered, trying to get the conversation back on track.

New Brunswick was far away, on another coast and in another country, well beyond the range of even the weather maps on American TV. But the incident, retold many times in the province's tech circles, also defies the image of Silicon Valley as full of global entrepreneurs who sought out innovation anywhere it sprouted. In those days of the early 21st century, the denizens of Sand Hill Road could be quite parochial. They didn't like to venture outside the continental United States, or any place they couldn't drive to in a day, or fly to directly. Toronto might work for them but not East Coast Canada, or, for that matter, Nebraska.

The New Brunswickers were told time and time again that they couldn't make it in the United States. An Ontario-based financier told them, "you'll never raise money in the U.S." Just another wall to crash through for Brian Flood.

The Boston area held another significant pool of risk capital, one that would seem more welcoming to folks from the Maritimes, which is just up the Atlantic coast from the old New England port city. There had long been a tight relationship between Boston and the Canadian East Coast. In the early 20th century, Eastern Canadians flocked to Massachusetts to find better jobs in mills and factories and many stayed. Maritime families typically had some cousins living in Worcester or Framingham. Canadian companies did a lot of business in the area — Irving Oil provided a big share of Boston's petroleum needs — and everyone cheered for the Red Sox.

But the Boston venture capital scene was culturally different than its counterpart on the West Coast, more conservative and risk-averse. The Silicon Valley crowd was much more open to innovation and disruption. It was a freewheeling business climate, and it showed in the financings that came out of that culture — Apple, Google, Facebook. Boston was the realm of big old institutions. Even the local tech companies like Digital Equipment and Data General were relatively big and slower to adapt. (Digital's long-time CEO Ken Olsen once said that "the personal computer will fall flat on its face in business.") And all the creative thinkers coming out of MIT and Harvard couldn't entirely break that conservative cultural bias.

What's more, familiarity bred contempt. Bostonians were more likely to look down on their country cousins to the north. Ian Cavanagh saw that as Brian Flood told his famous stories, reeling people into his yarns of Beaverbrook and UNB, he faced challenges with the investors on the East Coast who were dismissive of Atlantic Canada. In addition, they were more conservative in nature, while "the West Coast was less analytical and more emotive."

Q1 also needed some traction on its U.S. sales. It was hiring salespeople south of the border, people with contacts and networks who could complement the pitches being made by Flood, and increasingly Sandy Bird. They started picking up big contracts they needed — not just with Willis Marti and Texas A&M but with Texas Tech and other schools.

Flood and his travelling band would be in Atlanta one day, Boston the next, then off to Chicago. They used every possible personal contact in their Rolodexes. Flood had an indirect line to Trevor Eyton, the well-connected Bay Street player who was part of the team of aggressive dealmakers in the service of billionaires Edward and Peter Bronfman. Eyton was on the board of Coca-Cola in Atlanta, so Flood landed a meeting with him in Toronto. He would bring along the whole gang of kids, Chris, Sandy and Dwight. But no one owned a business suit, so he dispatched them to a Fredericton tailor who fitted them out. They all went in to see Eyton and he gave them access to Coca-Cola, a big breakthrough, which resulted in a sale.

Then they heard from one of their new salespeople, who had just gained access to a seemingly unattainable prize. Harvard University is one of the richest repositories of intellectual property in the world, and by the late 1990s, a lot of that knowledge — from medical research to digital copies of ancient manuscripts — was available on its electronic network. But it was also a nightmare to try to protect that information from attack, shutdown and outright theft.

The university network extended far and wide, beyond the campus buildings, the hundreds of faculties, departments and affiliates, to a wider web of global contacts, encompassing half a million distinct internet addresses. And the social-media revolution just augmented the concerns of administrators. Indeed, the threats were huge, from both inside and outside the Harvard community.

The university had its own one-off solutions to specific issues, but there was no overall solution that gave the university a map of the network, highlighting areas where there were dangerous anomalies. In fact, there was some intellectual resistance from those who argued the network should be an open forum of free discussion, not subject to the purview of the university. Some opposed buying products from private-sector vendors. But in the late 1990s, as viruses such as Code Red and Ninja grew more and more sophisticated, there was a hunt for an overall solution that provided both useful data and essential protection.

"It quickly became evident that security had to be part of network operations," recalls Jay Tumas, then Harvard's manager of network operations, a role that included the oversight of the system's architecture and design. He had to find a solution that would be functionally effective within a tight budget. He somehow came across Q1 Labs and got in touch with one of its new salespeople in the Boston area. Tumas went to see a trial of the product, now called QRadar, and he signed on — and he got a good price that suited his tough financial overseers.

It was a big deal for Tumas and an even bigger deal for Q1, even though it had to cut the purchase price by more than half, all the way down to $43,000. But think of the marketing possibilities in saying that you had sold your product to Harvard — it opened doors in corporate America. Harvard MBAs ran many of the companies Brian Flood and the kids were targeting, and constituted the leaders of much of the U.S. venture capital community. You could walk in the door of a VC and say, "Your alma mater chose us, and so you have that assurance."

Two decades later, Jay Tumas is still excited by the memory of the Q1 technology. Now a senior sales engineer with a cybersecurity company, he recalls vividly that "QRadar was obviously the best product on the market." It delivered what he calls "instant visibility" to potential problems, with the ability to whittle down the reams of traffic and data, focusing on a few key anomalies that could break the system. And the reports of data usage were valuable in answering questions about the use of broadband and future requirements. "At Harvard, I was a network purist, who wanted good solid accurate statistics on network traffic data."

Harvard was a global institution, which made it open to buying a security product developed in a foreign country. What's more, Jay Tumas's mother Dorothy was a MacDonald from Inverness, Cape Breton. ("That's pretty rare," he chuckles, "a MacDonald from Nova Scotia.") It did not make any difference where the company was located as long as it had an 800 number he could call.

He bought more than a product; he was also welcomed into the culture of openness. The Q1 team invited him into the discussion of the technology's evolution. In return, the voluble Tumas was an evangelist: "I talked to a lot of prospective customers for them over the years." He eventually moved Harvard onto a competing platform, which offered a feature QRadar lacked, but he always saw the Q1 Labs deal as a breakthrough relationship.

Q1's game was again seriously elevated when it started breaking into the U.S. government market. Another new sales hire got them into the U.S. Army and the Energy Department, as well as private companies like the *New York Times* and Sun Trust Banks. One of the challenges, Brian Flood recalls, was answering the questions *why should I buy it, and why should I care?* That was where the association with UNB was vital because the university allowed the Q1 technicians to gain access to its network and demonstrate the software in real time. Q1 people could show U.S. State Department types how an attack might happen. When the U.S. government chooses your security technology, that is something you can really ride in your marketing and sales.

It helped that Sandy Bird was coming to the fore as a salesman — in their sales pitches, Flood was the starter and Bird was the closer. "I called him the Chief Travelling Officer," Flood says. But the travel was more thrilling than they had hoped. The company was getting up to $800,000 in annualized revenue but burning through $200,000 a month. The U.S. venture capitalists were warming to their story, but Q1

Q1 team at UNB's Old Arts Building in 2003: front row, left to right,
Spencer, Bird, Flood, Newton. UNB president John McLaughlin
at centre, top row (Courtesy of Dwight Spencer)

was in a horse race with other cyber hopefuls, such as Arbor Networks,
which had come out of research at the University of Michigan.

The team scored a big breakthrough in landing VC interview no.
60 — it got to pitch its story to the world's largest venture capital firm,
NEA Ventures, which was led by its managing partner, Scott Sandell.
It was a high-powered meeting replete with an NEA partner who was
the Nobel Laureate in physics for 1978, Arno Penzias.

Flood went through his spiel. He referenced Beaverbrook, Churchill
and UNB, pointing out, for example, that NASA had cited UNB's
survey engineers for their mapping work ahead of the first moon
landing. At one point, Penzias interrupted to say, "So what do you do?"
Sandy Bird asked Penzias if he was familiar with a data flow coming
off the Cisco router. Penzias said no, he wasn't. Bird — who had no
university degree — went to the white board and took Penzias through
a highly technical outline of how Q1's product could monitor that data
flow. It was like the moment in the movie *Good Will Hunting* when

the unschooled savant, the MIT janitor, walks over to the blackboard and proceeds to solve a complex math theorem.

It was great theatre, but in the end, NEA said it would have to think about it. Bird and Flood didn't have that time. Money was running out.

The Q1 duo took an East Coast meeting with Polaris Partners, a VC firm in Waltham, just west of Boston. The Polaris partner they met was Mike Hirshland, a newly enlisted venture capitalist with an unconventional background. He had been a defensive end on the Harvard Crimson's 1987 Ivy League championship football squad. He had come out of Harvard Law with great prospects of a legal career and clerked at the Supreme Court with Anthony Kennedy, the conservative Reagan-appointed justice who later became the swing vote in the more polarized court of the early 2000s. Hirshland then moved to the Senate judicial committee where he got caught up in the efforts to break up Microsoft and its hold on the PC market.

It was heady stuff, but Hirshland was discouraged by the superficial politics of Washington, which was much more theatre than substance. Then he went to hear a talk by California's legendary venture capitalist John Doerr, and he was blown away by the possibilities. He concluded that helping launch new ventures would be a lot more fun than his likely future in corporate law. He made the move into venture capital and came aboard at Polaris. Even though he was joining a Boston firm, he saw himself more as a West Coast type of investor, willing to take a chance on bold ideas and creative people. And he liked to work with the early-stage companies.

Hirshland seemed to be a natural fit with a firm like Q1, and Flood went through the pitch and pulled out all the stops. Hirshland took it all in, but he was not convinced. He saw a lot of showmanship, but he really couldn't grasp the product differentiation that set Q1 apart. He began to canvas experts to validate the Q1 story by looking at the product and the business model — people who could tell him if this thing was for real.

As Hirshland pondered, the now desperate Brian Flood and Sandy Bird were gearing up for their next venture capital presentation on the other side of the continent— at Menlo Ventures on Sandy Hill Road in Silicon Valley. This was a big one. At its rate of spending Q1 would be out of money in a little over two months and the dream would be dead.

6. Here Come the Americans

Brian Flood was watching Sonja Hoel very intently, and he was not happy with what he was seeing. Hoel, a Silicon Valley venture capitalist, was being very quiet as Flood and Sandy Bird pitched her on investing in Q1 and its QRadar technology. It was 20 minutes into their presentation, and she had not asked a single question.

There was a lot at stake here — Hoel and her firm, Menlo Ventures, represented Flood and Bird's 64th meeting with venture capitalists. They were running out of time.

They were also learning the realities of venture capital, which appears to be a numbers-driven business based on hard stats — run rates, internal rates of return, market penetration, potential exit values. Indeed, these are all important but, as with many things in life, it is really about personal connections.

Brian and Sandy had no U.S. networks, but one of their angel investors did. Ian Cavanagh had worked in the Valley, and he was the kind of energetic networker that could get them through doors. He got them through doors at Menlo Ventures, where Sonja Hoel was one of the rising stars. And Sonja knew people on both coasts from her days at Harvard and with a Boston investment firm.

Ian Cavanagh, like Flood, was worried, but for a different reason. He knew that to pitch an idea to VCs, you need to follow the tried and true formula: present a certain number of slides, answer the questions and get out. Don't mess with the system. "VCs often think simplistically, and I told Brian to please follow the formula," Cavanagh says.

No chance that would happen. Brian was famous for his digressions into New Brunswick history, the saga of Beaverbrook and vignettes like the story of U.S. president John F. Kennedy's visit to Saint John. "If it's good enough for JFK, it should be good enough for you," he would say. This time was no different. Flood had begun with an extensive survey of the history of New Brunswick. "Sandy and I were shaking our heads, thinking, 'Jesus, Brian, follow the plan,'" Cavanagh recalls.

It turns out that Hoel's silence was an expression of concentration, not rejection. When the presentation ended, Cavanagh went up to her to apologize for the rambling presentation. He was relieved to learn that Hoel loved the quirky pitch and loved the product. She announced that she "got it" and would urge her partners to make the decision to invest in Q1. At one point, she suggested Menlo might do the whole Series B financing, an amount of maybe $10 million U.S.

Hoel, a blonde woman of Norwegian-American background who had grown up in Virginia, was hardly new to the world of cybersecurity investment. Still in her 30s, she had amassed a formidable record, starting fresh out of school and working for venture capital group TA Associates in Boston. One day, as recounted in the book *Alpha Girls* — about pioneering female venture capitalists — she saw an item in *PC Magazine* featuring a company that had cornered 60 per cent of the personal computer antivirus market and was about to sell itself to a bigger firm, Symantec, for $20 million.

Intrigued, Hoel tracked down the company founder John McAfee and was brassy enough to offer him a better deal, with the chance to get his growth capital and keep half the firm. McAfee agreed, ditched the Symantec deal and went public a year later for $42 million, from which the company spring-boarded into a huge valuation. After two years, as libertarian politics assumed a larger part of his attention, McAfee left his business to become a political activist prone to conspiracy theories. But the company continued, and in 2010 Intel bought McAfee Inc. for close to $8 billion U.S.

Sonja Hoel Perkins,
pictured here in 2020,
was Q1's breakthrough
U.S. investor in 2003
(Courtesy of the Perkins Fund)

But Hoel didn't get to ride that particular value rocket. When she initiated the McAfee contact, she was almost out the door at TA and on her way to Harvard for an MBA, which she thought she needed to become a venture capital partner some day. Her first home run came with her sitting in the stands. But she stuck to her dream and, after Harvard, decamped to California in July 1994 to join Menlo Ventures as a junior associate. This was where it was all happening.

Shrugging off the ingrained sexism of the Valley, Hoel became an astute investor who did some important deals, including cybersecurity offerings. She had, however, moved up a notch in her search. The cybersecurity industry was quickly broadening, looking for not just tweaks but wider protection. She wanted solutions that would fix problems, instead of just adding another security feature to a network. She looked for products that could turn the entire network into something more secure and less hackable.

This goal reflected both what businesses needed and what she felt in her heart. She had strong feelings about the role of security generally. "I think the biggest threat our society has is cyber-terrorism," she explained to me. "I've always thought that. For a while, it was kind of protecting networks and data," but as the threats got "bigger and bigger and cleverer, it frustrated me how much money was spent preventing bad problems but it was not finding new solutions." And she added, "As a woman, I was instinctively looking at safety and security, looking at how to be safe."

She felt the Q1 product took the game up to a new level. "I thought it was fascinating that you could actually see where stuff is happening on the network. It was an alarm bell, as if someone had just broken into your garage and was stealing your car. You could see on the network that someone is attacking your database or that there was weird behaviour," stuff that might be local in nature and not necessarily global.

"There were not a lot of companies able to do that. Most kinds of security programs were trying to keep the bad guys out — such as firewalls [and notices of] vulnerabilities — but once the bad guys got in, you really did not have a chance. This was being a lot more proactive."

But Hoel noticed Q1 had a challenge: "It had a pretty good engineering team and early success with customers," she observed, "but one of the concerns of the company was it was in Canada. How was it going to be able to hire a world-class management?"

There it was in a nutshell — the Canadian penalty, or more specifically, the New Brunswick penalty. It might be okay if the head office were in Toronto, which enjoyed direct air connections with the rest of the continent and where a cadre of proven technology managers could be found. But New Brunswick came with uncertain management depth and fragmented transportation connections to the rest of North America. You might be able to fly to Boston and New York, but anything else required acrobatic connections.

Sonja Hoel was interested in doing the deal, but she worried the company would have to be moved. Not only that, she observed that Brian Flood himself believed it could not stay in New Brunswick. At some point during the conversation, the Canadian team mentioned it had met Polaris and Mike Hirshland.

It turned out that Hoel knew Hirshland — knew him well. A friend of Hoel had roomed with Hirshland after his graduation from Harvard. There might be opportunity to team up. And Hirshland had been doing his own due diligence, and was coming around to thinking this Q1 Labs thing might work out.

But who would run the company? It is unclear exactly how Shaun McConnon came into the picture. He was certainly known to Sonja Hoel, who had once considered investing in a company McConnon had headed. He was also familiar to Polaris. And McConnon, in his late 50s, had a track record of cashing out big from cybersecurity startups. He had just come out of his second company, making lots of money for the VCs and himself. In total he had generated $400 million U.S. in proceeds from the exits of his two companies. VCs love these kinds of numbers and, despite their reputation for risk-taking, they love to work with people who have been through the startup tunnel and come out the other end. And he was available, biding his time at his home in Wayland, Massachusetts, just outside Boston.

As Hoel observed, Flood and Bird recognized they needed a Shaun McConnon–type too. This was the end of the line for the startup guys — here is where the pros came in. The future of Q1 Labs was hatched at McConnon's home in Wayland. The two Canadians made a kind of pilgrimage to try to convince him to become Flood's replacement, the second CEO of Q1 Labs; to keep from disturbing McConnon's wife, the conversation moved outside to the pool house.

That meeting was the impetus for McConnon's deep dive into Q1. McConnon liked Flood and his commitment, and he really liked Sandy Bird with his ability to explain and sell. He would never move to New Brunswick, of course, but the VCs were thinking Boston would be a better location, close to Polaris's oversight and to potential markets.

Hoel agreed with the move. "I'd never done that before, where we moved the company before we made the investment." She insists that she would never mandate the replacement of CEOs as a condition for investment. "As a VC I would never say I would invest in you, but you just can't run it anymore. That is the kiss of death — no one would want to work with you."

Her recollection is that Brian Flood made it clear he had never been a CEO before, and he was thinking he could not grow the company out of Canada. Says Hoel, "It is hard when you are not in a place of technology to get the right salespeople, the right marketing people. He made the choice and he didn't have the ego."

What's more, "The CEO we chose was not another version of Brian but someone who had proven himself two times in the security space and really knew that space. And the engineering staff stayed in Canada with Sandy up there running it." She thought it was one of first tech companies to use this outsource model, separating engineering from other operations. "You had incredible Canadian engineers working with American managers."

Meeting Hoel introduced Sandy Bird to a whole new kind of energy. He had noted that venture capitalists were often circular talkers. They never really said no to a pitch. It was often, "When you get someone else interested, we'd love to be in with them." The startup founders could spend their whole lives going around in circles, talking to VCs and never getting to the next step. At some point, they had to ask the question: Would you lead this round? And then they would get the real answer: Well, no.

It was different when they found Sonja Hoel. The velocity of questions accelerated, with sudden calls from Hoel to Bird's cellphone at his New Brunswick cottage on weekends. It was getting very real.

Right at the end, a Canadian alternative emerged. This was Ventures West from British Columbia, a respected pioneer in Canada's still-undeveloped VC industry. The Ventures West representative, Barry Gekiere, came forward with a term sheet — an offer — that was very attractive too. In fact, Ventures West was offering a slightly sweeter financial deal. It would have been a gentler transition and would not as likely have overturned the Canadian management team or resulted in moving the company.

But Brian Flood wanted to see his own self-immolation, and he wanted to richly reward his earliest investors, who might continue to back innovation in the province. So Q1 Labs picked the U.S. offer. Gekiere was puzzled and approached Flood later. Why was he turned down? Then he saw who was involved — the industry reach of the Polaris-Menlo Ventures team, and particularly Sonja Hoel. Gekiere could see why Flood and company made the choice they did.

Gerry Pond was torn by the dilemma. He was now chairman of Q1 Labs, and he would only vote on the choice of venture options if the other directors ended up in a tie. But he was part of the discussion. "It got down to, do you think our future would be better with U.S. investors or with Canadian investors in this kind of business?" The thinking was that most of the cybersecurity companies were U.S.-based and that's where the industry was headquartered. There were no Canadian players beyond a few startups like Q1. So the future would be better if Q1 threw in its lot with American investors, who could also deliver over the long haul.

But for Pond, the issue struck at the heart of the Atlantic Canada economic challenge: "When you are behind, how do you get ahead? At what point do you draw the line in the sand and say that for the economic future of the region and the country, we're going to keep this one in Canada? Maybe we won't get the same return short-term, but this is a company we want to build on, to be one of the foundations of a Canadian economy."

To this day, he believes if you keep playing the short-term game, you will never build a sustainable homegrown industry. If it's always a case of taking the best deal in the short term, which is always better for investors and their estates, how does the economy benefit?

"Gerry and I had philosophical differences about the U.S. venture capital," Ian Cavanagh recalls. "Gerry didn't like the fact that U.S. guys were calling the shots and the head office would be in Boston. I felt it was great to have a piece of a bigger pie, but the control issue bothered Gerry." But after all the talk, the fundamental question was where did you have the best chance of promoting and growing the Q1 product? "It had the best chance in the United States," Pond agreed.

The official announcement came on November 17, 2003, when Q1 Labs announced it had closed $14.4 million U.S. in Series B funding led by Polaris Partners and Menlo Ventures. It also announced the appointment of Shaun McConnon as CEO and emphasized his sterling track record with two previous startups. Q1 had never been a Canadian-registered company, but its core management had been based in Canada along with the Fredericton research and development program. Now the head office would move to Waltham, where Polaris was based. But R&D would remain in Fredericton and that was the crucial piece of the deal, in the eyes of the Canadian founders.

CRN, a tech news service, quoted Sonja Hoel: "This [product] addresses a real pain point by visually assessing the network and giving the administrator a view of the network and vulnerabilities. A picture is worth a thousand words." Which is exactly what Chris Newton was thinking five years earlier when he first conceived of his graphic product while labouring away in the dark corridors of University of New Brunswick.

It was a great thumbs-up to UNB and the province, but it also felt kind of empty for Canadian nationalists beyond the tech world. Was this another example of Americans coming in and grabbing assets, like they had done before with nickel, timber and gold? What did we really gain? It seemed like a classic story of Canadian resources — material or intellectual — being lost forever by taking the easy money. And yet Q1 Labs was not, strictly speaking, a Canadian company — it was a Delaware entity. And the global market economy is a harsh beast. You can do little to stand in the way of its inexorable conclusions: the Americans had the deep pockets and the existence of a rich cybersecurity ecosystem that could make this thing a success.

Venture capital itself is a double-edged sword. It provides the money to grow, yes, but there is that cost: the loss of managerial independence, the breakup of the founding team, the severing of relationships. Driven first by enthusiasm and adrenalin, the Q1 team always knew there was the possibility — indeed, the likelihood — that the VCs would push them to the sidelines, replaced by more seasoned managers, who would impose their own people, their own systems, their own ideas. Among the founding cast, some would leave but also some would rise in the ranks.

As news of the deal settled in, back in New Brunswick, there was a sense of satisfaction but also uncertainty. In the days after the sale decision, Jeff White, the rangy Newfoundlander and ex–college basketball player who was chief financial officer, recalls sitting around the meeting table with his colleagues and asking, "Okay, who goes and who stays?" White knew he could go, and the incoming team would want its own CFO in Waltham. White was fine with that — he was a veteran of the startup world, having earned his spurs with iMagic. And he would keep coming back, the next time as CFO for a company that did not even exist then, a social-media monitoring firm called Radian6.

Q1 maintained a dual-company structure: an American parent company with a separate Canadian subsidiary, a vehicle that allowed the much-diluted Canadian VCs to continue to keep their money in a registered Canadian entity. Flood moved into the figurehead role of the CEO of the Canadian subsidiary, but that was just a transition on the way out the door. Flood pledged he would never fall victim to "founderitis," the malady whereby founders cling to control, even when they have built the company beyond their ability to run it.

It was a scenario that could be spelled out this way: "You built a nice little castle here in your sandbox — now get out of the playground, the big kids are taking over."

7. Congratulations, You're Fired!

Shaun McConnon's face breaks into a smile. He's thinking about a comment he often gets — that he has a little chip on his shoulder. His response: "No, I don't have a little chip — I've got a big chip." He explains that he was brought up in a dysfunctional household with volatile parents. His father, who had been a tank commander under General Patton in the Second World War, drank like crazy. His combative Czech-American mother and hard-drinking Irish-American father fought like tigers. Shaun was born in Brooklyn, and at 16 he had to leave his Flatbush friends when his family moved to Virginia.

"But I couldn't take the bullshit anymore and the fighting in the house," McConnon says. So he turned around and hitchhiked back to New York, hundreds of miles away. But why the chip? He stayed in New York for three and a half months and nobody in his family called him. "That really pissed me off."

So he slunk back home to Virginia, not to be reunited with family but to graduate from high school and get away from them once and for all. He went to Roanoke College where he studied biochemistry. He thought of becoming a veterinarian, but he had to abandon that dream because of severe asthma. He found a job with the U.S. Food and Drug Administration but was fired after he fell asleep at his desk and, when admonished, responded to his manager with an unkind remark. He sold pharmaceuticals and hated it before landing a job he liked — at a computer company, RCA Computers, an offshoot of the fabled TV and recording empire. But that company got sold, and the new buyer didn't need him.

"I'm 24 years old and I've been let go three times. I'm going, 'What is wrong with me? I think I'm smart, I think I'm sharp, I've got a good degree and I've just been fired three times. I'm not feeling too good about myself.'" But he now had a track record with computers and ended up at Honeywell and then Data General, where he built his reputation as a skilled computer salesman. It was then that he found his home at newly formed Sun Microsystems.

Founded in 1982, Sun was the quintessential creature of Silicon Valley, a computer hardware maker that also developed the popular Java computing language. The company name came not from the hot California sun but as an acronym for Stanford University Network. It was the brainchild of Andy Bechtolsheim, a Stanford doctoral candidate in electrical engineering and computer science, and Vinod Khosla, an electrical engineer and Stanford MBA grad. (Bechtolsheim would later write the first cheque for the Google founders, which is how the Valley operates.)

They teamed up with another Stanford MBA, Scott McNealy, and added Berkeley-trained engineer Bill Joy as a co-founder. McNealy became CEO and the public face of Sun Microsystems, a brash salesman with a huge personality. He hired Shaun McConnon as his East Coast sales manager.

McConnon proved to be a skilled manager whose region accounted for half of Sun's sales, and he went on to get Sun established in Australia. But by this time Sun had got very big, and there was savage competition for the top jobs. McConnon's end came in a showdown over who would become the company's top sales vice president. McConnon was in Australia when he got a visit from a senior Sun officer. He figured this would be his triumphal entry into a senior role, but instead the message was that the company would give him a bit of time to look for his next opportunity. There was no room for him in the shuffle.

Reeling from the injustice, he went home to stew and started drinking a lot, but his wife, Bonnie, the product of a Tennessee farm upbringing, wouldn't let him wallow in his despond. "She came into my office and, using a Tennessee expression, said 'You can just sit in here and let the pigs eat you, or you can get off your ass and go out there and show them. And the only way you're going to show them, Shaun, is to be successful.'" That was the end of his purgatory.

He channelled a lot of that inherited chippiness into blunt talk and hard realism as he moved into the world of startups. He was approached first by someone who knew someone at a cybersecurity startup called Raptor that needed some help. Soon he was CEO, and he liked it. He could see his role as a mentor and strategist who could hire people to fill in his knowledge gaps. He sold Raptor to Cisco Systems, and he discovered he was good at selling companies. Then he joined another startup called Okena, and the same pattern ensued — build it and sell it. He was an aggressive negotiator, both for his adopted company and his own interests. When he came in with money and a track record, he always sought 10 per cent of the company.

He was looking for his next gig when Polaris and Sonja Hoel came calling. He liked the look of Q1 Labs, but the company had insignificant revenue and, in his harsh assessment, no management at all. Brian Flood was not a tech CEO, he concluded, but he appreciated that the company was being carried on Brian's back.

When you mention Gerry Pond's name, McConnon bangs his fists together. It was perhaps inevitable that the two warriors, almost exactly the same age, both mentors and investors, pioneers in their own regions and sectors, both let loose by their long-time employers but still with lots of fuel in the tank, would bump up against each other. They had different styles, but both were capable of blunt talk. Think of Pond as your lovable old uncle who could be a bit grouchy at times but always remembered you at Christmas. McConnon is your mom's second husband, a know-it-all outsider who bursts noisily into family get-togethers, but who in the end, you had to admit, had some good ideas. Pond and McConnon were original tough-love characters, both of them.

Pond, as Q1 chair, was naturally loyal to the people he had brought along. And there was a bit of the old Canadian-American sandpaper tension. Pond was on his way out as the American venture capitalists got to pick the new board. You'd think far-sighted VCs would want to work with someone like Gerry Pond, but he was considered expendable.

But Pond was also no innocent. He had been shoved aside after the phone company mega-merger. And he knew the arithmetic. McConnon, Pond says, "had done the exit to the big guys from a small company, a startup, and made a lot of money. He was well-regarded by the venture capitalists. They like to see people like that. He knew all the players in the security business."

To be fair, Pond says, McConnon was the right person for the day. "It's just that he had a personality that I didn't get along with." He was abrasive? "Abrasive is an understatement."

McConnon's view of Pond is simple, as well: "He's got a big ego, so do I." And these two strong personalities were perhaps fated to clash, given the circumstances.

McConnon's immediate need was management depth, particularly in the marketing realm. He didn't have to look far. Brendan Hannigan, a bright young Irish immigrant, was part of Polaris's bench strength of proven managers and entrepreneurs, who could be parachuted into a company in which the venture capital firm had invested. Hannigan, a graduate of University College Dublin in computer science, had lived in the United States since the early 1990s and had a broad feel for the industry, having worked at Forrester, the big research outfit.

McConnon met Hannigan in the lobby of Polaris's offices, went out to dinner with him and liked him right away, not the least for their shared Irish roots.

As executive vice president for marketing, Hannigan helped guide McConnon through the repositioning of Q1 Labs and QRadar. Both recognized there was no future for Q1 Labs unless it broadened its offerings. At the moment, it sat in a subsector of cybersecurity known

Veteran American tech executive Shaun McConnon became CEO of Q1 Labs in 2003, quickly putting his imprint on the company
(Courtesy of Shaun McConnon)

as anomaly detection. Hannigan and McConnon concluded that to grow and thrive, they had to extend their reach into a broader platform. It was much harder than they thought, and a project that was supposed to take two years consumed double that time. And the venture capitalists would get a little tetchy over that period.

Brian and Carolyn Flood remember going to a Christmas party at McConnon's home and hearing the new CEO proclaim that it would be a quick exit — 18 months to three years. A large player in the industry had already expressed an interest in buying, but it was too early to sell. That would turn out to be optimistic.

They continued to hire and promote people to fill in the gaps, including some New Brunswickers. The company hired a young engineering professional named Daniella DeGrace. She had the right track record, after years in the software business in Quebec and New Brunswick, including six years working in Paris. She was another graduate of Gerry Pond's iMagic team.

DeGrace was savvy enough to understand the power dynamics at Q1 Labs. She now believes that Shaun McConnon liked the novelty of a young woman in a senior job. "I don't think he had many female executives in his team, and so for him, that was a little bit of an element of pride that he had one." Her assessment of McConnon is that "he's an aggressive guy, he's very well-connected, knows where the money is." McConnon had a very clear goal — to sell the company at a targeted price.

As for Brendan Hannigan, "He was incredibly bright, a strong leader and really good at building the operations. Incredibly disciplined and structured." Brian Flood had already employed Chris Fanjoy, a native of the Miramichi with a strong tech resumé as a builder of MapQuest, the early online mapping product. He would bring a lot of the formal management rigour that the new majority owners felt they needed.

DeGrace notes that in the software industry, "there are a lot of different philosophies on how you're developing your product and what you believe your culture should be." The new organization felt it had to force discipline on the fledgling firm, and a culture clash was inevitable. It was like taming a beast, she says. "In the first phase, you're on a wild horse and you like the wild horse and you don't want to be tamed."

The taming went on. Within two years, the board and top management decided there would have to be cuts, including some of the Canadian old guard. McConnon did not get to the top of Boston's greasy pole by being a pussy cat. He and his team looked around and wondered why they effectively had two chief technology officers — Sandy Bird being the official CTO, and Chris Newton as the design guru in Fredericton. But Sandy Bird was willing to travel and Newton was not. And Newton was pulling down a fat salary for the times — estimated at $130,000 by Newton today.

Looking back, Newton understands the dynamics. "There was this big pile of energy and money put in, and they expected a certain trajectory." But a year or so later, "not much had changed despite the new CEO and the money, and that made the board nervous. All this was supposed to catapult us and they decided to make a bunch of changes and cut costs. I was one of the targets."

One day a senior manager walked into Newton's office in Fredericton and informed him he was being shown the door. Chris Newton, the most successful innovator in the recent history of the Maritimes, essentially was fired by the company he had created in the corridors of the UNB Computing Centre.

Looking back, McConnon says he had to let Newton go, "because he wasn't doing anything. And it wasn't a firing. It was a separation." McConnon says it was a matter of, "Hey Chris, you're not doing anything, your options are done. He was already thinking about the next company and doing all that stuff."

The fired founder — or at least the "separated" founder — is one of the classic tales of high technology. Many exiled founders, in their heart of hearts, welcome the transition so they can go back to their first love, developing things. Others openly seek their revenge. Apple's Steve Jobs is the role model for the revenge-seekers — he was shunted aside by the man he had hired, his CEO replacement, the former soft-drink marketer John Sculley. Suddenly tossed aside like yesterday's news, he went out to start new companies. And when Apple faltered some more, he returned rejuvenated to shove Sculley to the sidelines. Sweet revenge, indeed.

In Walter Isaacson's biography, released a few weeks after Jobs's death in 2011, the tech visionary recalled his feeling when in May 1985 he was told that he had no major strategic role in the company he had founded. "I felt like I had been punched, the air knocked out of me and I couldn't breathe."

It was the same sensation for Chris Newton. "It was a pretty big punch to the gut," Newton says. "I didn't see it coming either, which is not fun. It was my baby, so I was kinda oblivious to the fact that it could really even happen. I just took it as a lesson: it was business. It was my baby, but I sold it for investor money. Conceptually it was still mine, but not really."

Years later Shaun McConnon recognizes Newton's dismay. He had felt the same emotions at Sun Microsystems when he was let go: "Leave me alone. Let me be angry."

Newton says he felt like the ballplayer who helps his team win the

World Series and then the team releases him. His parting shot would be, "See you back here in the World Series next year, asshole." The firing was, at that time, "the worst day ever, and I felt pretty screwed over it, and all that jazz. But it turned out to be the best thing that could have happened. I was just stubborn enough to say, 'Okay, I will build another one and won't make the same mistakes.'"

Newton had by now laid out a few rules for his next startup: no large expensive product installations, no flying squads of salespeople and engineering teams on the road, no long sales cycles, no lumpy booking of revenues on the financial statement. Instead, the next company would buy into the new model of software as a service (SaaS), making programs available off the cloud as a subscription service, rather than a one-time "thing" to buy. Instead of elaborate onsite demos, customers would go on a website and do their own demos. They would sign up by the month, and if they stopped paying, they would lose the service. But if they liked it, most of them would continue to ante up, creating a nice fluid revenue stream.

A lot of other people were thinking the same way. One was Marc Benioff, the grandson of Russian immigrants whose father had run a men's store in downtown San Francisco. A brilliant technology salesman, he had worked at Oracle with its founder Larry Ellison, as Ellison's protege. But he later went off to form his own company, Salesforce, first with Ellison's blessing — and participation — but then in a bitter breakup between these two strong personalities. Salesforce's business model was built on the premise that you could download software out of the cloud.

Salesforce was founded in 1999, and Benioff and his co-founder Parker Harris led it into an initial share offering in 2004. Benioff was on a course that would bring him face-to-face with Chris Newton and his dreams. Benioff had this idea of the "marketing cloud," a broad platform that, in Salesforce's own definition, could consolidate customer relationship management in a single location, in a way that allowed personalized approaches to customers.

Meanwhile, Chris Newton's blue-sky thinking lifted him out of his funk. The angry stage was soon replaced by the get-busy phase. Newton was as always devouring information, looking for patterns. He became familiar with the "blogosphere," the proliferating legions of forums, blogs and posts that constituted the early days of social media. Facebook was still small at the time, and Twitter had yet to emerge. Some saw Newton's interest as a continuation of his study of flows: he was watching how ideas gain momentum and travel across the internet.

Five years after co-founding Q1, he was a bit older in years — a veteran of 33 — but infinitely older in self-knowledge. So he did what any New Brunswick technology startup founder would do when hitting a pause in their career. He heard from Gerry Pond, and he drove down to Saint John to see him. Could lightning strike again?

8. The Codefather and His Kids

The sleepy little village of Rothesay, New Brunswick, is one of the most deceptive communities in Canada. Under the cloak of a prim and proper Maritime village, of large but not over-the-top homes, tidy lawns, a village green and the twinkling waters of the Kennebecasis River, there swirls a maelstrom of wealth, influence and family upheaval.

This is Power Town, New Brunswick, the affluent bedroom community for gritty Saint John. Rothesay's quiet leafy streets are just a few miles away, but a world removed from the old port city with its stew of smells, smoke and steam, from the jumble of traffic around the Reversing Falls to those who scramble for a living on the mean streets of the city's south end.

Cynics around the province say that people who make their money from the grit and grime of Saint John steal away each night to the pretty little towns that surround the city, the most prominent of which is Rothesay. This is where the leaders of the forestry branch of the mighty Irving family own homes, the site of a private school that educates children of the local elite and close to yacht and rowing clubs where liaisons — both commercial and romantic — are hatched.

Rothesay is where, on July 14, 2011, police raided the home of stockbroker Dennis Oland on suspicions that a week earlier he had killed his father, Richard, a senior member of the Moosehead Brewery family, in his downtown office. It led to a murder charge of which Dennis was eventually acquitted eight years later, after a marathon of trials that agonized the Oland family. It fed the churning gossip mills of the province and disturbed the tranquility of Rothesay with the prying visits of out-of-town journalists and rubbernecking locals.

Elsewhere in Rothesay, down a little road that ends at the Kennebecasis River, you find Brian Flood's attractive waterside home. A stone's throw away from the Flood home, across the railroad tracks, there sits a tidy two-storey house along another quiet lane. It is solid but not imposing, befitting the unprepossessing standards of New Brunswick's establishment.

This is the residence of Gerry Pond, the most influential networker, mentor and technology power player in the province — indeed, in the Maritimes. If the McCains, Irvings and Sobeys are the Codfathers, surely Pond is the Codefather. There are other tech titans who through financial power and force of personality tower over a region — telecom giant Terry Matthews and, more recently, Shopify's Tobias Lutke in Ottawa, Jim Balsillie and Mike Lazaridis of BlackBerry fame in Waterloo — but few do it through such tireless exercise of networks and mentoring as Gerry Pond, who is not fabulously rich but quite comfortable.

After he was bumped from the chair position at Q1 Labs, Pond didn't waste a lot of time licking his wounds. He was busy forging his own identity in his post-NBTel incarnation. He had founded a technology firm, Mariner Partners, with some old NBTel veterans — Curtis Howe, the former chief technology officer; Bob Justason, the one-time engineering VP, and Jack Travis, an ex-president. Originally, Mariner had the mandate to run a telecom company in the Bahamas, but the deal foundered. Instead, the company was building a good business as a consulting and software development firm.

Pond had a bigger vision. He could see his new role as a change-maker, a continuation of his mission at NBTel. But this time, he would not be an "intrapreneur," creating little cells inside a large company, but a roving champion of independent entrepreneurs within a dense web of outside connections. Mariner would be at the centre of a cluster of companies, many in the Saint John River Valley, or the East Valley,

Gerry Pond shifted from the role of telephone company executive to becoming the most important angel investor and startup catalyst in Atlantic Canada (Courtesy of Paul Darrow)

as he called it, as opposed to the West Valley in Palo Alto. He and his partners would invest as angels, and would mentor and at times actively run companies as "entrepreneurs in residence," as godparents to the younger founders he counselled and supported — and constantly challenged.

Veteran innovation catalyst Laura Kilcrease does not know Gerry Pond but she admires his type. She feels this breed of business connector is absolutely essential to the development of innovation ecosystems — and Kilcrease knows how to build ecosystems. Born in England, she married a Texan and ended up several decades ago in Austin, the capital of the freewheeling Lone Star state.

The region had always been subject to wild swings in the dominant energy economy. And yet there was the potential to diversify the economy, building on a rich profusion of educational institutions around Austin — from the massive University of Texas to a large community college system.

Yet none of this was being connected when she came to town. Landing a finance job with a startup, she became a volunteer in the business community, working to build Austin as a technology counterpoise to the dominant oil and gas economy. She founded a pioneering technology incubator, one of the first in the United States, and helped form a vigorous early angel investor network.

Recently she has turned her attention northward. Today she runs Alberta Innovates, a provincially funded incubator based in Edmonton and aimed at bringing some of that thinking to Canada's energy linchpin. She points out that energy-rich Alberta has a lot of different technology options, both inside and outside the dominant oil industry. For example, research at the University of Alberta has made the Edmonton region one of Canada's leaders in artificial-intelligence (AI) professionals.

To build a tech ecosystem, Kilcrease says, "You need a godfather or a godmother," a Gerry Pond figure who acts as a role model in taking risks and lending a helping hand. "Humans don't like to take risk; they need to know someone is supporting what they're doing. It may not be with money, although sometimes it is. Maybe with expertise. Maybe an hour's meeting. Maybe a cup of coffee. Maybe a referral."

In many cases, it is simply the example of someone who believes in starting and investing in new companies, and has been successful. The thinking is, "So if they believe, why shouldn't I give it a go?"

She warns that building a strong ecosystem does not happen overnight — now considered in the top three or four tech centres in the U.S., Austin took about 25 years to build its own ecosystem of small and large companies, universities, angel investors, professionals and suppliers. But it happened because local business figures got other people engaged. "It also comes down to culture and the people, and their willingness to do things not for themselves but for the greater good, as well. Now, they may ultimately benefit, but it has to be beyond 'what's good for me?'"

Gerry Pond has the scars and the credibility, but he can't do everything. He's got to bring others to the table. And Pond has shown a gift for doing this, among people in his NBTel-Mariner group like Bob Neal, Jeff White, Bob Justason and Ian Cavanagh. You sometimes hear that he is less inclined to reach outside the region, to venture capitalists and connectors in other regions, who are crucial if Atlantic Canada is to escape the insularity that has been its downfall at times. Yet if you mention his name in business circles elsewhere, there is recognition that he is a name, a brand, that is admired.

Pond is called a lot of things, kind and caring but also crotchety and cantankerous, stubbornly contrarian in his thinking. (That's by the people who love him.) His personality is a little different than normally found in Atlantic business circles. He can be quirky-funny, with his quips and asides, but devastatingly honest. He can ask the hard questions, driving people crazy with his bluntness, but he is also unflinchingly loyal to his people and his province. Gerry's kids have followed him through every twist and turn in his business life, starting with NBTel and iMagic, then into a series of ventures he backed with his money and connections, and through a series of incubators and accelerators he founded or participated in. The Cult of Gerry is powerful and pervasive.

David Shipley, a cybersecurity company founder in Fredericton, remembers hitting an important milestone in his company, called Beauceron, and waiting for Pond's response. He learned not to expect coddling. His mentor's first comment was "Okay, what's next?" Says Shipley, "The kindest thing that Gerry can do for someone like me is challenge, probe and question."

The eye for talent is another of his gifts, combined with an ability to make connections with people. The motivation is always about tying the technology back to the community and to Atlantic Canada. Sometimes, outsiders feel he holds on to startups far too long, saving them for his little pool of New Brunswick investors. But Pond just scoffs at that suggestion and insists that, despite a preference for Atlantic Canada ownership, he will seek capital wherever it works best for the company.

More often, he battles the old images of Atlantic Canada as a quaint seaside society that lacks dynamism. He remembers back at NBTel when he launched the internet service called Vibe, based on Nortel's technology. A reporter from an Austin newspaper came, invited by Nortel, which had a big Texas operation. "They took a picture of me in front of a lighthouse, out near where I live. I said, 'Why do you want a lighthouse in the picture?' They responded, 'Well, you're known for that.'"

Pond complained that it didn't sound very high-tech to him. He adds, disgusted, "They wrote an article about this backwater province that had all this fancy stuff. And I was in it with a picture of a lighthouse."

He is almost comically old school, which charms his acolytes. The technology entrepreneur Daniella DeGrace remembers working with him at iMagic, when they were both in Paris, nailing down a sale. Part of DeGrace's mission as head of sales was to pitch phone companies, and their male CEOs, around the world. Pond turned to her and said, almost as a challenge, "Old guys like me don't like being sold by little women like you." DeGrace didn't flinch — she saw Pond as "my big teddy bear" who wanted the best for his people. She asked why his kind were so scared. Recalls DeGrace, "He looked at me and said, 'You'll do fine. You'll do just fine.'"

He is not a man of poetry, and he has a fairly harsh metaphor to describe his role of finding people and putting them together to build businesses: "My job is to be the hammer so the nails go in. The ideas are the nails."

One proven nail-supplier was Chris Newton, who showed up at Mariner Partners in 2006. Newton actually worked inside Mariner for a few weeks, while he pondered his next move. But he told Pond and company that he really couldn't go back to being an employee. He had some ideas about building a business around this new thing called social media.

Newton was looking for patterns that no one was seeing, or at least exploiting. He was a rabid watcher of the new wave of digital chatter, as expressed in blogs, forums and chat rooms. It was still early days

Daniella DeGrace during her Radian6 days. She was one of Gerry Pond's young acolytes on the New Brunswick technology scene (Courtesy of David Alston and Marcel LeBrun)

in social media — Facebook was still in the millions of users, not the billions of today. Twitter was just getting off the ground. The activity bubbled up from people who wanted to spout off about anything, such as governments, companies, political opponents. But there was a darker side too — revenge-seeking ex-boyfriends, pedophiles, abusers, white supremacists, all finding each other in a way they had never been able to, on a global network that reached into the darkest corners of the net.

Ian Cavanagh remembers a lunch with Chris Newton, where he outlined his idea of a technology that could monitor online behaviour by pedophiles. Cavanagh liked the idea but wasn't sure about the market. Police forces did not have a lot of money to spend on those kinds of things in 2005. Gerry Pond had a similar conversation with him and observed Newton had some of the same law-and-order instincts as his police-chief father. They took the idea to the local RCMP division, which told them it was a good idea but they couldn't afford it. Plus, it was a new and untested product at that time.

Still, Pond liked the way the conversation was going, and he had an idea for a connection that Newton should make. At the same time

Chris Newton was being fired at Q1, in another part of Fredericton, Chris Ramsey was coping with the fact that his employer, located on Canada's West Coast, had gone out of business. It was just the latest turn in the road for Ramsey, a Fredericton boy and UNB grad who had graduated into a job in Ottawa with Fulcrum Technologies, an information management company, and rose to a key product management role. Then Fulcrum was acquired and Ramsey had a chance to go to Boston but instead took a job a continent away in British Columbia. His employer, NCompass Labs, run by pioneering female tech entrepreneur Gerri Sinclair, was also bought in 2001 by Microsoft. Ramsey was on the move again to Microsoft headquarters in Redmond, Washington.

He then got a call from an old colleague at a new company back in BC, called AxonWare Software. He was offered the chance to come home to Fredericton, to work remotely with his West Coast colleagues and raise his kids in a family-friendly atmosphere. He felt he could even build a new house. But that all collapsed. Just as the first mortgage payment was coming out of the bank for his new house, with his wife six months' pregnant, he was on the phone with the top brass of AxonWare. They were shutting the company down and laying everyone off.

For the first time, Ramsey was looking for work, and he started researching the tech scene in New Brunswick. He got in touch with Steve Burns, a local cybersecurity entrepreneur. Burns knew a guy named Chris Newton, and he got them together. Newton was playing around with ideas too. And Ramsey quickly learned that all roads in New Brunswick technology lead to Gerry Pond.

Pond invited the two Chrises independently to the annual dinner of an organization called KIRA — KIRA is short for Knowledge and Innovation Recognition Awards. The two younger men spotted each other, sitting on opposite sides of Pond and their reaction was: "Hey, what are you doing here?" They started talking. Pond joined in, the three talked far into the evening, and the idea started to take shape. It was a Gerry moment, another product of his sly puppeteering.

Ramsey recalls that, just a few days later, "Chris and I drove down to Saint John and Gerry said, 'Okay, I'm going to fund this, and you're going to start a company.'" Chris Newton remembers it this way: "Gerry said, 'I'm in for $50,000' and looked over and said to [one of his Mariner colleagues] 'Are you in?'" Newton walked out with $100,000.

With Q1, he had started a business based on programs the university was already using. "With Radian6 there was nothing, zero, just a couple of sheets of paper, and something about monitoring social media."

The trio of Pond, Ramsey and Newton started meeting as a virtual company inside Mariner, but sometimes over coffee at a Tim Hortons at the top of the hill in Fredericton. To help push along the idea, they brought in Brian Dunphy, a smart software developer who had been one of Q1's first hires, and who was fired from Q1 the same day as Chris Newton was let go. The idea started to form with a fuzzy definition: with the rise of social media, there would be a demand from corporations and institutions for systems to monitor and report what was said about them.

Some of that service was already on the market, but in the form of clunky manual systems whereby a group of analysts would collect information and deliver reports periodically. Why not have a product that could provide a snapshot, in real time — something like Chris Newton had done in cybersecurity five years earlier?

Gerry Pond had someone else in mind who could help — a man named Marcel LeBrun, another of his nail-drivers who could construct a business. LeBrun was a little older, more battle-scarred than the rest, having built iMagic and watched that dream die inside the corporate structure of a French owner. It was an all-star team Pond was assembling — the best of the community he had built at NBTel and Mariner Partners, with a lot of UNB-taught expertise baked into the pie.

9. The Making of Marcel

When Marcel LeBrun was a university student, at the end of his first year at UNB, he experienced a moment of clarity, a realization of what was important in life. He came out of his final exams with the sense he had been measuring his significance in relation to stuff on the surface of life — marks, sports scores, achievements — but this was all secondary to his core beliefs, his relationship to God and the teachings of Jesus Christ. LeBrun had been raised as a French-Canadian Catholic but this had nothing to do with organized religion — this was his life and his mission. He became a person of faith.

It is hard to argue that this made him a better manager, a better CEO, but it likely imbued him with a beyond-his-years gravity and seriousness of purpose that his colleagues, employees and venture capitalists admired. Call it emotional intelligence, if you like. People would walk through walls for him.

He is also alert to the possibility of social enterprise, making good and being good. It is a nebulous term but finds concrete expression in the things he takes on with energy. Everyone who meets LeBrun is attracted to his combination of strong core values and a sense of humour. He is slim, almost wraith-like physically, with eyes that draw you in and an easy way of talking. And he knows how to position a technology company that is trying to find its place in the world.

Marcel is the descendant of a LeBrun who fought alongside French general Montcalm in the Battle of the Plains of Abraham, and after the British conquest, stayed to settle in Sainte-Geneviève, now part of Montreal. In more modern times, the family moved westward to

Cornwall, Ontario, where Marcel's dad rose from bike messenger to a manager in the American Optical Company. His father got relocated to Moncton when Marcel was 12, and after high school, the teenager ended up on the vaunted engineering and computer science track at UNB. When he graduated he did what any computer geek did in those days — he joined NBTel, and quickly entered the universe of Gerry Pond, as the Codefather was making the transition from head of human resources to chief marketing officer, and finally to CEO in the local phone company.

LeBrun quickly learned that "Gerry believes in people and takes chances on people." One of his first meetings with Pond was as a junior engineering employee. He was involved in a project someone in marketing had dreamed up — an enhancement to the voicemail product offered by the phone company. LeBrun had found a way to do the upgrade, and the company had done a small trial, but his group wanted to broaden the test, taking it to 3,000 homes. Because it was a $300,000 spending item, it had to go to the CEO. The head of engineering invited LeBrun to a group meeting with Gerry Pond.

Pond shot questions around the table before zeroing in on LeBrun. He noted the new add-on had actually introduced a glitch that downgraded one aspect of the voicemail service. Remembers LeBrun, "He looks at me and says, 'So you are the engineer who designed it. This is good, but you have introduced a deficiency in the network.' He is pointing a gun at me, but I was just doing what the marketing people asked."

Pond then said, "You have to fix it. I want you to know this is your job - no matter where you go in the company, you need to fix this deficiency." Pond had made him the CEO of this deficiency. LeBrun had to report to him and tell him how he was going to fix it.

"Later, the chief engineer took me aside and said, 'I think he likes you, and you own this thing. Whatever you need, you have a channel.'"

A lot of people became CEOs of their particular projects, with a reporting line straight to Pond. NBTel had its Living Lab hothouse of innovation, and new ideas kept tumbling out. It helped to have the New Brunswick government as a supporter and partner. The most potentially transformative product was the transmission of video by means of internet-protocol (IP) technology.

Running movies and TV shows through the internet doesn't seem so fresh now in the age of streaming, but NBTel's IP technology was ahead of its time. It could be the disruptive alternative to classic cable technology and held the potential for consumers to acquire their telephone, internet and TV services from the same vendor — namely, from NBTel and other phone companies.

This was the period, at the cusp of the 21st century, when convergence was all the rage, as communications companies battled to merge the proliferating content — music, print, video, movies and images of all kinds — with the channels that carried this content to consumers, the so-called pipes, such as cable and satellite TV, the internet, even newspapers, and increasingly the telephone. Anyone who controlled both content and pipes would reap huge rewards.

And there was another side to this convergence dream — to combine all the pipes that carried this valuable content into one bundled service. The cable companies and the phone companies were duking it out, both doing startups and acquisitions to position themselves, bidding up asset prices. Little did they know that Facebook and Google, as well as Netflix and Apple, would emerge to steal their lunch.

Pond put Marcel LeBrun in the spotlight as the head of this new unit called iMagic — the lead iMagician, so to speak — and as it developed, NBTel decided to spin out iMagic and bring in outside investors. There followed a partnership with Terry Matthews, and Marcel got a chance to watch another technology titan in action.

Matthews was a motormouth Welsh immigrant who had been recruited by Northern Telecom (later, Nortel) as a young engineer in Britain, and brought across the pond to work in Northern's semiconductor lab in Ottawa. As Northern phased out that business, Matthews and his Brit colleague Mike Cowpland founded a startup called Mitel, which originally imported lawnmowers, but then switched to making private telephone branch exchanges for business, a hot sector in the 1970s.

Out of a modest brick building, Mitel emerged as a forerunner in terms of technology public share offerings in Canada. Matthews parlayed that move into a prominent position in Canadian technology, focused on Ottawa where he built another telecom company, Newbridge, while emerging as an active investor. He was also a major figure in his native Wales, that land of depleted coal mines and gritty old towns. He was knighted Sir Terry and became the third richest man in Wales. Like Gerry Pond, he had a mission to bring new life to a struggling region.

Another key player was a young Toronto venture capitalist named Joe Catalfamo, who worked for Whitecap, a VC fund spun from the vision of Eph Diamond, a legend in Canadian property development as a founder of Cadillac Fairview. Catalfamo took his first flight ever to New Brunswick to check out iMagic and NBTel's Living Lab. He admired Gerry Pond and Peter Jollymore, the senior NBTel executives who championed the new technology. That visit began a relationship with the Pond group that would be long-lasting and fruitful for all, though there were some turbulent times too.

Catalfamo strongly backed the idea of spinning out iMagic, with Matthews as a co-investor, along with NBTel (soon to become part of Aliant, the newly merged Atlantic phone provider). His firm, Whitecap, came in as an investor. It seemed like a certain winner. At one time iMagic would claim a billion dollars in market value. "The technology was real, and it was ahead of the curve," Catalfamo believes.

And he saw something in the New Brunswick culture that unlocked the potential for innovation. There was a commitment to the old proverb "Necessity is the mother of invention." Pond and his NBTel colleagues held the belief that the only way to get ahead was to take the lead in technology. "It is no coincidence Radian6 and Q1 were born here," Catalfamo would say later. "How can you not be impressed with the innovation of these people? NBTel was an incubator before there were incubators."

In iMagic at its peak, Marcel LeBrun could watch all these bright minds, often older guys, around the table. But he ended up learning more than he expected, as iMagic went public in the fever of the high-tech bubble, just on the eve of the 2001 market crash.

He now concedes he was too focused on the goal of a stock market offering. The business was not grounded enough yet to survive a crisis. The crash came fast and hard. He remembers painfully that in March 2000, the tech-heavy Nasdaq stock exchange hit its all-time high, and iMagic was on its way to file its IPO with regulators.

By the time the IPO hit the market in November, the Nasdaq had lost almost half its peak value. There were 46 companies in the registration line for an IPO in Nasdaq, but only 16 got out the door and only six in their projected price range. "We were one of the six — one of the last tech IPOs for years." iMagic stock proceeded to swoon. Meanwhile, "our customers went into hibernation. All the capital budgets dried up, and all we were left with were trials." And technology trials do not make for a sustainable business.

Still, the media in Central Canada were discovering the New Brunswick phenomenon. In a piece in the August 6, 2001, *Maclean's* magazine, Danylo Hawaleshka wrote a story, "Converging on Your Living Room," with the introduction: "A New Brunswick firm is leading the highly competitive, global charge to combine the internet, television and telephone in one place."

The article continued: "At the heart of this fundamental realignment is a small company with powerful backers called iMagicTV Inc. Headed by chief executive and co-founder Marcel LeBrun, it makes software to send television signals over ordinary copper telephone lines." The piece suggested that cable competitors were sitting up to pay attention, while phone companies salivated over this new technology to take on the cable guys. LeBrun was portrayed as a cool operator: "The boyish 31-year-old father of three is eyeing the future and video-on-demand." It concluded, "Atlantic Canada, in many respects, is ground zero in the convergence war for consumers' hearts and wallets."

The article pointed out that Aliant, by now the merged combination of the four Atlantic phone companies, owned 29 per cent of iMagic, and was selling the service in Saint John and Moncton, bringing high-speed internet, TV and radio channels, and telephony to 2,700 customers. It quoted Gerry Pond, Aliant executive vice president, that there would be more services to come.

These were heady times, but the piece also noted that iMagic had gone public nine months earlier at $17.15 a share and, in the market meltdown, the price had been beaten down to about a buck.

Who killed iMagic? Some say it was simply ahead of its time. Others blame the Central Canada–based Bell system, which had a competing technology, and allegedly abandoned iMagic. What happened was the French giant Alcatel became a major partner. It had bought Newbridge, Matthews's telecom company, taking its interest in iMagic to 20 per cent. Having inherited that stake, and as the iMagic share price dissolved, it picked up the rest for a song in 2003, thus ending iMagic's life as an independent public company. The deal, which valued iMagic at $1.20 a share, was a blow to the remaining IPO investors but better than it might have been if the company had simply died.

Alcatel had another competing technology in the same space, and it let the two fight it out — survival of the fittest. Not surprisingly, it decided to pull the plug on iMagic. LeBrun stayed on at Alcatel for a couple of years to run a software division, but it was a company in turmoil, trying to digest a huge acquisition in the United States.

iMagic had been this bright fiery comet, blazing across the Canadian tech firmament, and it burned out. The people who had worked at iMagic and survived the Alcatel takeover eventually drifted away — finance specialist Jeff White, engineering and sales manager Daniella DeGrace, and marketing man David Alston, as well as ace engineer Jerry Carr. But they all kept in touch in the tech cocoon of

Finance executive Jeff White is one of the rare people who worked at all three pivotal New Brunswick startups: iMagic, Q1 Labs and Radian6 (Courtesy of David Alston and Marcel LeBrun)

New Brunswick. They remained at the centre of everything that has happened since then.

Marcel LeBrun left too, and went to work for a sales outsourcing company, one of the emerging businesses in the post-McKenna era. It was a tough business that required constant hiring and laying off, like a revolving door. It was just the nature of the business. One of his friends warned, "Marcel, it will eat you up." It had to be painful for LeBrun, but he was also talking to his mentor Gerry Pond about his next step.

Pond asked him to meet Chris Newton and offer any advice to the young second-time-around entrepreneur, who was playing with ideas about social media. "I liked Chris and I liked what he was doing, although I didn't quite understand how they would apply it to real business problem, and they didn't either."

LeBrun also liked what Newton brought to the game: insatiable curiosity and the ability to devour "tons of articles a day, like nobody else, and he reads and sees patterns." He saw that Newton was finding

Marcel LeBrun takes
a call at Radian6
after joining the
company as CEO
(Courtesy of David Alston)

"meta-patterns" in the movement of ideas on the internet. "He was watching how ideas were propagating online. He started to think about flow analysis of ideas. And would it be helpful for companies to know how ideas move through the internet?"

Gerry Pond had told Chris Newton that he had a CEO in mind for him. But at first he didn't tell LeBrun, who comments that "Gerry is pushy in the sense he would really challenge you, but he didn't order you. He just said, 'Go meet Chris.' But at the back of his mind he was thinking about how it might come together."

LeBrun helped shape the new enterprise's business plan and find the pain points the customers would pay for fixing. "I started talking to prospective customers and started getting excited about the potential."

By the time LeBrun came aboard, the company already had a name — Radian6 — but it was really "The Radian6" as in "The Dave Clark Five" or, more fittingly, "The Chicago Seven." They were six Timbit revolutionaries meeting over double-doubles and crullers. A friendly debate still rages over the exact identities of the original six, but it seems likely they were Chris Newton, Chris Ramsey, Brian Dunphy, Gerry Pond, Paul O'Hara (a Mariner manager who was the early CFO and who would die much too young) and Nick Breau, who left early and is now a self-help speaker and author (*The Power of Joy*).

Newton saw social media as a phenomenon that spanned the globe — essentially a circle, and radians are the angles that make up a circle. The meaning of the word "Radian6" would be not be understood by most people, and Newton liked that. It was a blank sheet on which the founders could imprint the meaning.

As the incoming CEO, LeBrun was constantly explaining the name. For a while, people thought it was a medical company with a radioactive isotope. But Radian6 would become a recognized brand in the rapidly emerging world of social media.

LeBrun brought a lot of ideas, and he put $50,000 of his own money into the pot. He got in touch with old colleagues, such as David Alston, an iMagic veteran who was working in a Saint John marketing agency. Alston, who was known for his tendency to switch jobs every few years, did not join at first, but in time he got itchy feet. LeBrun knew his friend's predilection for reinvention.

In fact, Alston had already been doing little favours for his friend LeBrun. He would phone up potential Radian6 rivals and, as a marketing consultant, asked if they would provide him with their sales promotion details, and he would take that information back to LeBrun.

Alston finally joined the team as an important piece of the puzzle, a boy from rural Sussex who brought marketing smarts, uncontainable chatter and a wicked sense of fun. He would don chicken costumes at company events, and his colleagues insisted he could speak a dialect of chicken language learned from his family hobby farm.

It was shaping up to be a reunion of the old iMagic team with Gerry as avuncular champion, Marcel as charismatic CEO, and David Alston, Jeff White and others joining up. A late entry was Daniella DeGrace, who had stayed at Q1 Labs but was concerned that the company was seeking a big exit with a corporate buyer, and she did not want to be part of a large organization again. She loved the energy and creativity of a startup. Radian6 was not retaining customers to the extent it needed to, and was looking for a "customer success" manager to plug the drain. One day, LeBrun called to ask her to join Radian6, and she quickly climbed aboard.

The momentum was building as Chris Newton ran into Jane Fritz, his UNB computer science professor, at their local Sobeys supermarket. "I've got the bug," he told Fritz. It was that old startup bug again. Would it be contagious?

10. Halfway to Impossible

In 2006, Matt Lauer was still the amiable face of U.S. morning television, the bland everyman who co-hosted NBC's *Today* show. This was long before he became a pariah in the #MeToo era as allegations about his history as a sexual abuser proliferated, and he fell in disgrace from one of the loftiest perches in American media.

One June morning, Lauer's guest was a blockily built 30-year-old with a shaved head and a goatee, named Vincent Ferrari. Ferrari was a blogger, with a big following that eagerly digested his comments about ham-handed governments and clumsy corporations. On June 13, 2006, he had phoned up AOL, the big internet service provider, with the intent of cancelling his service. He recorded the shockingly acrimonious conversation with a customer service rep. He posted it on his blog and, as they say, it went viral.

In the recording, an AOL representative named John comes on after a five-minute hold and hears Ferrari's request that his account be cancelled. There follows 15 minutes of in-your-face arguments by John as to why it was dumb to do this — interrupted only by Ferrari's constant refrain of "cancel the account," a request he made over a dozen times. John was persistent, rude and combative, and Ferrari calmly controlled, until John finally succumbed and agreed to cancel Ferrari's long-held account. Total time on the phone: 21 minutes.

The overpowering social-media response caught the attention of Matt Lauer and the folks at *Today*, as well as a number of other media outlets. Ferrari admitted to Lauer that he had heard about AOL's tiffs with other clients, and clearly was hoping to engineer a

gotcha moment. He got it, becoming a mass-media darling and AOL
a widely criticized villain, especially since its sales tactics had already
been the subject of inquiries and fines by regulatory authorities. The
blog and the Lauer interview are still cited as seminal moments in the
development of social-media marketing.

It certainly fell into the eager hands of a startup developing a tech-
nology that companies could use to track their social-media rating. For
Marcel LeBrun, the AOL public relations disaster became a sales tool:
"We could say to customers, 'Do you want this happening to you?'"

Many other companies were caught flat-footed. A blogger launched
a "Dell Hell" campaign, targeting the personal computer maker Dell
after a number of embarrassing moments, including the fallout from
its PCs catching on fire. Dell would become an early customer for
Radian6.

The flurry of widely publicized bad scenes was making global
corporations nervous, especially those with heavy consumer marketing
budgets. Radian6 was working on a platform whereby companies
could find out instantly what the online world was saying about
them, positive and negative, in the now-burgeoning field of social
media — early Facebook, very early Twitter (Instagram and Snapchat
would come much later).

Joe Catalfamo, the Toronto venture capitalist — who knew LeBrun
well from his iMagic days — was working with the Radian6 team. He
recalls that "Chris Newton said, 'I can create a model of this turning
into a social shitstorm.' And Marcel said, 'This is disruptive: look at
all these people together bringing down a company brand.'"

In Catalfamo's account, this had become a black swan, a sudden
event out of the blue, unpredictable and transformative, that would
change the landscape of marketing, and indeed the world. It was one
of those moments when the power shifted from corporations to the
people, Catalfamo says, rather grandly, but there was some truth to
that.

Radian6 jumped on it by creating a social-media monitoring platform. At the beginning, their product fell into the domain of the public relations industry. PR firms were already getting active in the monitoring field through human beings tracking the internet, picking up the conversation and then writing reports, not in real time but perhaps monthly. Others, in addition to Radian6, were starting to work on software to allow marketers to scan the blogosphere.

As LeBrun started talking to possible funding sources, he knew he was dealing with an already crowded field of potential rivals. Radian6 had to find broader applications of its technology, taking it, as he says, from an "oh-oh" problem to an "aha" problem — not just protecting companies from bad things but changing the way they did marketing, including customer service and relationship management. Over time, Radian6, he says, "became the voice of the biggest change in marketing in a hundred years. That was the key to where we really grew." The challenge was they also had about 300 to 400 potential competitors, as the market heated up.

Radian6 was on the cusp of the next thrust of social media. What if you, as a marketer, could turn the tables and use the social-media universe as your instrument, not your enemy, turning it into a strategic tool and relationship builder? It became a model of what LeBrun calls the "pull factor" — not pushing a product onto customers but feeling the power of the market pulling you toward it, ever onward and forward. He could feel the market pulling Radian6 along, and LeBrun and his team just had to keep their balance.

Chris Ramsey, the product management whiz in the Radian6 group, capitalized on that pull. Early in the life of the company, he had the idea of sending an email to the CEOs of the 100 biggest PR firms in the United States, asking if they were interested in the product Radian6 was developing. Ramsey figured they would get the typical low single-digit percentage response. "I came back in the office the next morning and I had a 30 per cent response on this email. And all these people saying, 'We're in, we're in, we want to see it.' And that's just how much pain they were going through."

Indeed, shortly after sending the first email, his cellphone rang and it was the CEO of Weber Shandwick, the biggest PR firm on the planet at the time. Weber Shandwick was interested in what Radian6 was building, and it might just join the Canadian company's early adopter program, a kind of advisory role that provided preferred access as the product became more refined. That put Ramsey and LeBrun into the orbit of a New York digital marketing phenom named Bonin Bough.

His first name is pronounced "Baw-nin," not "Bone-a" as in the French pronunciation or "Bone-in" as many of his fellow Americans like to call him. Bonin Bough's CV is as exotic as the name — a boy genius who headed the digital division of Weber Shandwick at age 30, who would devise social-media strategies at brand titans PepsiCo and Mondelez, and who would later team up with basketball great LeBron James to host a reality TV show about turning around inner-city Cleveland — a kind of *Dragons' Den* with social purpose.

The son of a prolific photographer who had captured the sights of New York in the fifties and sixties — and the lives of its African-American residents — the younger Bough captured the potential of the new world of social media. This Afro-haired product of the creative culture of Manhattan became the key figure in the story of Radian6 and its rise to become the global standard for social-media monitoring.

As Weber Shandwick's digital marketing chief, Bough met Ramsey and LeBrun when the New Brunswickers had nothing but a piece of paper, a concept and no prototype. He agreed to join the early adopter group, the only American at the time. Several months later, Radian6 produced a prototype, and Weber Shandwick became a full-fledged partner.

In a competition of three firms, Radian6 was miles ahead, Bough recalls. Still young and not burdened with preconceptions, Bough didn't care where the Radian6 team was from. "They had one of the most beautifully visual interfaces of anyone in that space; we just

Radian6 marketing head David Alston on stage with Bonin Bough,
Weber Shandwick's digital marketing chief (Courtesy of Derek Wilmot)

found each other at the right time." Other products, he said, "were
clumsy, did not feel new, did not feel fresh. These guys had a newness
to them and a totally different way to see and measure and track the
world that just felt better."

What Bough could offer was the immediate bounce from startup
to scale-up, providing access to a large global customer base that
was hungry for a product to gauge their social-media stock. In the
partnership, he was able to take the Canadian product to 20 countries,
19 languages and 60 corporate customers within a month and a half.
That established the mantra that has echoed through Bough's career:
startups don't have to think incrementally about scaling up — they can
explode overnight with the help of a big partner or customer. All they
need to do is offer exclusive, or low-cost, access to their product or
service, in return for instant growth.

More than a decade later, I caught up with Bough on a fall day
in Manhattan, in a Soho loft where he and a team of assistants were
sifting through digital images, part of a half million photos stored

away by his photographer father. As images flashed on the screen of Brooklyn Bridge, Central Park and this rich canvas of New York, Bonin was being filmed interviewing his 92-year-old father, Martin, about his camera, the shutter speed, the people photographed and what they meant to him. Bonin tore himself away from his documentary project to talk to me about the perfect partnership with Radian6. "We got something we could sell but we did a lot of heavy lifting for them." He smiles as he recalls LeBrun and Ramsey — "the dynamic duo," he says. "We spent a lot of time together; I was young and they were young." It helped his career and it certainly gave Radian6 a huge shot of momentum.

Chris Ramsey remembers the excitement of those early moments. This was going to be big, the Radian6 team concluded, and they put together a sales team to capitalize on the excitement. The key hire was Radian6's first sales representative, Rich McInnis.

McInnis was a graduate of Saint Mary's University in Halifax who got his sales chops peddling ads for the campus newspaper, unleashing a potential he didn't know he had. He discovered there was practically no restraint on what he could make in sales commissions. The campus gig netted him close to $60,000 in commissions in his final year. He then turned to selling cost-accounting software, moved down to the U.S. Northeast as a regional manager for the vendor, and thrived. But he came home with the idea of being part of a startup. He tried a couple of companies and met LeBrun in the process, who told him about Radian6, its market focus and early financing. On meeting the team, he told his wife, "I need to be part of this."

McInnis injected a shot of adrenalin into Radian6. At first, they were working in the National Research Council building on the UNB campus, where LeBrun, Newton and Ramsey sat in one small office with a cluster of desks mashed together. McInnis would join that group, often conducting his calls in the open. He was the total sales animal, cold-calling around the continent, fuelled by Red Bulls and Starbucks coffee. His colleagues would bring him lists of companies, which he would attack one by one. The cold-call patter went: "Yeah, this is Rich McInnis, I'd like to talk to who handles social media, like, who handles blogs?" There would be a pause, and Ramsey, often sitting beside him, would hear: "That's McInnis. Radian6."

"I called it dialing for dollars," McInnis laughs today. The spaces were so small, his bosses could hear every word in these first fumbling calls. So he just dove in. At one point, Radian6's young techies moved offices to a house in Marysville, once Boss Gibson's 19th-century company town. With each big sale, an excited McInnis would clamber up from his basement "sales dungeon" to the senior managers' top-floor loft. His bosses knew that the heavier his footsteps on the stairs, the bigger the deal.

Toward the end of the early adopter program, the Radian6 people took a booth at the biggest trade show in North America for public relations professionals, held in Chicago. Weber Shandwick was going live with news of its Radian6 partnership. As the press release went out, the interactive media director for a major ad agency walked over to their booth. Ramsey showed him a demo and, as he was walking away, the executive was sending out a Twitter message — Twitter was very new at that point — saying that the Radian6 stuff was amazing.

As the executive tweeted from 20 feet away, there was a surge of people toward the Radian6 booth. The Radian6 moment had truly arrived. "There was this swell of energy that started to build," says McInnis.

What partly fuelled that energy was the elegance of the product. Radian6 offered clients a dashboard to track and analyze social media. It meant a large advertising agency preparing a hundred-million-dollar ad campaign could use the dashboard to understand what people were really thinking, where their needs and interests lay, and the lifestyle elements that could be met by the branded products or services advertised.

The second part of the service was a console that allowed consumer brands to manage their interactions with people on various

Chris Newton and Chris Ramsey appear on the cover of
Progress Magazine, evidence of Radian6's growing fame

(Courtesy of *Progress Magazine*)

social-media channels — what the Radian6 crew called "engagement." The product offering often addressed basic customer service. Dell would use the console as a new channel into the company's call centre. A negative tweet about a Dell product experience would get picked up in seconds and routed to a social-media call-centre employee who would use the console to reach out to the unhappy person and help them out.

Another ingredient was Radian6's vibe. Business gurus have observed that "culture eats strategy for breakfast," and Radian6's culture was remarkably freewheeling and progressive, even for a tech startup. The senior team sat in the same room, with desks that they would pull together for instant meetings around any issue.

In Ramsey's memory, "The people that worked for any of us would just walk in with a problem and say, 'Hey, I've got this going on.' It would just be a conversation. People weren't intimidated. They'd just walk in and say, 'I need help.' And we would all help them solve it. It was a lot of fun, a shorts and T-shirt kind of place. There was no stuffiness. Lots of Nerf guns in the development operation, ultimate Frisbee at lunch." Sort of like Silicon Valley? "Not really intentional, it just happened that way. It was just a 'be yourself' culture."

David Alston excelled in the Radian6 marketing role, because, he says, "Marcel trusted me and kind of gave me lots of rope to hang myself with." They would be joined by Jerry Carr, another iMagic veteran who headed up engineering and was known for his managerial smarts and prodigious work ethic. And of course, Chris Newton was having the time of his life.

Brian Dunphy, as a member of the team, got to watch Newton doing what he wanted to do — solve complex problems. He was bowled over by Newton's obsessive work ethic: "He's one of the hardest working guys I know." Dunphy saw that Newton was a decent programmer, not a star, but he could research his famous patterns and flows all day long.

"For a university dropout, he was highly, highly intelligent. And you could never really win an argument with Chris, not because he was always right but because he would wear you down." Dunphy saw a creative dynamic at work. In a startup, a developer like Dunphy has to be the realist who says, "Well, that's impossible." But Newton would challenge the developers to the point where "we would start doing halfway to the impossible."

Outsiders were beginning to discover Chris Newton's achievement. His one-time Miramichi schoolmate Jody Glidden had three startups under his belt when he ran into Newton — it was probably 2005 and it was either in an airport or a coffee shop, Glidden can't remember.

Glidden said something like, "Hey Chris, how are you doing?" Newton replied that he had this thing called Radian6, and it was doing really well. Glidden didn't know anyone else from the Miramichi who was into startups and who was successful at them. "Chris sort of came out of nowhere."

Radian6 had a different model than Q1, one that allowed it to concentrate its team in New Brunswick, thanks to the new distribution mode of using the cloud and software as a service (SaaS). In a sense, Radian6 capitalized on its strong New Brunswick provenance, while taking on the big players in its U.S. marketing. Local and global at once.

Sophie Forest, a venture capitalist who would later loom large in this story, points out that the Radian6 team, tucked away in Fredericton, was in its own little cocoon, "which to some extent, was positive."

Chris Newton would gather competitive intelligence, coming into board meetings with long lists of rivals, including 50 new ones in a month. It could have been distracting, indeed overwhelming, if you were in the Valley. You would be running scared, looking over your shoulder. But in Fredericton, Forest says, "they were just doing their thing. They were really down-to-earth: 'Let's build a business, let's sell, let's get revenue, let's grow.' And I think it helped them a lot."

Instead of listening to the noise about competitors, and harbouring worries that others were doing better than they were, they could focus on employees and customers. "So they built the best product because that's the only thing they cared about."

And they were smart, she says. At some point when they were growing really fast, they had to scale up the sales effort by building an internal team — people on the phone doing demos and sales. So they recruited from a traditional pool, the people who had worked at copier companies like Toshiba, Canon and Xerox. The idea was this group knew how to sell, and they could be trained in the intricacies of the Radian6 product.

And Forest was pleased to see that the entry price to buying the product was very low. "So you could basically buy the software for five hundred bucks or whatever a month, which a marketing employee can put on their credit card." When a customer had got used to using it, and was now depending on it, it would become a bigger sell. Then it needed authorization from above, but by then the customer was committed.

Employee turnover was negligible. New Brunswick workers, even high-in-demand techies, do not move around much. There is not a lot of poaching. Tech entrepreneurs point out that if they were doing business in the Valley, or in Toronto, they would expect employees to head out after work to watering holes, run into people from other companies, and before the night was over, they would have an offer in hand.

But in Fredericton, employees might head out to the Snooty Fox, a favourite pub, and never run into another tech worker or manager. Not that they would likely move if they did. Loyalty is big in that part of the world.

Radian6, being so far ahead with social media, could be innovative. David Alston remembers a turning point when the company knew it was a known brand. It was working with marketing consultant Chris Brogan who was one of the top influencers in social media — people followed so avidly by so many, they could shape buying trends. They decided to do a video webinar series, which was daring at the time because video on social media was still unexplored and technically hard. They called each program a "Twebinar," described as "a webinar and Twitter mash-up where conversations take place in real time before, during and after the webinar, on Twitter."

They would go out and interview key people in the social-media space as guests. The concept was a hit because Radian6 now had the profile to pull in the top social-media thinkers for interviews — like the best-selling author Tim Ferriss, someone so unconventional that he first met Alston while walking on his hands, something he was learning to do at the time.

As a result of the series, Radian6 was clearly one of the in-crowd in terms of social-media relationships. "We kind of entered the circle," Alston recalls. "We're like, 'Wow, this really worked, so let's keep doing things that are outside the box.'"

It was still a little company based in New Brunswick, but people really didn't know that, or care. "We were in the cloud, so people would think we're in California, people would think we're in Toronto. Generally, people would never think we're in New Brunswick. We were proud of [being from there], but we weren't out there beating our chests. It was just about Radian6 and our community of people that we connected to around the world, that had the same view of the world in terms of how social media was going to transform marketing for good."

The New Brunswick culture of self-effacement, of not tooting your own horn, became an asset too. The company had a rule that no matter who you were in the company — an executive, a marketer, salesperson or a conference speaker — you wouldn't go into a conversation and start talking about Radian6. "We were always talking about where the industry needed to go — that kind of thing'" Alston says.

"We saw that if you were going to generate content and you were going to generate leadership, you weren't going to start bragging about yourself and talking about yourself. If people believed in where you were going and what you believed in, they would want to get to know you."

Like Q1 Labs, Radian6 was able to tap the local angel network, led by co-founder Gerry Pond and his cohorts. There was some government money, including an injection from the New Brunswick Investment Foundation — a government seed-money source — taking the founders close to a million dollars in early financing. But that funding was evaporating, and there would have to be a round with venture capitalists.

But this was different than the Q1 Labs scenario. The company was headed by a bunch of people who had been through the wars at iMagic and Q1 Labs, had travelled through what VCs call "the valley of death" and survived. And the company was different. Both Newton and LeBrun wanted to avoid their past experiences with very expensive sales processes. This was SaaS, and the sales process was mostly online or by phone.

LeBrun recalls that "Chris and I had a list of things we would never do again — and things we would always do." LeBrun would never again send engineers on planes to demonstrate the software, "which we did at iMagic, and it was expensive. The sales process to decide if you even had an opportunity cost a lot of money. Radian6 cost nothing."

LeBrun says the length of the path to value was critical. Other companies, even those with better products, might find the path too expensive and long, and the company would not survive. The powerful pull of the market allowed Radian6 to grow astonishingly quickly. It experienced triple-digit growth every year, moving from a million dollars in sales the first year to an annual run rate of $25 million within a couple of years. In 2009, the company turned profitable, having been cash-flow-positive almost immediately.

This speed amazed the seasoned board members around the table. In fact, it unnerved one director, a Californian and a veteran of tech startups. He worried that the company was not spending aggressively enough and had too much money in the bank. It should be plowing more back into the business, he said. It bucked the model of Silicon Valley whereby startups seeking capital would be expected to lose tons of money.

Forest remembers LeBrun would respond to these concerns by saying, "I know, I know, but I can't help it." He couldn't hire fast enough to increase the rate of spending, and all the time the revenue was pouring in. "It was a machine they couldn't stop." It was no doubt helped by the lower costs of doing business in New Brunswick and the low turnover of people. LeBrun was prudent — after all, he had been through the iMagic experience, and he was content with a bit of safety net.

But how do you capture this whirlwind? In his early 40s, Bonin Bough is today a veteran of startups and has seen them come and go. He invests in a portfolio of fledgling companies that he advises. He says there is a window for a single-purpose kind of company, a time to sow and a time to reap. "It is hard to become a much broader player if you are doing so well. You get too stuck on your legacy code," he muses. You are so focused on making it better, you cannot see how to shift into new products and new markets. Pivot, it is called, and it is the hardest thing to do in technology, particularly when your original product is so hot and demanding of attention.

Radian6 had widened its offering — from a monitoring device to a sophisticated customer relationship management tool. But by the dawn of 2011, Bough figured, Radian6 was near its peak. If his friends from New Brunswick waited any longer, they might not be able to capture the high exit valuations that were there for the taking.

11. Selling Radian6

Montreal venture capitalist Sophie Forest had been working on a deal to sell Radian6 for three months, and she worried the whole thing could go up in flames. The Radian6 team was trading proposals with the buyer's people. Every time her group sent a proposal off to the pursuer's head office in San Francisco, its lawyers would mark it up and shoot the thing back with their next list of demands. This had been going on for a month, and the tone had turned testy, with the whole deal seemingly sitting on a knife-edge.

The would-be buyer was Salesforce, the explosively fast-growth software phenom from the West Coast, controlled by the dynamic Marc Benioff. Salesforce, a little more than a decade old but already a giant, helped pioneer software as a service (SaaS), where programs are made available as a subscription, plucked from the cloud. It was on the acquisition prowl and in 2011 this innovative company in Fredericton was in its sights.

By now a veteran investor in her early 40s, Forest understood the mergers and acquisitions game. First, the bigger company hooks the management of the small company with the dream of a big exit, a role in a much grander business, taking its technology out to a wide market, and guaranteeing to keep on employees. The two parties talk first in expansive visions, and the charm offensive sweeps the usually young managers off their feet.

Then it gets left to a committee of the startup's board and management and the acquirer's corporate development team to do the transaction, and the whole thing quickly bogs down in minutiae. After so much praise, the dialogue might turn negative, with the big company demanding all kinds of terms and conditions, and the small one responding with wounded pride. The once charmed managers wonder when the deal will get done, if ever.

That was the state Sophie Forest felt had been reached with Salesforce. The sticking point was not price in isolation but the devilish details that could alter the price in the end. Forest felt they could sink the deal. Whatever, there are other deals out there — after all, Radian6 was a pretty hot property. But for so much work to just go up in smoke, it would be hard to take, and the synergies with Salesforce were so apparent.

Then she heard that Benioff had asked LeBrun to come to San Francisco for a face-to-face talk, and he was heading out right away. Given the tenor of discussions, Forest worried the message from Benioff would be that he was pulling the plug. "I had been working on this for three months, full-time. And then, all day, I'm thinking, like, 'God, the transaction is off.'"

The dark-haired, wise-beyond-her-years Forest sat on Radian6's board, representing one of its investors, Brightspark Ventures, where she had carved out a role as the Montreal partner of this innovative venture capital firm. She was that rare female in her job. She had worked for years at the massive Quebec pension fund investor, Caisse de dépôt et placement du Québec (known widely as "the Caisse"), and on behalf of the Caisse, had invested in a Toronto software business owned by Mark Skapinker, a South African–born entrepreneur. Skapinker made his mark when he built and sold a company called Delrina, best known for its WinFax product, which allowed computers to transmit documents to fax machines. After the sale of Delrina, he formed another startup in which the Caisse was a lead investor and Forest was on the board, the only woman.

When Skapinker sold this last of his startups, he pivoted to a new role as a venture capitalist and with a partner started up Brightspark as an early-stage investor. He then proceeded to recruit Forest, whom he knew and admired. She liked the Brightspark approach to early-stage investment and the fact that Skapinker was a family man who wanted to make sure that Forest could have a successful career while maintaining a life balance with her husband and two young daughters. Brightspark would be a Toronto-Montreal firm with an eye on both startup communities.

The story of Forest, Brightspark and Radian6 is a classic tale of how venture capital can work at its best, and how it can be both a funding source and strategic counsel to a young company. The veteran VCs and Radian6's young leaders established a close, almost family relationship, but also hard-edged in its financial expectations. This is a relationship that can make or break a startup, and Radian6 benefited immensely.

It started with Joe Catalfamo, whose name winds its way through this story. Formerly an investor in iMagic, he was now a partner with BCE Capital, at that time the phone company's venture capital arm. He knew LeBrun and Pond well, and he had become Radian6's guide through the maze of venture capital. At the start, he had tried to get some American VCs to fund the Canadian startup, but they turned him down. This would be an all-Canadian play.

The Brightspark connection had its origins in a meeting in 2005 at the Procter & Gamble building just north of the 401 expressway in Toronto, where Brightspark had its offices then. (It is now located in the MaRS incubator space at College and University in downtown Toronto.) The first contact was Salim Teja, an energetic vice president and partner in Brightspark. He was Tanzanian-born but Edmonton-raised, a business grad from Western University in Ontario, who in his 30s already boasted an impressive career, including co-founding a West Coast U.S. startup that he had exited.

Catalfamo approached Teja, saying he had seen this very interesting opportunity led by a CEO that he'd worked with in the past, but it was very, very early stage. In fact, all they had was a PowerPoint presentation, Catalfamo said, but the CEO was tremendous, and he'd like Teja to see the opportunity. Says Teja, "As a venture firm, when you get a referral like that through a partner in the ecosystem, you want to take that meeting."

Catalfamo introduced LeBrun, who walked Teja through his background and the work that he had done at iMagic, followed by the ten-slide pitch. As a venture investor, Teja was looking for three things: Why this opportunity, why this team and why now? "And if those three things line up, then you have an unbelievable opportunity."

The opportunity looked impressive, he felt. Social media was going to emerge as a mainstream marketing and communications channel. Brands were going to struggle with the process and needed tools to manage it. They were already showing signs of being caught off guard and suffering for it.

LeBrun took Teja through the bad experiences of companies like AOL and Dell — Vincent Ferrari played a role in the narrative. Teja thought these stories were very compelling. He believed the social-media problem would only snowball and get more challenging.

So the "why this" made sense, but "why them"? Teja liked that the co-founders Newton and LeBrun were experienced entrepreneurs, as well as being technically adept. Then it became a function of "why now." Teja's take is that "we felt that the timing was right because the market was developing so quickly."

Teja also felt this product would address urgent pain points for a customer. "When we look at businesses, we often think to ourselves, 'Is this company providing a vitamin or a painkiller?' A vitamin helps companies get better around a particular strength, and painkillers solve an urgent problem. And you always work better when you can start with a company that's coming in with a painkiller, because customers pay attention. And this was sort of exactly what we saw with the framework of Radian6."

Teja came away impressed, but knew his partners were going to ask why they would invest in a company in Fredericton. Was there the talent out there to do this? Could the company tap into an ecosystem that would help it grow? He hopped on a plane with Joe Catalfamo, went out to New Brunswick, doing a quick immersion into the research at UNB. They spent a lot of time with Chris Newton talking about his technical vision.

Teja liked what he heard but had to sell it to his partners, Mark Skapinker, Tony Davis and Sophie Forest. They agreed that "the team was compelling, the problem was compelling, and the technical vision for the solution was very, very compelling." The one caveat: they would only do this deal if Teja agreed to sit on the board and go to New Brunswick to keep an eye on these guys.

Forest, as well, was impressed with the complementary skills of LeBrun and Newton. "Chris Newton was more like the mad scientist, very innovative, very creative. Marcel brought more operational experience. We really like repeat entrepreneurs. That's where we've been very successful in the past. So they fit that bill really well. And then we ended up investing in the company."

It was initially a $4-million Series A investment with Catalfamo's BCE Capital (soon to be spun off as a company called Summerhill) as the lead with an injection of $2 million, with Brightspark providing $1.1 million and the BDC coming in with $900,000. Later, the trio would follow up with another $5 million. It was a relatively small amount to be invested ahead of a potential knock-the-socks-off payday, but Radian6 had not needed a big infusion of cash — it was spinning off so much of it.

Even when they did the follow-up investment, Forest says, the money was never spent. "It stayed in the bank account. It was more like they were getting low on cash, and then they started being profitable, but we didn't want them to worry, so we did the round. But they never used it. They really didn't need it."

It was, as they say, the beginning of a beautiful relationship that blossomed as Radian6 gained increasing traction, and as social media began to blossom. As co-founder Brian Dunphy likes to say, "Radian6 rode the back of Twitter." By the time Radian6 had cracked the brand-name market, garnering half of the Forbes 100 as its clients, the takeover suitors were starting to line up. In the early cases, the money or the synergies didn't work. LeBrun and his co-founders did not want to get ahead of themselves.

It was inevitable that Salesforce would enter the discussion. Radian6 had mutual customers with Salesforce, and they began to integrate their offerings as Radian6 moved beyond marketing into the full customer relationship. And that set the stage for higher levels of dialogue.

The whole culture of Salesforce can be encapsulated in its hosting of the biggest tech trade show in the world, the vast annual Dreamforce extravaganza in late summer in San Francisco, a kind of Woodstock for technology geeks. It attracted tens of thousands of vendors and users for three days of texts, cloud computing and rock 'n' roll — Dreamforce always had a good rock band for its gala.

LeBrun remembers being invited to Salesforce chief executive Mark Benioff's house in San Francisco the day after Dreamforce 2010. Business is very personal, and Benioff and LeBrun clicked. Even before negotiations began, the two men — the grandson of Russian immigrants and the descendant of a French soldier in 18th-century Quebec, from different edges of the continent — talked about a deeper relationship between the two companies. The biggest impetus for joining the two companies came from clients, including the powerful Bank of America, which felt that Salesforce needed to bring Radian6 into its orbit.

Benioff is very people-oriented, and is one of the tech world's most outspoken social progressives, a true product of his Bay Area roots. "When he does acquisitions, he acquires people," LeBrun says. And in that early meeting, he recalls Benioff asking his corporate development team — the people who do acquisitions — "Are we thinking of doing something with these guys?" LeBrun himself answered, "I think they want to know if you like me first." That started the relationship. They did like each other.

LeBrun and his co-founders had agreed that the goal was to have fun every day and the business would follow. If a big exit comes, fine; if not, fine. "One lesson from iMagic is you can't put the exit too high on the priority list. It happens if you do the other things right, but it is not good to set out to do that — because then you do unnatural things for the business. From the day we started iMagic, we said we would exit in x number of years and we did, but we had no business doing it. We built the business too much on doing that, but at Radian6 we built the business to deliver value for customers."

In time, Salim Teja had left Brightspark's partnership for roles with new startups and helping forge innovation at Indigo Books & Music, before taking a leading role at MaRS, the hub of Toronto's innovation community, located strategically close to the University of Toronto and the Ontario Legislature at Queen's Park. Sophie Forest took his spot on the Radian6 board and became a key point person on the Salesforce file.

She saw the familiar mating game evolve with Benioff and his team selling their vision to LeBrun and his team. Then the temperature cooled, with her team crossing swords with the Salesforce lawyers. At that point LeBrun told the board he had been asked to meet Benioff once more in San Francisco. For Forest, it was a pivotal moment: Was it game over?

Looking back years later, LeBrun can understand Forest's concern about the future of the deal. But his recollection is quite different from hers. He explains that Benioff is an intuitive leader, driven by his relationships and the human interaction. To gauge the human element, he wanted to see LeBrun face-to-face.

After receiving the request, LeBrun got on a plane the next morning and went to see Benioff again in his home, where the Salesforce CEO asked him about his goals and his dreams. LeBrun wanted his team to be well integrated inside Salesforce, and to continue to have employment. And he wanted Benioff, in time, to deem this the best deal he had ever done. It was a conversation that, in LeBrun's view, operated in a parallel universe to the nitty-gritty details of negotiations. This was personal, and it was perhaps even more essential to the deal than the normal back-and-forth. And Benioff apparently liked what he heard. The deal went ahead.

There had been a number of earlier meetings over the deal's terms, which LeBrun considers typical in such negotiations. For example, there was some concern over the distance between San Francisco and Fredericton and whether the integration budget should include a private plane to travel back and forth regularly.

At that point, Salesforce had not done much acquiring of companies outside the Bay Area. The plane kept being added to the budget and then removed, until the parties agreed that trips would be kept in the budget for a year while the two companies went through their integration. It had never been a deal-breaker, but it underlined the challenges for a small Atlantic company and a large Pacific company to get together. The deal got done, for $326 million U.S., consisting of $276 million in cash and $50 million in shares — including $10 million in cash and $4 million in stock to the founders. Sources say there were more trailing payments, taking it up to almost $380 million, but for Salesforce, the reported lower number would be an easier sell to shareholders. Some critics were saying Salesforce was paying too much. Looking back, most analysts say it was justified, given the synergies.

All the Radian6 investors wanted a big price, but Forest noted a certain restraint in Gerry Pond. Forest remembers a discussion with Pond. "He is in Florida and he tells me, 'You know, Sophie, I have enough change in my jeans.'" In Forest's memory, Pond said the amount of the sale didn't change anything for him. "I'll do whatever the guys want to do, but I want the company to stay in the Maritimes."

A team of Radian6 managers had been working non-stop during three months of negotiations, taking on tasks after their regular shifts. Others got pulled into the picture. Kim Saunders was working for

Radian6 in Saint John. She had been hired out of the same marketing agency as David Alston, but had evolved into the role of human resources head at Radian6.

When she had joined, there were 20 people. Three years later the head count was up to 325. She had a hand in onboarding more than 250 people, sitting in interviews as she tested their resilience, work ethic and — that elusive but important factor — a sense of humour to work with this relaxed, fun-loving team. And by her reckoning, the company only lost a handful of people during a three-year period, a reflection of both the compelling work culture and the Atlantic tradition of loyalty.

One morning she had come up to Fredericton from Saint John, and she felt a certain excitement in the air. Marcel LeBrun invited her and a colleague into a meeting room. The company was being sold to Salesforce, he confided, and there would be an exhausting month of due diligence conducted with the utmost secrecy.

The momentum built toward mid-March 2011 when the announcement would be made. Scattered among three cities, Fredericton, Saint John and Halifax, employees would be summoned to breakfast meetings where they would be told the news. Brian Dunphy, who headed a software development team, was pinged one night when he was at the movies with his wife. He stepped out to take the call and was told everyone in his team had to be at the Wu Centre at nine o'clock the next morning.

The meeting was as much an adventure for the team of Salesforce managers who came for the event. At one point, one of the jet-lagged visitors asked Saunders how he could get a coffee at 6:00 a.m. in cold dark Fredericton and she said, "Well, there is Tim's." Welcome to Canada!

The Radian6 employees filed into the Wu that morning and watched as Marcel LeBrun took the stage. There is a tradition of online "sales bells," mass messages sent out to mark sales announcements.

LeBrun asked what was the biggest sales bell the group had seen. The response came back with deals in the hundreds of thousands of dollars. Think bigger, LeBrun said. "Salesforce for $326 million."

Dunphy lost his mind with excitement, but he saw concern on the faces around them: Would their jobs be safe? "I had been knocked around so much it didn't worry me anymore," Dunphy says, and he knew there was a good market for software developers.

Life had to go on until the deal closed and, meanwhile, there was the first-ever Radian6 users' conference in Boston. It would, of course, have to go ahead, and it would be a command performance with a lot of Salesforce stakeholders attending the event.

Jerry Carr was the point man to make sure the conference went off without a hitch. He watched LeBrun mount the stage to do his keynote. "I was sitting in the audience and I looked at my phone and I saw trouble." He discovered the system had crashed for the demonstration, and he scrambled to the control room. A nervous Chris Newton rushed into the room to ask what was going on. Carr confirmed the worst, and they messaged LeBrun: "Stall, Marcel!"

"Which he did masterfully," Carr says. "He went up on stage and told a few stories and made it feel very seamless. And then once the system was back and running and we validated it, we messaged him again and said, 'Okay, go!'"

Brian Dunphy was one of the conference attendees, and he had a lot riding on the Salesforce deal. "I was damn near broke at the time." He was finishing renovations to his house and had taken on freelance assignments. He would work at Radian6 from 9:00 a.m. to 6:00 p.m., then go home for a nap and work on freelance coding till 3:00 a.m. He and his wife were living on credit cards.

At the users' conference, he was told he might need a sports coat or suit. After the show, the team would be going out to San Francisco to meet the Salesforce group. He went to a tailor in Boston, got fitted up, but as he went to pay, the credit card bounced. Dunphy managed to find another card to cover the cost.

Marcel LeBrun in action
at the 2011 Radian6 users
conference in Boston
(Courtesy of Derek Wilmot)

When the deal finally closed and the money came in, Dunphy suddenly went from insolvency to multi-millionaire status, one of many such transformations created out of Radian6 and Q1 Labs. People used the money for houses, cottages, putting the kids through school, buying a car, sometimes a very nice one — some of Fredericton's young tech boffins had a weakness for Porsches. And some started reinvesting in what they hoped would be the next Radian6.

For Dunphy, the sale to Salesforce was a financial lifesaver but also a career-maker. Eight years later, the burly, likeable Dunphy would be recognized as one of the deans of the New Brunswick tech community, a seasoned leader who was heading a global team of developers in the event-management space. And as an investor in startups himself, he is an inspiration to every coder working feverishly in his or her basement, fuelled by coffee and trying to make ends meet.

Peter Moreira, the business journalist, writing in his online newsletter *Entrevestor*, cited the estimate that appeared in the allNovaScotia online service — that 12 New Brunswick investors received $68.4 million in payouts from the deal. "That means a dozen Atlantic Canadians with a history of investing in startups have tens of millions of dollars, which bodes well for the next generation of startups in the region as they will likely invest again." It was not a Silicon Valley number, but it was a great start.

Some institutional backers made off with a good haul, helping to validate their strategies. One early investor, the New Brunswick Investment Foundation, a government fund to provide seed money, scored big-time by believing in LeBrun and Newton. In 2006, it joined Pond and his friends in providing $50,000 to Radian6, and followed up two years later with $277,000. In the Salesforce deal, it walked away with a return of $9.25 million.

And no one did better than Summerhill, Brightspark and the BDC. When the Radian6 transaction was awarded deal of the year by the Canadian Venture Capital & Private Equity Association, the press release pointed out the magnitude of the bonanza for the VC firms involved. The original investment generated an internal rate of return of 142 per cent and a multiple of 22.8 times the original amount. A multiple of ten is considered a winner; Radian6 more than doubled that score in five years.

When the dust settled, Sophie Forest was trying to make sense of this success for Brightspark. What made it work? Certainly, the management and the product, and the galloping market. But what made such a rare event was two things you can't control — luck and timing.

She recalls, "They were just ahead of the curve. And they were smart enough to keep on being ahead all the time, probably because they were in their own bubble. They didn't really realize that they were leading this market by that much. So they kept on running and always looking back as if somebody was catching up. And the culture made them really humble. They were just working hard and making it happen, and not getting ahead of themselves." Again, culture was eating strategy for breakfast.

"Sometimes startups get early success and then they forget that it's only a quarter of the road — there's still so much to do. In their case, they were just heads down, let's do it. No ego. They were paying themselves very small, decent salaries. There was no excess."

LeBrun would say, "Go for your biggest customer first," which is what Radian6 did. It is hard to ignore the low-hanging local fruit and tackle your toughest market first. Like Brian Flood, Forest feels a lot of companies in the Maritimes shy away from that approach. "They sell to smaller local customers that have a lot of empathy for them."

"It's easier, but it's not real life," Forest says. After selling to the local market, once you go out to pitch international clients, "you don't get the empathy you once enjoyed." She adds, "They don't care about you being from New Brunswick; they just care about the best product."

When you go after the big global companies right away, you are up against your real competition in the world. Then, she says, "you can come back to your home market with confidence." That was what Radian6 did.

The Dreamforce conference for Salesforce's users and vendors was held in late August 2011 at the Moscone Convention Center in San Francisco, drawing hordes of techno-geeks to the sounds of metal rockers Metallica. The now acquisitive Salesforce had bought a couple of other companies, and the Radian6 guys got to hang out with the other founders. Dunphy kept thinking about how Radian6 the previous year had paid tens of thousands of dollars for a table-sized booth, and now the company had 1,000 square feet and was part of the team. He and Newton were standing in the middle, and Dunphy saw this bright glow of triumph in his colleague's eyes.

Dreamforce was also the occasion for the ritual deal-closing dinner. Joe Catalfamo had marked the occasion with little trophies for the principals, "nothing over-the-top," he insists, just a memento for "the enormous sense of pride for Canada." LeBrun and his team held a final Radian6 party and got Alston to wear a chicken suit. "Marcel always thinks it's pretty funny," Alston says.

For LeBrun, it was another step in his learning. As he had emphasized in his 11th-hour meeting with Benioff earlier that year, his great hope was that after Salesforce had more deals under its belt, he would hear Benioff say Radian6 was the best purchase he had ever

At the final Radian6 party, Marcel LeBrun brings on a chicken-suited
David Alston one more time (Courtesy of Daniella DeGrace)

made. It was important for the credibility of New Brunswick and
the Maritimes. "I didn't want word to leak out in the Valley, that 'we
bought his East Coast Canadian company and it didn't work, so we
won't do that again.' I wanted them to know they got good value, and
I wanted to make sure the team was integrated, so this wouldn't go
away."

Two years later, LeBrun got his affirmation. At a Dreamforce event,
someone asked about Radian6's role, and Benioff said it was the best
acquisition Salesforce had made to that point.

Gerry Pond was, of course, pleased. He felt that Salesforce was
committed to Atlantic Canada, and that the Radian6 deal established a
beachhead for the software giant on the East Coast of North America.
There were no assurances, of course, but he liked the commitment.

It was Pond's biggest deal, even to this day, and he estimates it
probably earned him more money after-tax than he had made in his
entire career at NBTel. And he did it in five years, as opposed to his

more than 35 years at NBTel-Aliant. "It allowed me to do things I had never dreamed I could do," he says.

He would be able to invest in a wider range of startups in East Valley Ventures, his angel investor network. He could help in the fight against poverty in the region. He could assist the province's universities and help build incubators like the Pond-Deshpande Centre, with a mission to balance commercial and social enterprise. He did not need the usual CEO toys, but he craved to make a difference, and he would. "I became a whole person with that money," he says.

Surely this windfall, and all these people who reaped such rewards and were now seasoned veterans, would generate more startups in Atlantic Canada. All eyes were on the founders and, particularly, Chris Newton.

12. The Most Ridiculous Year Ever

In 2011, Chris Newton was on a roll. He was still under 40 years old, and he had co-founded two groundbreaking tech companies. Now one of them had graduated into the spectacular category, having just been sold for around $330 million U.S. in its fifth year of operations. In New Brunswick, the business landscape is dominated by private family companies, whose value is concealed from the public. But everyone knew the approximate value of what Newton and his pals had created at Radian6. The numbers were mind-boggling — 142 per cent annual rate of return for investors. Chris's other company was doing well — but its progress had been slower than that of Radian6.

All this was exoneration, vindication, a resounding "Take that!" to all who had doubted him. The way ahead looked clear. Newton had a chance to follow in the footsteps of the best of the Silicon Valley serial founders. He was looking at two years or so working for Salesforce — there was even talk of moving to California with LeBrun. Who knew what would happen after that? Another company, another home run? Maybe a bunch of them. No wonder there was a glow in his eyes as he attended Dreamforce.

In his new role at Salesforce, he needed to add some insurance coverage, and that required a medical checkup. Newton had a mole on his back and his mother had told him, as mothers do, that he should get it checked out. So he went for his insurance checkup and the doctor took an interest in that mole, saying it should be tested. The results came back — melanoma cancer in the third stage.

Life has a way of getting in the way of career, money, ambition. Newton's mantra was "Every pain point is an opportunity." He had prospered from others' pain points. Now he was faced with a personal pain, and it would mean a re-examination of his life.

He had barely started at Salesforce when he went on short-term medical leave. There ensued a bunch of surgeries; a big patch of skin was taken out of his back; all his lymph nodes removed under his arms. There was radiation treatment and chemotherapy, and finally long-term medical leave.

When he got the news, he had to tell his parents. He was close to his father, growing up in a police family and even working for Dan in one of his post-retirement businesses, as a security guard in the Miramichi. An emotional Chris got his father on the line and told him the alarming test results. Little did Chris know, but Dan Newton had also just received a cancer diagnosis and was building his resolve to tell his children. But when Dan heard from Chris, and detected his son's level of stress, the stoical father decided to hold on to his own bad news.

Marc Benioff, the co-founder of Salesforce, stepped up. Benioff was known to be very employee-centric. A huge philanthropic donor to health care in the Bay Area, he said he would get Newton in to see a melanoma specialist. Newton flew to California and learned of an immunotherapy treatment that was in trials in the U.S. but had not yet been tested in Canada.

The doctor said he would get Newton the drug, but the young Canadian couldn't acquire it in Canada (though the drug subsequently became available). Instead, he had to go to a location across the border in Maine and take it back to Fredericton. He would drive to Houlton, Maine, every six weeks to two months for the new drug, for which he would pay $10,000 per trip. Benioff offered to pay for the drugs, but Newton felt he had already been richly compensated for his shares, and now he would be sidelined by his illness. It was on him to pay the drug bill.

Newton was at home bandaged up from surgeries, being cared for by a nurse who came in every day, when his friend Sandy Bird called in fall 2011 to say Q1 Labs was being sold to IBM and the price was good — it would end up at $600 million U.S.

Chris couldn't help but smile. "I'm on the phone with Sandy, and it was the most surreal year ever. I had lived a pretty normal life until these two companies [were built], and the peak point of both them was that same year. It was the most ridiculous year I will probably ever have." And a life-challenging health crisis at the same time.

Indeed, the Q1 Labs story had been quietly proceeding, with the development team in Fredericton under Bird and the senior management and sales team in Waltham, Massachusetts, under Shaun McConnon. It was typical for VCs to exit within ten years on the outside — anything over eight and the investment was getting long in the tooth. It was eight years and counting for the American venture capitalists that had joined the Q1 transaction. Some were fretful but others were hanging in with the goal of, maybe, a $600-million exit.

And the CEO Shaun McConnon had Brendan Hannigan on board to help achieve that goal. The two executives contracted an analyst from the consulting firm Gartner to help show where they stood in the cybersecurity space, and where they needed to be. There were various categories of products, and Q1 was in the section called NBAD, for network behaviour anomaly detection. It was a declining piece of the market.

But there was another broader technology platform with more promise, called SIEM, for security information and event management. "Events" are any transactions monitored on a network, such as a credit card swipe or access card tap. According to Gartner, a SIEM system can "analyze event data in real time for early detection of targeted attacks and data breaches." It can report on such data for incident response, forensics and regulatory compliance.

To grow the company, Q1 had to diversify the offering of its QRadar product to include SIEM. It was a huge challenge. Gartner did periodic reports on the SIEM sector, including four-quadrant charts with "ability to execute" up the vertical axis and "completeness of vision" along the horizontal. In 2006, Q1 sucked at both and was buried in the losers' quadrant in the lower left.

Hannigan was adamant that they had to combine NBAD with SIEM, and nobody had ever done that before. It was projected as a two-year project, but it took four. According to McConnon, "I kept praying, 'Please God, just give me a year, maybe two, where nobody else does this.'" Nobody ever did.

McConnon has kept posters of the annual Gartner charts; they are still in his office today in Boston. Q1 kept moving ever rightward and upward until it was gaining fast as a SIEM leader. By 2011, revenues were up to $75 million, and Q1 had turned the corner on profit.

But the product pivot had required additional financing. Approximately seven months after the Series B round, on June 29, 2004, the company raised $11 million U.S. from a group comprising its Series A investors and newcomer Globespan Capital Partners. Less than two years later, it raised another $9 million. The time was fortuitous, as the global financial crisis of 2007-2008 followed soon after.

McConnon had stepped back from the president's role, retaining the title of executive chairman and making way for Brendan Hannigan as president. The new marketing head would be Tom Turner, a raw-boned Yorkshireman whose softly modulated accent — a combination of English North Country and Bostonese — belied his hard-nosed rugby-playing obsession. Turner was into his second company with McConnon, and there would be another in the future. It became the CEO's style — he took his guys with him from one startup to another.

His acolytes were well-travelled, with Hannigan, a Dubliner, and Turner, from Thirsk, a Yorkshire market town where his parents ran the bookshop and their biggest revenue source was the local veterinarian named Alf Wight. Wight was the author of a best-selling series based on his country vet practice, written under the pseudonym James Herriot. The books inspired a popular TV series shown on the American PBS network. Tourists would flock to the Turner shop to buy Herriot books, such as *All Creatures Great and Small*, then land at the vet clinic's doorstep to have Wight autograph their copies.

As the Q1 marketing lead, Turner found the travel connections from Boston to Fredericton frustrating. He watched the airline service dwindle away: "First there were two flights a day. And it went down to one flight a day, and then it went down to one flight a day on an Indiana Jones plane. And then you had to go through Halifax, so at that point, you might as well drive."

His team would drive to Fredericton in a van, seven or eight people, stopping for wireless access points, which became more intermittent as they worked their way north — a bonding exercise, he says with a chuckle. There were stories about a memorable trip in Shaun McConnon's Bentley, cruising well over 100 miles an hour and worrying about whether McConnon could slow down in time for the border crossing.

The thinking was that Q1 would have an initial public offering, and it had contracted an investment banker to start the process. But IBM had stepped into the picture. The old mainframe company was now a services powerhouse, intent on making cybersecurity a core part of its business. Sonja Hoel's take was, "We had filed to go public, and IBM kept asking about us. We kept saying no, and they said 'we really want to buy you,' and they finally gave up a price we could not disclose, but it was high enough." Someone later leaked that it was in the area of $600 million.

As Sandy Bird was relaying the news to Chris Newton, Shaun McConnon was making another call. Brian Flood had left Q1 long before. He and Carolyn had been at their daughter's White Coat Ceremony at McGill University's Faculty of Dentistry, during which third-year students receive their official white coats, marking their transition to training in a clinic. When they got home to Saint John, there was a message on the phone from Shaun McConnon to call him back. Brian looked at Carolyn and wondered if this was the call they had been waiting for.

Flood and McConnon had not talked much over the past few years. There had been a legal dispute at the end, and Flood's exit was messy. But the two still admired what each other had done. Eight years into the VC control — and more than a decade after Q1's founding — Brian was thinking, "This is about the right time for an exit."

Brian called McConnon back and got Carolyn on the line too. McConnon confirmed the company was in play. Carolyn said, "Shaun, you should be very proud of yourself." It had been a leap of faith, Carolyn says, looking back. "Well before there was an exit, there were a lot of people who were starting to lose faith — they did not think this was going to work." Some of those people blamed the Floods for selling out to American interests. Brian had stuck to his guns — that the project needed the abundant U.S. capital to achieve the payday that was deserved, and from which New Brunswick would ultimately benefit. There was tremendous emotional release in that telephone call, which melted the heart of the alleged tough guy, Shaun McConnon. He could feel the mixture of relief and joy in Brian's voice.

The Q1 deal was welcomed by Sandy Bird and Dwight Spencer, who would join IBM, emerging as key figures in Big Blue's unfolding cybersecurity strategy. Bird, in particular, would thrive, as he headed the Fredericton development lab that became a fundamental piece of the IBM cybersecurity business. It was the perfect transition. And Spencer remained a valuable customer-facing manager who combined a grasp of technical language and abundant people skills.

Two deals, two paths. Q1 Labs won the venture capital association's award as deal of the year for 2012, following in the wake of Radian6. It was a tribute to BDC and NBIMC, who did the first VC financing, after the choir of angels. (The deal was done in the same calendar year as Radian6, but because of the deadline to qualify for the award, it slipped into the next year.) Peter Moreira summed it up in *Entrevestor*: "Q1 was a great deal, but not quite as stellar as Radian6. Q1 attracted nine rounds of financing totalling $42 million over eight years and produced an internal rate of return — the key ratio in determining the annual return for investors — of 32.8 per cent and a multiple of 9.0 times original investment. That's fantastic, but it pales in comparison to Radian6, which had an IRR of 142 per cent and total return of 22.8 times."

Shaun McConnon was revelling in his third big exit deal, and he would go on to another startup, seeking the same kind of outcome. The hard-living veteran warhorse was recruited by a Boston company, BitSight, first as an adviser to its younger founders, then as CEO. BitSight occupies another area of cybersecurity: security ratings — it can do an assessment of a company's ability to resist a cyber attack.

Interviewed at BitSight in 2019, McConnon was hoping for an exit event in a couple of years and a billion-dollar valuation. He had taken up writing, as the author of a sci-fi novel *Supremis*, all about a superior form of being, and he was pecking away at a memoir, which he calls *The Last Entrepreneur*.

He sees himself as a survivor of a dying breed, the kind of business player who works for others, not for the quick financial hit. "The old school entrepreneur basically thinks about his investors, his employees and his customers first. If all those do well, very well, so does he." As opposed to a lot of young entrepreneurs, he says, who are entirely consumed by making money for themselves, and customers be damned.

In Boston, McConnon has become the ultimate battle-scarred survivor in a world of bright young things. A tech news service, Pando, saw him as "one of these guys that you bump into on a street in Boston" and assume he's some old salty dog or a lifer from the streets of Southie — Southie being the historically hardscrabble, now trendy south end of Boston. "Only later do you find out he's one of the under-the-radar legends of the tech industry."

Sonja Hoel is a survivor too. Much had happened in the eight years since she first invested in Q1. Her star kept rising at Menlo. At 39, she married a Bay Area restaurateur named Jon Perkins, and they had made plans to adopt a baby with a willing birth mother, a young friend of the family — as described in the book *Alpha Girls*.

But in 2008, just ahead of the baby's arrival, Sonja Hoel Perkins was diagnosed with advanced breast cancer. Shaken, she went ahead with the adoption, just as she was facing a debilitating round of chemotherapy. She returned to Menlo Ventures after a six-month leave and got back into the groove. After another series of radiation, she managed to beat the cancer. She decided not to participate in another Menlo fund, although new deals came to her attention, including a ride-sharing startup called Uber. As Hoel urged her colleagues to back Uber, Menlo Ventures came in as lead investor in a Series B round estimated at $32 million.

The Q1 deal had been satisfying, another feather in her cap. The returns enabled her to win the investor of the year award in her firm. "Q1 was a total home run," she says, although she notes there have been other companies she has backed that scored capitalization in the billions of dollars.

She moved on from Menlo Ventures to operate her own firm, The Perkins Fund. Shaped by her life twists as a mother and cancer survivor, she is a prominent Silicon Valley feminist and activist. She works with Broadway Angels, a kind of all-star team of leading female investors, and Project Glimmer, which supports low-income teenagers and young women, often with gifts of jewellery, makeup and gift cards, giving them a better self-image as they advance their lives.

As an investor, "I work with the most optimistic people trying to make the world a better place." Q1 is one of those situations. "It really saves businesses, if you think about personal credit card information and CEOs whose data gets breached. Those are the kinds of companies I want to get involved with." But, she says, "I had to decide what I wanted to do in my life, and I needed more time with family. I have more influence now than ever with Broadway Angels — we see all these deals, and we've done more for women in these ventures." She adds, "The companies I invest in are going to be history-making companies."

Cancer shaped the lives of Sonja Hoel (now Perkins) on the West Coast and Chris Newton on the East Coast. Newton never knew his

An uncomfortable Chris
Newton poses for a *Globe
and Mail* photo shoot in 2011
(Courtesy of David Smith)

dad was ill right up until Dan Newton died in late 2011. He had not
told Chris and his sister about his illness. Patty Newton (now Patty
Phillips) shakes her head: "I was disappointed his dad didn't tell him;
the kids were heartbroken they didn't have a chance to talk. He kept
quiet to the end."

Meanwhile, news of the twin deals spread all the way to Toronto,
where I was working for the *Globe and Mail's Report on Business*. I
started to put together a story that would reflect this core message:
"The deals, for Radian6 Technologies and Q1 Labs, are transforming
the image of New Brunswick from a have-not province dominated by
pulp, petroleum and potato barons to an innovation hotbed populated
by smart young techies and risk-embracing investors."

I called up Chris Newton in Fredericton. I was struck by how
low-key he was — after all, this fellow in his late 30s had become a
hometown hero through his two great companies. Surely, he would
be whooping it up, but I sensed a certain sadness and a feeling of
distraction. I didn't know how much.

Newton remembers those days well, as he experienced what was,
for New Brunswick, a media onslaught. When the newspapers and

magazines sent out photographers, they did not know that he was badly cut up, covered with bandages and scars under his clothes. "Nobody knew I was sick."

There was some inadvertent dark humour. One media outlet wanted a full body shot of Newton. He had just had his lymph nodes removed, and there was fluid building up. So the doctors attached drainage bags to his arms. He had no place to hide them, so he stuffed them down the front of his pants. "I figured that if they were going to show me bulgy somewhere, it might as well be down there," he says now, laughing.

He goes often to his mom's house near Moncton, where he sees framed newspaper stories on the wall, displayed in the manner that a hockey mom might celebrate the big games of her prodigy son or daughter. He sees what his mom sees — the shots capturing his success — but he sees something else too: "Oh yeah, that was the day I had all those bandages and my shoulders pinned back — they'd taken a ten-centimetre bit out of my back and stapled my shoulders."

Yet he was able to beat the cancer (although he knows he can never be entirely sure it won't resurface). He pulled back from the startup world, spending time with his wife and young family. During his prolonged retreat from business, Newton would often be asked, now that he had hit two home runs, whether he would ever hit a third. He replied that there have already been three. The third was conquering cancer. Some friends see the Radian6 deal as delivering a perverse benefit, vastly more important than the money. If Salesforce had not bought Radian6, Newton would not have gone for a checkup, might not have had the mole tested in time to be successfully treated and might be dead today.

13. A Cambrian Explosion

Growing up on Cape Breton Island, and studying computer science at the local university, Gavin Uhma was oblivious to the trials and triumphs of Chris Newton, Gerry Pond, Marcel LeBrun and the tech revolutionaries in New Brunswick. Uhma was the classic computer-obsessed kid, a decade younger than Chris Newton but similarly glued to a screen for long hours; he played with video games before graduating to the language of software programming.

Like Newton, he was a young geek in a region unassociated with advanced technology. Similar to the Miramichi, Cape Breton is naturally beautiful, but also blessed with its own rich mélange of Acadian and Gaelic cultures. Industrially it is known more for its moribund coal and steel works than new technology — even though the telephone pioneer Alexander Graham Bell had a summer house in Baddeck, where he set up a lab and explored heavier-than-air flight, the genesis of Canada's first piloted aircraft.

The stories of Q1 Labs and particularly Radian6 would intersect dramatically with Gavin Uhma's life, serving as a catalyst in his emergence as a 20-something startup legend in Nova Scotia and a central player in the Halifax technology community.

The Halifax venture capitalist Patrick Keefe sees the Radian6 and Q1 exit deals as triggers for "a Cambrian explosion," the economic equivalent of the evolutionary burst of energy 500 million years ago that spawned new organisms, including the ancestors of today's human species. Similarly, Radian6 sparked an explosive chain reaction and Gavin Uhma was among the forces set in motion.

As a kid, in a household with two sisters and his mother as sole provider, Uhma was uncommonly entrepreneurial. While others in his Grade 3 class might have been trading peanut-butter-and-jelly sandwiches, he was selling Tic Tacs in the schoolyard. By the time he was studying at Cape Breton University in Sydney he had graduated to more sophisticated enterprises, putting together computer parts with memory chips, and operating PC sales and service and web development businesses.

He was always jumping into projects before he knew what he was doing. He recalls, "I would spend three months learning something, and then I'm saying, 'Oh, I'm going to start a company. This is so awesome that I can do this now.'" The enterprises yielded mixed results, but he became comfortable with exploring the edges of possibility.

On a student internship in Ottawa, he had a lot of time on his hands in the evenings and began playing around with the idea of being able to record a cursor's movements as it navigated a website. "I don't know why I was doing that exactly, but I thought, 'Okay, if I capture exactly the position of the mouse and the timing of the mouse, then I can put it on a timer and I can play it back and it looks exactly like the motions I just took.' And it was just kind of fun to be able to do that."

Two years later, in 2008, he was back in Sydney and still tweaking his "fun idea." At a tech event, he ran into a Prince Edward Islander named Jevon MacDonald, a well-travelled entrepreneur who had co-founded a Charlottetown computer service business called silverorange, which had embraced the open source movement and, in fact, originated the famous Firefox logo for Mozilla.

After an unsuccessful foray into another PEI startup, MacDonald had helped build businesses in Toronto and Austin, Texas. With five web-based startups under his belt in his 20s, he was now a roving entrepreneur-in-residence with Innovacorp, the provincially funded seed-capital source.

Up to then, Uhma's understanding of the tech world was that if you had an idea, you pitched it to government, and you tried to drum up enough funding to survive. MacDonald had a bigger vista in mind — private venture capital, global linkages and "more fast-moving, highly funded, capital-intensive kind of stuff. And it was just different from the world that I grew up in in Cape Breton," Uhma recalls.

The two exchanged emails and the slightly older MacDonald began to see Uhma as "a kid who was totally brilliant, working in a basement in Cape Breton, but he didn't have a product sense in his body." They were a match made in heaven, a kind of Newton-LeBrun duo, Nova Scotia style. MacDonald could see the potential of developing Uhma's idea for the enterprise software market, and he knew some of the players, including Salesforce founder Marc Benioff.

From Uhma's days playing with his cursor in Ottawa, the idea had graduated to selling a program to marketers of web-based software, who could use the technology to guide customers through their sites, tracking their movements remotely as prospective clients learned the functions of the products they were thinking of buying.

Along with a couple of other Cape Breton University alumni, David Kim and Kirk MacPhee, Uhma and MacDonald founded a company called GoInstant that, within a few months of being formed, raised $1.7 million in seed financing. The company had yet to earn a dollar of revenue, but in this first round of financing had already attracted funding from Silicon Valley venture capitalists, including Yuri Milner, the Russian billionaire who was the biggest single investor in Facebook. It was testimony to MacDonald's wide network of relationships.

One of MacDonald's old contacts, Marc Benioff, had been following him on Twitter and wondered what he was doing. Benioff was just coming off the Salesforce takeover of Radian6. Benioff saw the GoInstant product presentation and was immediately interested in the company. He emailed MacDonald, and before long, the four young Maritimers sold GoInstant to Salesforce for $70 to $80 million U.S.

In pure dollars, the GoInstant deal was only a fifth the size of the Radian6 haul, but it was, in a way, just as significant. This out-of-the-blue exit deal was another validation of Atlantic Canada, and Halifax in particular. A lot of factors were involved — Uhma's tech vision, the partners' complementary skills and MacDonald's ability to see a product that would appeal to the enterprise market, plus his nimble navigation of his network of contacts.

Uhma and MacDonald both agree the example of Radian6 loomed large in their story, as a shining beacon of what could be done. When you are a young startup founder, seeing someone break through a barrier gives you permission to try it, MacDonald explains. And young founders are naturally competitive. When they see an event of that scale, they instinctively want to beat it.

The deal also opened up a relationship with Marcel LeBrun. MacDonald consults LeBrun constantly and sees him as the most accomplished CEO in the Maritime technology space.

Kim Saunders, the Radian6 human resources chief, says GoInstant's progress is an example of what Radian6 accomplished for the Maritimes. The Fredericton firm mapped out the route for becoming a successful startup in the region. It got easier to be noticed, a big help in hiring employees. "Everyone in the tech world knows Radian6. Everyone wants to be Radian6."

What's more, Radian6 had provided an entry point for Salesforce in Atlantic Canada, and in the country as a whole. Once Marc Benioff was comfortable with Canada and had established a base with Radian6, he invested in a Toronto company, Rypple. GoInstant was the natural next step. In a sense Radian6 begat GoInstant, and the two gave Salesforce an important step up in Canada.

MacDonald believes that Benioff relished the injection of fresh thinking into Salesforce, a challenge to the dominant West Coast culture that had been its nurturing ground. He particularly liked the infusion of Atlantic Canadians into what had been until then a San Francisco–Silicon Valley creation. "Our group was sent in to break stuff," MacDonald says, with the freedom to make change happen in a big organization. It was a special time that GoInstant and Radian6 helped fashion.

In Halifax, that dynamic was further cultivated, as the local Radian6 office combined with GoInstant's people to give Salesforce a significant presence in the city, along with its offices in Fredericton and Saint John. The excitement of those takeovers has faded somewhat over the years, and yet among those three locations, the San Francisco-based giant provides a solid core of jobs — "a few hundred," according to one company source in 2020.

Yet some industry leaders say that, after the takeovers, Salesforce's role locally has been disappointing, because the company placed so many key roles in other centres, and integrated Radian6 with other new acquisitions. The major focus for its marketing cloud activities became Indianapolis, where Salesforce in 2013 acquired a significant company, ExactTarget, for $2.5 billion U.S. After the shining potential of Radian6, Atlantic Canada seemed to have been passed over.

Yet Salesforce has had a positive impact in the Maritimes, and remains an economic driver. Many of its jobs in the region are engineering roles that feed into the company's global research and development effort. There are also customer service types who have worldwide responsibilities, as well as positions in marketing and sales.

Salesforce is a continuing builder of skills and connections, as people move in and out of the organization with seeming ease. The culture remains fiercely entrepreneurial. Sources say there is no stigma attached to leaving the company and heading out to work in a startup, and if it doesn't work out, moving back into Salesforce for a career.

Uhma and MacDonald also provide sterling examples of how the Salesforce deals created ripples. After working at Salesforce — side-by-side with former Radian6 employees — they became figures in the emerging startup scene. It started as a question of office space. Before the sale to Salesforce, GoInstant had occupied an office that was much larger than needed. Uhma and MacDonald played with the idea of splitting this office in half and making room for other startups to come in. One of the biggest problems for early-stage startups is finding that first office. It is a huge distraction to check out potential office spaces, make a decision and negotiate terms.

"So if you could establish a place that's not an incubator, but much simpler, just a space for offices that has good internet and the lights are on, and you just have to pay one bill and you don't have to worry about [office-space] management, that would be a pretty good thing," Uhma says.

The idea helped give birth to the Volta startup hub, now on three floors of the Maritime Centre in central Halifax, home to a parade of companies and a focus for mentoring, investing and all kinds of services on site. There are equivalent spaces in Fredericton, Moncton and other cities, but there is nothing in the Maritimes to match Volta's scale and density of startup activity.

Listed as a co-founder of Volta, MacDonald has entered another realm of movers and shakers, as a fellow of the Creative Destruction Lab (CDL) in Halifax, the Atlantic Canadian arm of the highly success- ful startup training and mentoring program pioneered at the Rotman School of Management at the University of Toronto. MacDonald is part of an advisory and founder group that includes names from the old power elite in Atlantic Canada — Bragg, Steele, Sobey, Rowe, Dobbin, Risley and, yes, Gerry Pond again.

When this group of more conservative, seasoned business leaders signs on, it indicates that startup enterprise has moved into the main- stream, with the safe established brand of CDL offering assurances. The CDL model provides opportunities for young companies to raise capital, not just from the program's all-star team of local mentors but from investors outside the Atlantic region.

Meanwhile, Gavin Uhma, still in his mid-30s, has contributed to the startup scene at Cape Breton University, and he and MacDonald are on to their next new ventures in Halifax. As Uhma says, "I'm just a big geek. And I like trying to immerse myself in emerging tech and try to understand it. And then I generally find my opportunities from that."

Inspired in part by GoInstant's story, this budding tech community has provided a shot in the arm for Halifax, which, despite its status as the major Maritime city, had been reduced to a relatively sleepy business centre. In the historical pecking order of the Maritimes, Halifax had tended to treat the other Maritime regions as mere colonies, feeding human and financial resources into a city with a grand history as a commercial port, a military sentinel on the Atlantic and the home to six universities, including the much admired Dalhousie.

In the early 21st century, it could be argued that tiny Fredericton, when combined with Saint John just an hour away, was a more vibrant technology centre. Fredericton shared many of Halifax's advantages as a provincial capital, as the home of a major power company (NB Power) with a big employment and procurement footprint, plus a strong university research component. But the Fredericton–Saint John nexus had something Halifax seemed to lack — Gerry Pond types who could lace together business and academia, drawing in political leaders and top civil servants for community-building projects. As greater Halifax-Dartmouth's population exceeded 400,000, four times the Fredericton census area's populace (and seven times that of Fredericton's urban core), it was underachieving.

Coasting on its heavy government, university and military presence, Halifax was stymied by a kind of commercial inertia, despite the presence of some household-name entrepreneurs. Its plight was symbolized by Barrington Street, arguably the "main street" of the Maritimes, but lately a depressed zone of closed shops with paper-covered windows.

Yet, the emergence of an innovation culture, flowing partly out of the GoInstant deal, helped fashion a turnaround. Another factor was the effort of civic leaders in developing a large back-office capability for the hedge-fund industry, and in luring other financial services and industrial firms to the city. A group of public figures, professionals and entrepreneurs stepped up to the challenge, including corporate networkers such as Chris Huskilson, the retired head of Emera, the provincial power company's parent.

Others credit the removal of constraints on downtown development, a big ship-building contract and, more recently, the designation of Halifax by the federal government as the hub of an Oceans Supercluster, a public-private undertaking to feed off the region's maritime industries. The Oceans Supercluster gained momentum from a single deal. About the time of the GoInstant sale to Salesforce, local tycoons John Risley and Robert Orr sold Ocean Nutrition Canada, a global producer of Omega-3 health products made from fish oil, to a Dutch company for $540 million.

For Risley, it was a continuation of the deal-making that began decades earlier when he and his brother-in-law sold lobsters out of the back of a pickup truck and parlayed that business into Clearwater Seafoods, a force in the local fishery industry. In the wake of the Radian6 and Q1 Labs deals — which were conventional tech exits — this one was "outside the box," Risley says. It made people take notice that you could build these sexy new companies in so-called old industries.

Ocean Nutrition did not inhabit the typical ocean sectors of servicing offshore oil, fishing or even fish farming. "People expect ocean startups in those silos," Risley says. Ocean Nutrition was a world leader in a nutritional field, and Risley caught the usual flack about selling out to a foreign company. He doesn't apologize for it. Indeed, some head office and research jobs have gone, he says, but the Dutch owners continue to invest in local production. "Creating jobs in rural Atlantic Canada is very much a function of the oceans economy."

Risley is one Atlantic tycoon who bridges old and new, reflecting his restless, driving personality. He figures he has invested in twenty startups over the years, including five to ten in his early-2020 portfolio. While making money is a passion, he is increasingly interested in preserving an industry or building a community. He sees his most recent investment in that light, as part of the group that bought

Canadian satellite technology champion MDA for $1 billion, with plans to repatriate its head office from the United States back to Canada.

Risley says, "As I get older, I get to allow my arm to be twisted into spending more time and money investing into community-building, including outside Atlantic Canada. [I'm] hoping to convince people that all the bright minds out of U of T and the University of Waterloo don't have to go to Silicon Valley. And that is what we want to do with MDA." But he adds, "You have to be a cool business, and if you are not a cool business, they will pass you by."

There are a lot of cool businesses congregating in Volta, and in other Halifax cubicle farms, part of a burgeoning tech scene, which combined with vibrant university life and a downtown coffee-and-pub scene, makes it an attractive place for young entrepreneurs. What's more, there are direct flights to Boston and New York, a big advantage over Fredericton.

The tech deals changed the narrative for Patrick Keefe, the son of a Halifax tavern-keeping and brewing family, who through a series of serendipitous events had ended up as an important investor in high-tech Atlantic Canada, as one of the general partners in Build Ventures, a public-private venture in early-stage investing.

Keefe in his youth had an academic bent and attended Oxford as a history student — his area of concentration was international political history with a focus on the Suez Canal crisis of the 1950s. His father died and Patrick, on returning to Canada, worked in the family business, which besides the Granite brewing business also included a portfolio of restaurants and commercial real estate. Then Patrick's wife had an opportunity to become a medical resident in a Boston hospital, and he followed her south, enrolling at Harvard for an MBA and then moving into consulting work with Boston Consulting Group and to venture capital with Atlas Venture, a prominent Boston firm.

When his wife's residency ended, they came home to Halifax. By right-place, right-time circumstance, he became co-owner of a joint venture to expand Starbucks coffee shops in Quebec and Atlantic

Canada. When, as expected, Starbucks bought him out, he joined Innovacorp, the local seed-capital investor. Among his moves was hiring Jevon MacDonald as entrepreneur-in-residence.

The next turning point was the 2010 publication of a report on the state of Nova Scotia's economic development efforts by Université de Moncton political economist Donald Savoie. *Invest More, Innovate More, Trade More, Learn More: The Way Ahead for Nova Scotia*, otherwise known as the Savoie report, focused on the work of the various development agencies. It also highlighted the need for an independently run venture capital fund to stimulate startup activity, jointly funded by public and private sources.

The report was embraced inside government, and Keefe became deeply involved in the conception of the venture capital fund, whose limited partners would include provincial governments. There was some heavy lifting involved. "Provincial governments investing in an independently managed investment fund is counterintuitive," Keefe says. "They are making a financial commitment but have no control over the financial decisions."

The project was in danger of losing momentum when in 2011 the Radian6 exit hit the news, followed within the year by Q1 and GoInstant. Those events fostered a favourable environment for the fund to launch. Keefe was in the right place at the right time, as a Build Ventures founding partner. Build Ventures was able to close the first fund in 2013 for $65 million and another in 2020 for about $50 million, and has invested in a broad group of companies in four provinces.

Keefe, also a co-founder of Volta, sees several major outcomes from the Radian6 deal. First came the pure dollars that the deal generated. In particular, "Gerry Pond took a significant amount of personal capital and rallied a group around East Valley Ventures. They recycled that wealth in the ecosystem, investing at a ferocious pace."

This angel investment opened up a pipeline for the Build Ventures portfolio of early-stage investments. Its roster is replete with such

Gerry-built company names as Smart Skin, Resson and Fiddlehead Technology, as well as companies headed or supported by graduates of the Pond school of startup management.

Radian6, along with Q1 Labs, also injected talent, not just at the founder level, but in the ranks of vice presidents, directors and heads of departments — people like David Alston, Daniella DeGrace, Rich McInnis, Jerry Carr, Kim Saunders, Jeff White and Greg Picot (formerly at Radian6, now Eigen Innovations' president), who would lend their expertise to the next generation. "Those fingerprints are everywhere across our portfolio," Keefe says.

When Matt Hebb, the founding CEO of the Oceans Supercluster, needed a bit of finance capability in the early going, he called Gerry Pond and chatted about it. Before long, Jeff White, the utility CFO for tough finance jobs in the Atlantic startup universe, was on board, adding his instant credibility. He was at both Radian6 and Q1, as well as East Valley Ventures, and so it was assumed he knew a thing or two about the finance role. He would later move on to head the New Brunswick Investment Foundation.

Keefe talks about the concept of "entrepreneurial recycling," which these big exits encourage. People achieve success in their respective startups, and become world leaders in their technology fields. When the exit comes, they join the acquiring company like IBM or Salesforce, which are good places to hone their crafts. Then, after the requisite period of golden handcuffs, they become free to have a massive impact by jumping into these new companies.

But there is another important outcome that is more intangible — the cultural impact on the region, the idea that you can actually do this from Halifax, or indeed anywhere in Atlantic Canada. "On any measure we punch above our weight in producing valuable tech companies," Keefe says, noting the low population and small venture capital base.

In terms of catalytic impact, it creates a burst of "holy shit, we can start a company here!" That spirit is hard to measure, but Keefe sees it happening over and over. As we talked, his new fund's first two

investee companies were being led by major actors in the Radian6 and
Q1 stories.

Another factor that has changed is Atlantic Canada's profile in the
world. It is a different environment than when Brian Flood and Sandy
Bird first went to Silicon Valley, caps in hand, begging for venture
funding. At that time, Keefe recalls, the big money in Silicon Valley,
or on Bay Street and Wall Street, felt there was no way you could
make money from venture capital in Atlantic Canada. But times have
changed, and now the VCs in Toronto and farther afield are coming
to Halifax.

The Radian6 transaction, followed hard by Q1 Labs and GoInstant,
provided the "stake in the ground that this is a real region where things
can be done." But the challenges remain. A lot of the players in the
ecosystem rely on a single payer, which is government. Among the
agencies, there is a competition for resources, with often self-defeating
overlap in services provided. Government funding is a double-edged
sword — a good supply of early non-dilutive capital, but a constant
gauntlet of bureaucratic procedures for entrepreneurs to pass through.

Jevon MacDonald is now running his new startup, Manifold, which
provides a cloud-based one-stop interface for services catering to
software developers. He believes the next phase of innovation should
take the focus off government dependence and ease the heavy hand of
the state on the tech sector.

MacDonald worries that the region's entrepreneurs spend too much
of their time trying to satisfy government requirements for funding,
when they should be out there innovating and selling. Outsiders to the
region say Atlantic Canadians are way too obsessed with government
funding, he notes.

"The economic development approach of government does not
work in this community," he says, in terms of the economic impact
and the costs to both the recipients and the public. It is a waste of
money and has not had the expected impact, he argues.

MacDonald, still only in his late 30s, would take the government entirely out of direct investing, because he believes the agencies and their fund managers lack the private-enterprise structures and processes to make good decisions. The processes they use create a lot of friction in the system. He also would like to see governments get out of program-based spending for technology startups because these programs get locked in, and when the game suddenly changes — as it inevitably does — they are left hopelessly behind.

The number-one thing government could do, he says, is subsidize a regular flight to San Francisco, where you could get on a plane on a Monday morning and be back Friday and not spend endless hours in transit. Nowadays the business founder comes home totally exhausted, and he or she can't run a business that way. And, he argues, many tech startups do have to connect to California personally.

Above all, "we've got to get out of entrepreneurs' way," he urges. It means a different approach to economic development in an urban technology centre like Halifax, versus the rural communities, which may need a more direct stimulus approach. Too many times, the cookie-cutter model of government funding has failed.

Another challenge: people talk of a well-educated and motivated talent pool, but there is a desperate shortage of sales personnel in Atlantic Canada. Radian6's sales rep Rich McInnis — now employed at Salesforce in Halifax — says there is some talent, but not in abundance. It needs more nurturing in universities and an overall attitude adjustment in society. The sales role in Canada, and particularly Atlantic Canada, is stigmatized, still associated with slick come-ons. Yet it is fundamental to building companies. In an organization like Salesforce — which actually incorporates the skill in its company name — sales is a driver of strategy.

Gerry Pond built a career as a non-techie with a sales capability. Now he sees it as a lifetime goal — one of many — to lift the sales function to a higher level of respect. He has been the financial backer for a new sales stream in the MBA program at the University of New Brunswick's Saint John campus. "What I was trying to do was get rid of the very embedded history of sales being bad," he says, and the antiquated image of a salesperson as a used car guy in a flashy jacket. Even used car guys would reject that image today.

Little startups with young geeks and tech purists make for nice, inspiring stories, but you need the Rich McInnis types out there pounding the pavement and plying the phones, with an enormous hunger for the next deal. The kind of person who, like McInnis in his Radian6 days, would be on the phone with customers, working beside his pregnant wife who was confined to bed rest. To save time, while he relentlessly worked the phones, she was feeding data into her husband's laptop computer.

Like Jevon MacDonald, Patrick Keefe sees the danger of geo-graphical isolation, and emphasizes the need to jump on a plane and get out of town. "If you sit here and don't spend time in a vibrant and entrepreneurially dense area like San Francisco or New York, your learning cycles are slower and your timelines are stretched out." Companies have to have a regular process of getting out face-to-face with customers, suppliers, investors, researchers. "That is what we urge them to do — get out of here." In building Radian6, he notes that Chris Ramsey, as the key product manager, seemed to spend his whole life on the road.

Gavin Uhma has taken this advice to heart as he embarks on his new company, Dropout Labs, which focuses on securing data using artificial intelligence and cryptography. To keep fresh with contacts and technology, he and his family spent two months in San Francisco recently but came back home to Halifax. He and his wife have three kids who had to start school.

His company deploys machine learning and cryptography, which are very specialized skillsets in Atlantic Canada, or anywhere in the world. So he has adopted the idea of a distributed team. He has some people in Halifax, but the rest are scattered. "Time zones still matter. So we have a nine-time-zone rule. There are nine time zones from Paris to San Francisco, and we'll hire within those time zones but not outside of them."

It helps that he can fly directly from Halifax to Toronto or New York non-stop, but a trip to San Francisco is a serious commitment. It's often a week-long expedition — two days of travel and three days of meetings. "So I'm trying to figure out how I can manage my work-life balance, live in Halifax but then still have a team that's going to be able to tap into the markets that we need to tap into."

Uhma accepts that being in Halifax imposes a logistics disadvantage — indeed, it is the same to be anywhere other than San Francisco, New York, Toronto or other major centres. "But you can make it work. In some cases, it can be an advantage because you don't have the same distractions that you otherwise might have." He notes wryly, "We don't have awesome startup events happening all the time."

Yet there is another concern held by more detached observers — that the startup deals, pioneered by Radian6 and GoInstant, fostered a fast-in, fast-out mentality, a constant churn of new companies that depart before they're ready, and their positive economic impact becomes muted over the long term. But in Keefe's view, the small exits are essential for — deal by deal — creating an upward spiral that, in time, will pay back with seasoned managers running larger companies.

"You don't create multi-billion-dollar companies out of thin air," he maintains. "I agree we need the big ones, and it can still happen, but I wouldn't look at an exit as a missed opportunity but another step along the way."

14. Cyber Cyber Everywhere

It was 2016, and Steve Lund was settling into his job as New Brunswick's economic development chief, when he was invited to Israel to see what that embattled nation was building in its cybersecurity sector. There are always abundant reasons for going to Israel, that much-studied model on how a small economy overachieves in technology leadership, and cybersecurity is one of its critical clusters. Lund also knew New Brunswick had a solid foothold in computer security from its Q1 days, and a research focus from the local university, UNB. Surely, there would be lots to learn in Israel.

On that trip, the Israelis put on a show for Lund, who had in 2015 become CEO of Opportunities New Brunswick, the Crown corporation mandated with supporting business growth in the province. One of the highlights was a visit to Beersheba, a city in the desert where the government was partnering with industry, academia and the military to create a cybersecurity community.

"They were building a cluster and really figured out how to do it," Lund recalls, clearly impressed. He saw how cybersecurity was pervading daily life — as a big idea that was being nurtured, with no cost spared.

The U.S. technology giant IBM had a presence in Beersheba, and it invited Lund to a briefing. In the presentation, the IBM officials displayed a loosely assembled organizational chart of their cybersecurity business. Lund looked at it in amazement. Everything in the organization had lines flowing back to one place — Fredericton, New Brunswick. He knew there was something going on in his backyard, but in this desert setting, 5,000 miles from home, he found out just how much. Fredericton was a brand name in the cyber world, and yet it was hardly known in Canada.

That revelation in Israel inspired Lund as he became a key driver behind a new agency called CyberNB, dedicated to leveraging this homegrown expertise into more companies, more research and a wider pipeline of talent. As of late 2019, he estimated Opportunities NB and CyberNB had helped create 500 cybersecurity-specific jobs and was projecting close to 300 more based on the expected growth of New Brunswick companies.

A key focus in growing that talent is education. New Brunswick is an enthusiastic participant in CyberTitan, a high school program that originated in the U.S. but flourishes in Canada with a national competition. CyberNB helps bring training in cybersecurity to middle and secondary schools; there is an IBM-backed day of cyber-immersion specifically for high school girls. The schools have taken up the curriculum challenge, with an emphasis on coding and security awareness. It's almost as if a third language is being added to the province's linguistic tapestry, the language of cybersecurity.

New Brunswick is shaping up as a test case. Can a lightly populated province focus on a single, but broadly influential, technology area and leverage that strength into global significance? Will successive governments continue to support that program in the face of extreme budgetary constraints and shifting political winds? (Lund himself left his job after his five-year term, as his agency's mandate changed.)

There is no denying cybersecurity is a vast area of enterprise, serving corporations with billions of dollars of data at stake and con-sumers experiencing the dread of a credit card hack. The movement toward the "internet of things" just heightens the concern — IBM has observed that it secures the safety of more than 21 billion "things" in the world, from digital fridges to smart wristwatches to critical infra-structure. And that figure has become rapidly out of date. Each day, it monitors 70 billion security "events," from a credit card purchase to a swipe of a building access card. In response, the tech industry has spawned a dense thicket of cybersecurity tools and vendors.

Unlike Israel, New Brunswick is not surrounded by enemies, but it does face a crisis: an economic one. Although cybersecurity is no panacea, the province has decided it is a broad avenue that could help pave the way to a better future. Cybersecurity is one of three technology foundations on which the province hopes to rekindle stagnant economic growth. The other two are digital health systems — appropriate to a region facing a public health-care crisis — and "smart grid" systems that allow more efficient digital management of power assets at a time of sustainability priorities. And of course, cybersecurity links into these activities, as well.

The strength of cybersecurity in New Brunswick today can be traced back to Chris Newton's office in the late 1990s, to the UNB Computing Centre, and the formation of Q1 Labs. Newton was, of course, long gone from Q1 Labs by the time it accepted a takeover offer from IBM, which resulted in a $600-million U.S. payday for the backers of the company.

By this time, Brendan Hannigan, a well-liked Irish-American executive, was president of Q1 Labs and Sandy Bird was chief technology officer, leading the development team in Fredericton. An estimated 100 or so employees worked in Fredericton (about half the total employment) when IBM bought the company, and for a number of them, the immediate celebration was tempered by apprehension.

Some were familiar with the Alcatel takeover of iMagic — a few had worked for iMagic — and how the French company said all the right things about the value of the technology, the commitment to the people and the New Brunswick community, and on and on. But Alcatel didn't live up to that commitment, and it let iMagic die. People came out of iMagic wary and cynical about big company promises. Would IBM, another multinational buyer, do the same?

Brendan Hannigan wondered about his future role. It was clear during the acquisition process that IBM liked Q1 Labs, liked it a lot. Then one day in 2011 the senior IBM executive in charge of the acquisition visited the Q1 office in Boston, and he and Hannigan went out to lunch.

The conversation went along these lines: IBM was not only buying Q1, it was establishing a whole new division around security. Over the years, IBM had collected a bunch of different cybersecurity products, located in disparate areas of the company. The plan was to take all these different "point products" related to security, and consolidate them in one division. And Q1 Labs was going to be one of the anchors for this division. "I need someone to run it, and I want it to be you," the executive told Hannigan.

"I said 'Sure, I'll do that.' I figured, 'I'm not going to get a chance to go and do something like that again,'" Hannigan recalls.

It became clear that IBM valued Q1, and it did plan to make QRadar the core of its new security division. Q1 would become the hub of development shops from Belfast to the Gold Coast in Australia. According to one Q1 officer, now with IBM, the idea was "Let's bring it all under one halo of a product," which in this case was QRadar with its broadened mandate for managing security events.

Thus, the Q1 Labs senior people would become senior people in IBM's security universe. What's more, IBM would expand its Fredericton presence substantially over the years. It was not a perceived betrayal, as in the case of Alcatel, but a model of how a massive multinational can become a change-maker in a little city far from its base in Armonk, New York.

"A lot of people thought IBM would move everything out," Dwight Spencer says. "But they didn't just want the technology — they wanted the team." Above all they wanted Sandy Bird and Brendan Hannigan, Spencer says — although they undoubtedly wanted Spencer too for his specialized handholding abilities.

The progress of Brendan Hannigan tells the story. He had helped take Q1 Labs to revenue of $75 million U.S. a year, and it had turned profitable in its final years. When he took over the new security systems division of IBM in 2011, all its constituent businesses added up to an estimated revenue of $800 million a year. When he left four years later, to pursue other interests, it was a $2-billion business — touted as the industry leader in security intelligence tools for business.

Accordingly, the Fredericton office exploded in growth, experiencing annual double-digit percentage gains in staff numbers, topped by 50 per cent in 2014, and then by 75 per cent in 2019. IBM does not disclose numbers, but the estimate, widely used in the New Brunswick community, is that the development unit employs about 300 people in Fredericton and a small team in Saint John. In early 2020, IBM projected employment will grow another 25 per cent by 2025. (There are other IBM offices in the province, but they are largely service units, not development labs.)

Three hundred or so people does not sound like a lot, but it is meaningful for a small community. And these are well-paid, highly productive jobs. Consider the payroll effects alone. If you assume 300 people are working for the former Q1 Labs, with an average developer's salary of $80,000 — the norm for the industry — it would add up to a $20-million-plus injection to the local economy every year.

The Fredericton office is a pinprick in the global universe of IBM, but the QRadar product still sits at the core of its cybersecurity business. It means QRadar is now the most globally influential New Brunswick–created brand — indeed, the biggest brand to come out of Atlantic Canada, eclipsing such venerable names as Irving Oil and McCain fries. Yet, it is largely invisible to the wider public, only existing as digital code and subsumed in IBM's complex networks. No splashy ads on transport trucks, billboards or *Hockey Night in Canada*. But in the world of corporate security, QRadar is golden.

The growth of that business has meant the Fredericton development lab has literally burst its seams. Located in a bland strip-mall structure in suburban Fredericton, it has kept expanding its space, until there is no more room. IBM had to move a contingent of people over to the nearby Knowledge Park, the office subdivision tailor-made for tech companies, and there is still a small office in Saint John.

In 2020, the company was expecting to consolidate its operations by taking up a floor in Fredericton's new Cyber Park complex, a 135,000-square-foot structure that will serve as a focus for the city's cyber community. Built at a projected cost of $35 million, it is the house that cybersecurity built, a monument to the pioneering work of people like Dave Macneil, Chris Newton and Ali Ghorbani. It will enjoy high-level security, which means the technology infrastructure will keep on ticking even under extreme duress. The province's emergency measures organization will be on the top floor.

"IBM likes Fredericton, because Fredericton continues to deliver," says John Burnham, who has spent more than a decade with Q1 Labs and IBM. Burnham was hired by Brendan Hannigan at Q1 Labs to help build QRadar's "buzz and brand," particularly by honing its image for the all-important community of technology analysts. He helped redefine the clumsy SIEM moniker, building the idea of a "security intelligence platform." He stayed at IBM where he now plays a similar role inside the security division.

As an outsider to New Brunswick, Burnham credits the Fredericton story to a strong local talent pool. When he joined Q1 Labs in 2009, he quickly discovered that New Brunswick was among the leaders on the continent in terms of density of broadband penetration to both home and office. It was not just about streaming Netflix to your home — "It means being able to work at high speeds on coding, wherever you are." Another product of the McKenna vision.

A lot of IBM's Fredericton presence could be traced to Sandy Bird, the kid from across the river who was by now a gold-plated brand name in cybersecurity. Bird is the ultimate adaptable man. He had quit his regular university degree program to work with Chris Newton and Dwight Spencer on securing UNB's networks. At Q1 Labs, he had thrived as the closer for Brian Flood in pitches to venture capitalists;

he had collaborated with Shaun McConnon and Brendan Hannigan in the transition to a wider cybersecurity platform; and he joined IBM as the chief technology officer for its security systems division, where he helped build QRadar into the foundation of a global business.

He understood why IBM liked Fredericton. It experienced very low attrition among its talented work force compared with other places it did business. In the New Brunswick way, people are so dedicated to the companies they work for that they won't leave, even if the remote fields look a lot greener. It was sometimes frustrating to try to hire for a position, Bird says. After a raft of interviews, top candidates might bow out because they could not bring themselves to leave their existing employer.

Contrast it to California, where your intellectual capital just gets up and walks out the door all the time. IBM likes places where the product knowledge stays for years. Walk through the IBM development labs with Aaron Breen, the director of development for IBM Security Intelligence, and he points out the hardy core of Q1 veterans. Breen himself is a Q1 Labs veteran — indeed, a product of that old iMagic. He, like a number of others, has thrived inside IBM.

For Sandy Bird, the travel was constant between Fredericton and the team he was building in Israel — the team that Steve Lund got to know about. That work was based on his expanded role as a thought leader among IBM's nearly 400,000 employees, a worldwide contingent about the size of greater Halifax-Dartmouth. He was, in the words of the IBM website, "one of the company's all time technical giants."

In 2014 Bird had become an IBM Fellow, an honour held by only about 300 people in the 100-year history of the company. When Bird reached that status, there were only 89 active Fellows. The program included five Nobel Prize winners and five winners of the Turing Award, often called the "Nobel of Computing." The IBM website extolled Bird: "The chief technology officer for IBM Security Systems, still in his thirties, has been elevated to the highest echelon of IBM technologists."

Sandy brought a bit of New Brunswick humility to the game. When he was joining the elite Fellows group, he noted that among his colleagues, there was a scientist developing a chip that mimicked the brain of a mouse. He kept thinking, What am I doing sitting beside this guy? In no time it all, it was clear that Bird belonged.

Dwight Spencer had stayed with IBM too after the acquisition and was known as "principal solutions architect for Q1 products." He liked the role, as he continued to do the customer-facing work, dealing with the new buyers' challenges with the technical platform. He had basically spent 17 years grappling with QRadar. "I knew all the little corners of the software. I grew up sharing those experiences of what QRadar was trying to do." It was his baby.

If Sandy Bird and Dwight Spencer were the corporate stars of the cybersecurity world in Fredericton, Ali Ghorbani was the intellectual doyen. His career had blossomed since arriving as a young Iranian grad student in 1987. Indeed, his life tracks the emergence of cyber as a core strength in the university and the economy. In the 1980s he specialized in artificial intelligence and neural networks, but then turned his gaze to cybersecurity. He accepted his first PhD student in about 1998. "That was the start of cybersecurity at UNB — in New Brunswick, I would say."

He actually taught Chris Newton and Sandy Bird — although he barely remembers them amid the hordes of students. When they went off to found Q1, as part of the founders' agreement with the university, he conducted research that led to a broadening of QRadar. The Q1 team would meet with him every week.

"We did a lot of work from a research perspective on their solutions," Ghorbani says. "We added some additional capabilities, and built a whole new system. Initially we called it 'simulation of network attacks,' which was later renamed by Q1 and IBM as 'risk management systems.'"

By then, he had established UNB's Information Security Centre of Excellence, which at the time consisted mainly of IT researchers doing information and network security work. But it took on a broader mandate, growing into today's Canadian Institute for Cybersecurity, with government and corporate partners.

Today, the institute is an academic leader in network security, with about 60 affiliated researchers. It does technical work in areas like intrusion and malware detection, but there are also researchers in biomedical advances, cyber law, sociology and terrorism.

Meanwhile, Ghorbani is an entrepreneur himself; in 2012 he co-founded, along with three of his PhD students, a company called Sentrant Security, operating in online advertising fraud detection. They sold it in 2017 to Nielsen, the consumer research group, which relocated the business to Toronto. He notes the new owner did not find it easy to travel between Fredericton and the source of much of their business in New York.

In 2013 he established another company called Eyesover, which operates a platform that eases the process of research and "issue discovery" for policy-makers and politicians. Two of his former students are the co-founders, and a former New Brunswick cabinet minister is the CEO.

Eyesover emerged from research Ghorbani had conducted on social media, back in 2004 before Radian6 was founded. There had been a provincial election, and the sitting government was toppled. One of the key issues that emerged late in the campaign was the debate over a toll on the highway between Moncton and Fredericton.

Ghorbani observed that the issue helped defeat the incumbents, and yet why didn't they see it coming? How about a system for discovering issues that you don't know about? He called it "opinion mining for issue discovery," or OMID. Ghorbani built a business around it.

Along the way, he was involved in pushing out the boundaries of cybersecurity networking, including UNB's participation in Global EPIC, a cybersecurity "ecosystem of ecosystems," developed first by

Israel, the UK and Canada. The region's profile is starting to emerge, says Ghorbani. "I believe we're well known across the country now as a hub of cybersecurity talent development and research."

This is the environment into which David Shipley landed, with his own extensive CV — soldier, journalist, university website specialist and now cybersecurity entrepreneur. He came along at the right time, in the trail of Q1 Labs, IBM's presence and the Ghorbani era at UNB. He is the perfect creature of the emerging ecosystem.

Shipley's nomadic career gave him the rare ability to see the big picture, a capacity often lacking in technical minds. Leaving military service to attend university, he later joined the *Telegraph-Journal* in Saint John, an Irving-owned newspaper. It was a period of upheaval for Shipley: he lost his mother to cancer and dealt with other profound personal challenges. Leaving newspaper work, he moved over to the University of New Brunswick in a website marketing role. "It was a fantastic job, particularly for the change of pace, and I needed it."

Shipley's life took on a moment of clarity on Mother's Day in 2012. He had become close with the IT Services team at UNB, though he was not part of it. On that day, he got up early and walked his dog, a newly acquired greyhound, obsessively reading his emails as techies are wont to do. An email popped up from a "hacktivist group" intent on creating mayhem with a message. They had hacked a broad range of global and Canadian institutions, including the Toronto Police Service, the National Film Board, Harvard University and the University of New Brunswick.

It was not devastating. They did not acquire social insurance numbers or student grades, but they got some budget information and a password. The group taunted the organizations that had left their networks exposed. The mass email scolded: "Your site is terribly vulnerable and I suggest you patch it." The message told administration offices, "Information leaked is only to demonstrate how pathetic your security is." Shipley called his friends in the IT department and said he thought it was legitimate and the university had to deal with it. Shipley spent that entire Mother's Day Sunday, "much to my wife's displeasure," working on the incident with the team.

The university weathered the experience and enhanced its preparedness. "It was an awakening for all of us here," says Terry Nikkel, the UNB associate vice president who heads IT Services, the same department that once employed Chris Newton. Shipley impressed Nikkel, who recognized that he had a certain unique set of skills. Shipley sees his strengths as a combination of parts: "The military strategic thinking about the world in that adversarial way, and the journalism side, being able to quickly process complex information and distill it to its essential parts. And I was the natural nerd."

So Nikkel recruited Shipley away from web marketing, bringing him into his team, where the former journalist got the technical tools he needed. "I gave him quite a bit of leeway so he could try different things," says Nikkel.

Specifically, Nikkel and the university allowed him to simulate phishing expeditions — fraudulent emails aimed at employees and designed to extract private information, including sensitive business details whose exposure could cripple an organization. Human frailty is often the biggest challenge to organizations' security — for example, "people clicking on things they shouldn't," Nikkel says. Shipley's behavioural work eventually morphed into a company, Beauceron, dedicated to helping organizations assess and address the exposure of their employees.

Shipley once explained to the university information office that he was aiming to create digital sheepdogs. "Our clients go from being a sheep to becoming a sheepdog. In honour of that effect, we named our firm and our technology after a sheepdog from northern France, the Beauceron."

Shipley is grateful to the founders of Q1 Labs for leading the way, and to UNB for having learned from those experiences. "A great deal

David Shipley of Beauceron Security has become a new-generation leader in New Brunswick's cybersecurity ecosystem

(Courtesy of Beauceron Security)

of the success we've enjoyed to date as a company in New Brunswick is the result of being able to drive down a paved road when it comes to entrepreneurship."

He credits the university for having grown in its handling of intellectual property. Because he and his team were doing work on their own and building their platform, they got to own all the intellectual property. "We gave UNB a perpetual licence to the platform. As long as we're in business, if they want to use it, they've got it — for faculty and staff. It was a win-win for both parties."

Shipley continues to explore the behavioural aspect of cyber-security, in educating users and C-suite executives about the dangers of cyberattacks and how to develop an informed response. Today Beauceron is getting a reputation globally — and it sits at the core of the nascent cyber industry in New Brunswick. There are still not a lot of players, but it is happening.

Terry Nikkel likes to point out that his IT Services group at UNB has essentially created two companies, Q1 Labs and Beauceron. The common stereotype is that universities spin off companies related to research conducted by academics. That does happen at UNB, and yet two of its most influential spinoffs came from people on staff solving real-life problems for systems and services.

In Shipley's view there had been two strong narratives in the province over the past 30 years. One narrative was the McKenna revolution; it was followed by the second narrative of Q1 and Radian6 and their great successes. The province needs these stories, because, he says, New Brunswick has been dogged by a culture of failure. "This is the albatross around our neck. And that holds back a significant number of people that would be entrepreneurs."

Is cybersecurity the next winning narrative? The Toronto venture capitalist Salim Teja knows the New Brunswick scene — he was a VC investor in Radian6. He agrees Canada needs to be focusing on cybersecurity, just as it needs to be more visible in artificial intelligence and quantum computing. "But what we haven't done yet [in cybersecurity] is build a strong ecosystem. So we need an incredible depth of talent from a research perspective. We need an incredible volume of startups that are doing innovative things in the cybersecurity space. We need to be able to attract customers and capital in order to help these things get commercialized. I think that we're still early in that process."

Is it possible to build that critical mass in Fredericton? "I'm not sure that the ecosystem is large enough there," says Teja. "And does it have enough hooks into some of these emerging areas like AI that truly differentiate us [in Canada] as an ecosystem? I think we've got to link some of these things together."

The challenge is that cybersecurity is a vast area, where a single company, a single region, has trouble attracting attention. Ghorbani emphasizes the need for a tighter focus. "We do not have the resources and means to do everything," he concludes. That is particularly important because there are bigger players with more money to spend, not just in Israel or elsewhere abroad, but in Ontario, Quebec, Alberta and British Columbia.

If the institute, for example, is pulled in too many directions, "then we don't do a good job, and we cannot afford to do an average job. We have to do a job that says 'wow,' like Radian6, like Q1. So if we don't do 'wow,' we'll be the same as the others." In his institute, Ghorbani is advancing the development of critical infrastructure protection — from military bases to power plants — where he believes the province has a competitive edge. "We want to be known across the country for this niche. We're not going to do all the other ones because we don't have the resources."

The intersection of smart grid power systems and cybersecurity for critical infrastructure is a potential sweet spot that could draw corporate players to the New Brunswick scene. Siemens, the German-based engineering and industrial giant, was first attracted by the smart grid activity and the ability to work with NB Power. Along with UNB, the two companies set up the Smart Grid Innovation Network, which allows the testing of smart grid technology by dozens of New Brunswick firms. Meanwhile, the university is doing a study for Barbados Light & Power — which is owned by the Nova Scotia power utility Emera — on how to implement smart grid systems for the island's stretched power system, aimed at getting to 100-per-cent renewable energy by 2030.

"Building a smart grid and cybersecurity go hand-in-hand," says Faisal Kazi, president and CEO of Siemens Canada, whose company was also drawn by the spirit of collaboration and experimentation in the New Brunswick community. The result is a cybersecurity centre that will complement the smart grid work and help develop technology for global markets.

IBM and Siemens have both been beneficiaries of job subsidies, the source of a continuing debate that winds its way through the industrial history of Atlantic Canada. Tech founders and managers say the subsidies can deliver a vital boost to a new and promising company or an incoming knowledge giant. But skeptics wonder if they deliver lasting economic impact, and there have been painful examples of lack of accountability. The subsidies may make it harder for established firms to vie for scarce IT talent. Yet governments in a have-not region see such subsidies as a key competitive tool to bring in higher-tax-paying jobs. It is a tough global climate, whereby multinationals can just as easily locate their research centres in India, China or Estonia.

Will multinational machines like IBM and Siemens continue to see New Brunswick as a valued player in their plans? Global shifts in competitiveness and internal corporate developments are unforesee-able. A home-based company may be a more loyal foundation for a local economy, yet it can prove to be a weaker base for penetrating the global economy. IBM's security systems division, for example, has been a great horse to ride out into the world. For now, the incoming players are the best game in town — until the young local stars develop into something much, much brighter. There are people in Atlantic Canada who intend to make that happen.

15. From the Ashes of Nortel

In the wake of the spectacular collapse of Canada's Nortel Networks, the west-end Ottawa campus of the former telecommunications champion emptied out and the parking lots became a wasteland. One day in the mid-2010s, drivers passing by the complex must have found it odd to see a lone man standing in one of the lots, sobbing.

Dhirendra Shukla had worked 12 years for Nortel, much of it in that now-abandoned building. Nortel had shaped his adult life, since he had come to Canada as a 22-year-old Indian-born engineer. He had watched as a cascade of circumstances — flawed governance, inept leadership and public indifference — conspired to fashion Nortel's shocking demise, the largest bankruptcy in Canadian history.

For Shukla, Nortel embodied the Canadian dream, a global knowledge machine that hired and trained people, registered thousands of patents and put Canadian technology on the map. By tracing Shukla's life and career, you begin to grasp how much Nortel meant to the Canada brand, as the best-known Canadian company in many corners of the world, a magnet for young men and women in this country and internationally.

Now, on this day, Shukla was back in Ottawa, where he still had family, having flown in from his new home in Fredericton. On revisiting the Nortel site, he was overtaken with emotion. "I stood in the parking lot and cried."

He and many others had worked day and night to save that company, but it seemed no one cared. "If Canada is going to move from a resource economy to the intellectual economy, you can't lose iconic institutions like that because there's nothing to replace it. Young people had nowhere to go. That whole place was just empty." At one point a car came into the lot and the bewildered driver said, "Can you give me directions? I'm lost." That summed it up for Shukla.

As a telecom manufacturing and systems giant, Nortel once employed 93,000 people around the world, and in the go-for-broke casino of the late 1990s tech bubble, it reached a market capitalization of $250 billion U.S., at one time accounting for a third of the value of the Toronto Stock Exchange. It went on an acquisition rampage in the overheated atmosphere. When the tech bubble burst, Nortel collapsed into insolvency and a garage sale of assets; it yielded a small fraction of its former valuation, even in its saner years.

Creditors and former employees waged a long and bitter battle over those assets, while lawyers and bankruptcy professionals took their fee cut, an outrageous $2 billion U.S. More than 6,000 patents were sold off to a consortium of international bidders, including Research in Motion (RIM), the one Canadian participant, then riding high as the company behind the BlackBerry smartphone.

Nortel, once called Northern Electric, could trace its lineage to Alexander Graham Bell, the Scots-Canadian-American inventor of the telephone. In the end, its death triggered a massive looting of an intellectual storehouse, and governments failed to lift a finger.

The death of Nortel left huge gaps in a lot of communities in Canada and around the world, places like Brampton, Brockville, Belleville and especially Ottawa, for many years its research and development core, where Nortel was a central part of the private-sector balance to the federal government's overwhelming presence.

Yet, Dhirendra Shukla was able to find another life mission, and he pursued it with typical vigour, focusing on the training and mentorship of engineers as startup entrepreneurs. He took on the leadership of the 20-year-old UNB program called TME, which is officially the J. Herbert Smith Centre for Technology Management and Entrepreneurship, and he built it into a fertile breeding ground for new enterprises.

Ex-Nortel engineer Dhirendra Shukla leads discussion in UNB's
technology, management and entrepreneurship program
(Courtesy of Cameron Fitch, UNB Media Services)

He arrived in New Brunswick just before the Radian6 and Q1
Labs exits. It was great timing, as he became a central player in
the development of a flowering — call it a cluster, an ecosystem, a
laboratory for making and building companies. He was able to use
the Radian6 and Q1 founders as resources and mentors. He was
channelling the spirit of Nortel into building a technology community
that could replicate what had been lost to Canada.

There are a number of pieces in that cluster that, to an outsider,
seem perplexing in their number and variety for such a small community — although the insiders insist the various parts are complementary.
Nancy Mathis, herself a veteran of startup experience, runs the Wallace
McCain Institute (WMI), which works with owners and managers to
build sustaining peer networks. The WMI alumni group is a rich tapestry of New Brunswick business, from the family behind the large
Armour Transportation business in Moncton, to the owners of Mrs.
Dunster's, the bakery group in Sussex.

Gerry Pond had teamed up with Desh Deshpande, the UNB gradu-ate who has built tech companies in the United States, to found UNB's Pond-Deshpande Centre, mixing early-stage commercial purpose with social mission. And there is Propel ICT, a pan-Atlantic accelerator network, with Pond as a co-founder, that is aimed at giving new com-pany founders the tools to test and develop their ideas quickly, using a virtual training model. Add to this Planet Hatch, a co-working space for new businesses, with operations in the Knowledge Park office com-plex, designed to house the New Economy of Fredericton.

In the middle of all this, Dhirendra Shukla landed as a walking-talking idea machine, and an irrepressibly enthusiastic Canadian nationalist. His eyes positively sparkle when he talks of his adopted country — its space, its beauty, its opportunity. He believes in the Canadian idea of opportunity combined with enlightened social policies, and Nortel was part of that ethos.

Shukla may seem over-the-top with his unvarnished enthusiasm, but John McLaughlin, the former university president who works with him, says he is "the real thing," an innovative and passionate agent for change. That makeup springs in part from his global upbringing. Shukla's father was a mining engineer who led his family into different parts of the world. Hired by a British company to work in Zambia, he moved his family from India to Africa when Dhirendra was seven.

He was a fortunate boy in his Zambian village school, unusual in being able to afford a textbook. And yet he always stood third or fourth in his class, ceding the top slots to less affluent textbook-deprived students. When he hears of New Brunswickers complaining of their sad standing in the world, he remembers those other students, who had so little and achieved so much.

Dhirendra went on to London, England, for high school. When he was 12, the family took a vacation to Canada, and visited Montreal, Ottawa and Toronto. He fell in love with what he saw. Years later when he finished his master's degree in engineering at the University of Bradford, his father asked what he intended to do with his education.

Dhirendra said he had chosen Canada. He came to Ottawa on a holiday, and he landed a job offer at Nortel.

He loved working there in the good years, but as Nortel began its precipitous descent, it became a demoralized workplace. That turned Shukla to thinking about how things could be done differently. "How do these startups do these things, while we struggle at large institutions?" He wanted to channel his energy into something positive, to "absorb myself into a different world while things around me were collapsing." He started working on a PhD, and looked at the methods and motivations of company builders. He surveyed about 150 founders across Canada, including a New Brunswicker named Marcel LeBrun, who had helped build two tech enterprises.

In the throes of Nortel's collapse, the TME leadership job came up at University of New Brunswick, and Shukla promptly applied. "Not in my wildest dreams did I ever think they would hire an old techie from Ottawa who had just come from a collapsed company." Not old, but at 36, feeling old.

Shukla arrived in Fredericton in summer 2009 and began his transition to academic life. At one point, he encountered a new colleague, who, with the best of intentions, tried to prepare the young Indo-Canadian for the harsh realities of life in New Brunswick. The conversation went along the lines that "they will never accept you. No one will remember how to pronounce your name." The colleague thought he was helping Shukla, who shrugged it all off. And it turned out New Brunswick was very welcoming. He had found a new cause, not in an anchor company like Nortel, but in the quest of young entrepreneurs.

When a legacy giant crumbles, the great hope is that it is an act of creative destruction, that new companies and ideas will flower in the same soil as the withered giant. Companies have indeed formed from the ashes of Nortel, founded sometimes by people who once worked there — although many, like Shukla, got almost nothing in final compensation. But none of these companies has the heft of Nortel.

In Ottawa, there is a new tech champion, Shopify, a booming e-commerce juggernaut, which has proven to be a generator of angel investing, similar to the role Salesforce and IBM played in funding "Gerry's Angels" in New Brunswick.

In the *Globe and Mail*, Brenda Bouw described "the Shopify angels" as a group of employees and founders, some of whom had formed companies bought by Shopify over the years. They "are using the proceeds to help fuel Canada's next generation of entrepreneurs."

Thanks to Shopify and others, Ottawa remains a vital technology community, even if it lacks the excitement of earlier decades when it was dubbed "Silicon Valley North." There are several Silicon Valleys North in Canada today. Ottawa still has much going for it — the federal government and National Research Council, two universities, a vibrant community college, a fabulous place to live with its federally funded parks and nearby ski hills in the Gatineaus.

Fredericton is often dubbed "little Ottawa," and it has many of the same attributes. It is a pretty city of government and universities, with a highly educated workforce, somewhat protected against the winds of economic cycles. Amid this comfortable way of life, risk-taking was not always encouraged. And yet, suddenly, in the first two decades of the 21st century, Fredericton gave birth to a flourishing startup culture. The question is: Can those startups make it past the early stages and create sustainable growth amid all this publicly funded comfort?

There is a yawning gap in size between the new companies and the traditional mega-players like McCain Foods and the various Irving companies. John McLaughlin underlines what is still missing for a dynamic economy. "The sweet spot is the $100-million growing enterprise. We don't have them in New Brunswick." There are the billionaires, and the micro-enterprises, and few in between.

Filling the gaps is Dhirendra Shukla's mission. His TME program had been launched in 1988 with a $5-million donation by J. Herbert Smith, a UNB engineering grad who was the first Canadian to run General Electric Canada. Smith felt he owed his great career at General

Electric to the engineering giant's vaunted management training programs, which seeded young people with an early grounding in the fundamentals of leadership. If a certain management knowhow could be embedded early into the DNA of graduates, he felt it would become part of who they are, just as they launch their careers.

Shukla continues Smith's mandate, with the added emphasis on the students actually founding companies, using today's lean startup methods and local mentors. The program had launched only one company in the 20 years before he arrived. In less than a single decade under Shukla, the expanded program has spun out 135 new companies with a survival rate of more than 60 per cent so far.

Under Shukla, with the help of John McLaughlin, and the stewardship of Eddy Campbell, the energetic mathematician who was president of the university from 2009 to 2019, UNB added a master's degree to the TME program. Many enrollees are international students drawn by the global reputation of UNB.

The influx of international students is a key building block of New Brunswick's plan to expand its population, enhance its skills and develop a larger entrepreneurial sector. Post-secondary education is one of the province's strengths — indeed, it ranks high among Atlantic Canada's strengths. UNB, Université de Moncton, St. Thomas and Mount Allison universities, plus the New Brunswick Community College and the Collège communautaire du Nouveau-Brunswick, all fill crucial demographic and economic roles. (There are also a couple of smaller niche institutions.)

The education opportunities were what attracted Kumaran Thillainadarajah, a Sri Lankan–Canadian who has travelled a tortuous route to become a company founder and a linchpin of New Brunswick's economic future. When I approached him for an interview, it was a busy time — he was a new Canadian citizen and in the summer of 2019 he was getting married.

Our interview took place in the basement of the old Post Office building, a sombre structure on Queen Street, in the heart of

Fredericton's historic downtown. The building captures the two Frederictons — stolidly institutional and wickedly innovative. You step down into the basement lab, where a squad of software developers are fixed to their screens.

I spotted Thillainadarajah at one of the desks, a strikingly handsome man in his mid-30s with a well-worn passport. He was born in Nigeria, lived in England, then in Trinidad and the Maldives, before returning to his family's base of Sri Lanka for high school. He arrived at UNB in 2003 to study computer engineering. His well-educated, well-travelled family had charted a life plan for their smart son: graduation as an engineer, followed lock-step by employment in a large and established firm. Little did they know.

During his final year of engineering, he was helping out on a summer research project run by Felipe Chibante, the energetic Fredericton native who holds UNB's Richard J. Currie Chair in Nanotechnology. Chibante needed student bodies for a project sponsored by the Institute for Biomedical Engineering. The hope was that minuscule nanomaterials could be added to rubber to make a mechanically stronger covering for prosthetic limbs.

Chibante watched the young computer student, standing at the cluttered workbench in the nano lab, studying the electrical properties of this covering. Thillainadarajah realized that they could make a sensor with this rubber. Indeed, there was a "eureka moment" when the light bulb literally went off — Chibante pressed the sensors to adjust the conductivity, which caused a connected light bulb to brighten and fade.

Thillainadarajah thought, "This is really cool. But I don't know what to do with it." Indeed, that would be the challenge for the next decade of his life — he had a solution, but he did not yet have a product.

After the summer, he went back to school and started taking some TME courses "sort of just for fun." On a whim, he wrote a business plan around this rubber sensor he had devised with Chibante. That was the beginning of the company Smart Skin, conceived as the developer of a sensor that could give amputees a sense of touch.

The young computer scientist met his first entrepreneur, Chris Ramsey, who described his life journey to a TME class, how he left a good job at Microsoft to take a shot with this really small company that failed and then he joined another startup, Radian6. "That's so crazy," Thillainadarajah recalls thinking. "Like, my family would probably kill me if I did that. But then fast-forward to a year later, I was doing something probably more crazy."

A TME instructor, Mike Oliver, urged Thillainadarajah and Chibante to enter business-plan competitions, and they actually won their first one with a prize of $500. It allowed them to build a crude prototype. They took the prototype to another competition, which they also won. They built a better prototype and entered it in another contest.

They did not win that next one, but the judges came back with important feedback: this was a great technology but probably prosthetics wasn't the right product — too much R&D, too little return. It was a hard message, given that the duo had been working for a year on the prosthetic skin. They would have to pivot to a new market.

They entered the Breakthru Competition sponsored by seed-capital provider New Brunswick Investment Foundation, and they pitched their Smart Skin as a platform for a number of potential applications. "We could do gaming, we could do mobile phones, we could do a bunch of things." They did well at Breakthru and came away with a $50,000 investment commitment by NBIF.

Thillainadarajah was still a student, but NBIF's then director Calvin Milbury was saying that, to obtain the investment money, the company should have a full-time CEO. But what would the young immigrant's family say? This was not part of the plan for their son. Yet he quit his UNB degree program without a degree. Maybe for a year, he thought.

One deciding factor was Gerry Pond, who met with the young student when he had nothing but an idea. The first time they had lunch, the veteran investor offered him a small loan. "I actually declined it because I thought it was crazy to take someone's personal money," Thillainadarajah says.

A friend gave him a dose of reality, explaining that offering this loan was part of Pond's job as an investor. The young man went back to Pond to tell him he would take the money. Pond introduced him to his network, people like his old NBTel colleague Bob Neal, who has served as a mentor through the life of Smart Skin.

At one point Thillainadarajah and Chibante turned up at *Dragons' Den*, the popular CBC TV reality show built around funding start-ups. Chibante recalls his 22-year-old colleague was nervous and the segment introduction took three takes to get down. Finally, the presentation went ahead. They focused on the potential for the rubber skin as a smart covering for cellphones. They got funding commitments from two of the Dragons, but the segment never ran on TV, and the entrepreneurs did not receive a follow-up call from the investors.

By this time, Chibante, originally a 20 per cent owner, was stepping back from the company, dealing with a new funding commitment to expand his work at UNB. He would remain a shareholder, adviser and friend. Throughout this time, Thillainadarajah was becoming aware of the special environment of Atlantic Canada for starting companies. "People want to help you because they want to see you succeed." In other areas, they might ask first what they could financially get out of it.

He gives a big nod to public funding agencies, which take a lot of heat from free-market purists but stepped up for him. The National Research Council's Industrial Research Assistance Program (NRC-IRAP) was critical in building prototypes. The Atlantic Canada Opportunities Agency (ACOA), through its business development program, helped him to get in front of customers.

Among the prototypes, the team constructed a model of a golf grip testing machine, which if successful could help golfers improve their game. That involved making a simulated golf club, which "almost looked like the gun from *Ghostbusters*, with a huge backpack and all these electronics off it. It had all these wires."

The team tested it in the lab with everyone taking a swing, but there were no real golfers among them. Through Bob Neal, they visited a golf school in Florida, lugging the outsize prototype. With the very first swing from a serious golfer, cables went flying in all directions. The violent impact from the swing had not been factored into the prototype. Back to the drawing board.

The most promising application came by accident at a networking event, when the young startup founder ran into an entrepreneur from the packaging field. He told him about the urgent need for packaging line sensors, particularly in beverage bottling. Smart Skin found a corporate customer at a large beer plant who took an early prototype. The product was a kind of proxy for a bottle going through the line, measuring pressure on the glass containers — when they would break and when they would not. In the span of a very short period, Smart Skin saw its sensor could help the plant reduce the breakage of glass bottles and do it economically.

"The economic opportunity for us was huge, much bigger than everything else that we were working on. When we saw that data, we decided to forget everything else that we were working on and just focus on packaging." Still, the team recognized it might yet return to the other applications.

It was not an easy road, and Smart Skin took about a decade to get to the commercial product stage. Thillainadarajah says that, at some point, the board decided it needed fresh blood. It hired a new CEO, who had some experience with packaging and had worked for J.D. Irving, the industrial family's forestry and paper products business. "He's familiar with the industrial environment we deal with."

The founding CEO became chief technology officer, focusing on development of the product. And a new market has been identified — packaging for pharmaceuticals. Smart Skin gained a new investor as well, Schott, the big German glass company. It continues to explore the potential for its sensors. "I think year over year, more than 75 per cent of our revenue comes from new products that we didn't have the year before."

As for his family, "I think now they're okay with it because they see that I'm doing all right." For a while, he figures, his immediate family told the extended family that he was still in school. "They thought it was just a phase or something."

One of his larger concerns is how to break down the barriers for young immigrant innovators like himself. When he started Smart Skin, by day he was focusing on the business, but by night he was trying to figure out how to legally stay in the country. It was an immense struggle because there was no well-worn trail at that time.

Things improved with the introduction of the Atlantic Immigration Pilot, a program that streamlines the road to permanent residency, including through a startup program. Immigration is a priority in Atlantic Canada that transcends politics and party lines, as reflected in a State of the Province speech by Premier Blaine Higgs in early 2020. He asked for the federal government to raise the maximum immigration limits for New Brunswick to 10,000 a year from 7,500. Higgs set a goal of growing New Brunswick's population to a million people by 2040, which he said would have multiplier effects, in raising the province's gross domestic product by $15 billion and adding 100,000 jobs.

Thillainadarajah sees Smart Skin as the perfect company for New Brunswick. All its work is being done in the province — from the production of sensor material to the research and the final assembly. As it develops, it is facing the next big hurdle: scale-up — the jargon used in the business world for elevating a small company into a larger commercial enterprise, with exponential growth and extensive market reach.

Academic studies show that high-growth companies deliver disproportionate economic impact for the entire ecosystem, but getting there is very hard. Radian6 and Q1 Labs scaled up to a point but were sold. Can New Brunswick develop more companies to land in John McLaughlin's "sweet spot"?

They won't be the size and status of Nortel. Dhirendra Shukla still thinks wistfully of the former telecom giant and the missed opportunities. A flourishing ecosystem needs both big and small organisms. "If you don't have large iconic companies that act as a foundation, that act as a distribution channel, act as a champion, then these bubbling startups are not going to be able to survive. And they will all be pulled down south."

Shukla is the rare mix of ideas and energy that would be an attractive catch for other innovation centres, from Waterloo, Ontario, to Cambridge, Massachusetts. But his work in New Brunswick is not over, and his passion is undiminished. "I'm doing it because of the sheer love of the game, love of the place, love of the people."

16. Old Dogs, New Tricks

More than a decade ago, Shawn Carver and his business partner Dave Baxter were starting up their data analytics firm in Moncton, and they were hunting around for ideas. Then they had the kind of small-world encounter that exemplifies the East Coast. One of the partners attended a local event where he met Nestor Gomez, a technology manager at McCain Foods operations, based almost 200 miles away from Moncton in little Florenceville.

They had not much in common, it would seem. The young entrepreneurs' company, Fiddlehead Technology, was new and untested, based on math and data science. McCain Foods was an old family company in rural New Brunswick, a pillar of the Saint John River Valley potato economy, a processor of frozen fries and other foods.

Yet it was also a global brand marketer, with consumers and business relationships as far away as China, India and Australia. McCain Foods fit the young Fiddleheaders' needs in another key way. "We were looking for a reference company in the region that could present a problem, and we would help solve it," says Carver, then in his early 30s. He had been born in Moncton, worked a while as a consultant in Toronto and come home to his roots.

Gomez was the lead in McCain Foods's new startup and entrepreneurship program. The company was rolling out a strategy where it would strike alliances with small enterprises with interesting technologies. Because the McCain family and company have both roots and presence in the Maritimes, McCain Foods was more likely to work with entrepreneurs in Atlantic Canada, although it looked elsewhere too.

Gomez and his bosses, including CEO Max Koeune, also liked the intangible factors the two young men brought to the game. After a few meetings with Carver and Baxter, the McCain managers felt a sense of commitment, both to the duo's own vision and to the success of McCain Foods as a company.

Carver and McCain Foods have since travelled down a mutually rewarding road together, with Fiddlehead, named after a beloved local edible fern, providing consumer forecasting solutions for McCain and then casting a wider net by using their McCain work as reference points. "We simply wouldn't have the company today had McCain not taken a chance on us," says Carver, Fiddlehead's president. (Baxter is no longer employed at Fiddlehead, but has retained his ownership interest.)

It has meant rare access to a large global company and its challenges. Coming off the first series of meetings, Carver and Baxter were permitted to spend several months interviewing McCain people throughout the organization, before identifying ten potential application areas for their work. In narrowing down the list, McCain Foods realized there had to be outside demand for whatever application was developed and took that into account. Fiddlehead came up with tools that allow marketers to understand consumer trends for anything that might be found in a grocery store.

McCain Foods provided more than a cheque book. It was a relationship whereby the larger company's managers would hop on to phone calls with prospective clients. Fiddlehead got to work for companies such as Maple Leaf Foods — controlled by another branch of the McCain family — and the global dairy giant Saputo. Data analytics firm Nielsen Canada became a reseller of a product developed with McCain Foods, putting Fiddlehead into a much bigger game.

It is a test case for the role that big legacy companies can play in the development of startups, giving the mature company access to new ideas at a reduced cost, while lending the newcomer instant access to a significant partner and to markets that otherwise would take much longer to penetrate.

McCain Foods has forged a relationship with not just Fiddlehead but Eigen Innovations, a company that uses artificial intelligence and data connectivity to help manufacturing companies improve efficiency. Based in Fredericton, its CEO Scott Everett just happens to come from a Saint John River potato-farming family.

Born out of collaboration between Everett and his UNB professor Rickey Dubay, Eigen Innovations has extensive ties with the automotive industry. Everett believes its competitive edge comes from the fact that its largest customers are located outside Atlantic Canada, and McCain Foods too has that global reach.

McCain has taken an equity interest in a vertical farming business called TruLeaf, with a head office in Halifax but taking its name from the Nova Scotia town of Truro where it was conceived. Vertical farming is the practice of growing crops in vertically stacked layers, in controlled environments that produce year-round, often under LED lighting and using hydroponics and aquaponics.

McCain Foods also has invested in Resson, one of the darlings of the local tech scene, a company that combines drones, machine learning and analytics to allow farmers to make better and more productive use of their acreage. The company is another that has sprung out of the UNB hopper — co-founder Rishin Behl was an Indian-born mechanical engineering student who linked up with local entrepreneur Peter Goggin. Resson has also received equity investments from Indian farm equipment giant Mahindra and agriculture biology titan Monsanto, now part of Bayer.

McCain executives sum up the relationship with this seemingly diverse group of startups this way: the food giant can provide product valuation, and access to both subject matter experts and McCain's data, to make sure what the entrepreneurs are addressing is a real problem. And McCain Foods will do customer reference calls, as Fiddlehead discovered.

What does McCain get? Access to advanced technology at an affordable price, and not necessarily by making big investments, which is the case when working with large companies. The relationship should work for both sides, one McCain executive says: "If these companies help us, they'll do it at an extremely motivated level. They really want to develop their product, so they'll bend backwards to figure out what's the best product, what's the best turnaround time for the next version. They're not like the large companies, where you're one out of two thousand customers. You *are* the customer. And if these guys are smart, they'll figure it out."

Gomez is an architect of the strategy, a graduate in computer science from the University of Havana, with more than a decade's service with McCain. He calls the collaboration strategy MIGHT, for McCain Inspiring Growth through High Technology.

The hub of McCain's own technology infrastructure lies in tiny Florenceville, home to about 60 per cent of the 250 IT professionals the company employs worldwide. You could say that Florenceville is the central nervous system of IT for McCain globally. About 20 per cent of the IT workforce comes from outside the province, often newcomers to Canada, making for a very diverse labour force in the rural community. IBM has also established a separate Florenceville office, servicing McCain and other clients.

The role of legacy companies in a region can be critical to its economic development, beyond providing jobs in the short term. And McCain is not the only example. Another model developed in Idaho, another forested region with big economic inequities, old family companies and a heritage of growing potatoes. And like New Brunswick, Idaho is far off the beaten path in a region often overlooked in the chronicles of innovation.

Boise, the capital and the largest city in Idaho, is the home of Micron, one of the top global suppliers of integrated circuits, or computer chips. Micron started as a classic story: four guys in a basement designing chips. They reached out to local angels, including J.R. Simplot, the founder of a potato processing and food empire

— essentially, the Simplot company is the McCain Foods of the United States. Simplot invested $1 million, and that launched Micron.

Micron no longer manufactures chips in Idaho, but its research and development centre is in Boise, and there is a legacy of technology innovation that still looms large in the state's economy. Boise is one of the startup centres of the New American West. Simplot's involvement is the cheque-writing model, while McCain speaks to the potential for a deeper co-development relationship.

The McCain project injects a more integrative model in what is often seen as a binary divide of old legacy companies in Atlantic Canada versus new startups, of extractive and processing businesses versus those built on intellectual capital. Indeed, there is something counter-cultural in the new tech startups, which are often formed, built and sold for exit prices within a few years. They are fleeting and transitory, while the tradition in New Brunswick and much of rural Canada is to build long-term ventures — at least, until the resources are too expensive to exploit. Some ancestor drives a stake in the ground with a mill, factory or refinery, not just for five years but, it is hoped, five decades or more. The sense of permanence is ingrained in the company's self-image.

The Irvings trace their story to a sawmill in Bouctouche in the 19th century, when the first J.D. Irving established himself. The McCains were potato farmers and seed potato exporters long before the brothers Harrison and Wallace opened a frozen fries plant in the late 1950s. The Olands trace their beer-making origins to a backyard in Dartmouth, Nova Scotia, where their ancestor Susannah Oland, a recent immigrant from England, brewed beer in her garden shed starting in the 1850s and laid the foundations of today's Moosehead. The Ganong family has been making chocolates in St. Stephen since 1873.

And yet the question remains: are these old titans building future industries in the region or just perpetuating old power bases? They may in fact be smothering innovation, leading to the thesis that the old families are too ubiquitous, too powerful, that in their drive for domination, they trample the budding shoots in other patches. Can a successful company be too successful for its region?

The Irvings are most commonly at the centre of this debate, alternately savaged for their domination of rural economies and admired for their street smarts and front-line efficiency. The debate often lacks nuance. First, "the Irvings" are not monolithic, having over the past 15 years undergone a wrenching unravelling of ownership structures that K.C. Irving had set up. They are no longer a solid front, but three distinct units, with varied sub-units, and many different players involved.

The Irvings attract controversy in part because they are obsessively private and, in their long history, have shown a willingness to crush competitors and sideline critics. Also, they own the major English-language news sources in the province — just a rounding error in terms of their entire business, but a source of constant distraction. The biggest story in the province is often about the Irvings, and the main source of coverage is the Irving-owned media. It is a combination fated to create tensions.

Meanwhile, there is some disdain for the kinds of businesses the Irvings are widely perceived to run — commodity-based with low margins, where success is built on driving costs out of the system. Some say it would be too bad if the highest value-added product in the province were toilet paper — a reference to their Royale tissues — rather than advanced technology. Others see the genius: few products are more recession-proof than toilet paper. Toilet paper is the most sought-after grocery item during a crisis, whether it's the oil shock of 1973-74 or the recent pandemic.

What's more, in all their businesses the Irvings are good at applying technology to operations, and the secret of innovation often lies not merely in invention but in application. They also train good managers, who become a leadership resource, occasionally for the little startups that need help in growing. As a company moves from the raw tech stage to larger markets and bigger financings, a senior manager with an Irving track record can be an asset.

John Risley, the financier and fishery mogul in Halifax, is one who appreciates the Irving forestry arm, in particular. He concedes there are fewer of the old economic anchors, like NBTel, that hired people out of university and put them through rigorous management training. The traditional businesses today do not have those kinds of budgets.

Yet Risley sees the forestry-shipbuilding-food giant J.D. Irving Ltd., led by hard-driving Jim Irving Jr. (along with his brother Robert) as an exception. Jim Jr., the son of J.K. Irving, also known as Jim, understands that his traditional businesses — from sawmills to retail — have to make smart use of technology, and focus on how it can contribute to the cost profile.

Risley argues that a region needs traditional established business throwing off cash to support new technology enterprises. In the Irving forestry operations, that cash comes from operational effectiveness. "Why do Irving sawmills supply products to half the Home Depot stores in the U.S.? Not because they love Jim Irving but because the Irving company offers lower cost and better quality than any of their competitors."

Indeed, as you travel New Brunswick, you find the Irving companies are quiet enablers to some of the new companies. Ryan Groom's Kognitiv Spark, which makes mixed-reality tools for organizations operating in remote locations, signed the J.D. Irving company as its first customer. McCain too has been a supporter in the early stages. Both McCains and Irvings were customers of an earlier security company he ran. "A lot of times, you are not a prophet in your own hometown," Groom says, "and so it is nice to see that."

Of course, the Irvings *do* want to crush competitors — they are fourth-generation survivors in the ruthless art of capitalism. And they should probably do even more to support the little sprouts in their big backyard. But they are not passive in the tech ecosystem. They are players.

The Irvings are saddled with a Goliath-like mystique even in New England, where the energy and forestry operations are well represented. The *Portland Press Herald* in 2014 published a report seemingly gobsmacked by the commanding Irving presence: "They control somewhere between 200 and 300 companies — because they are privately held, nobody really knows the exact number."

According to this report, "They are the largest landowner here in Maine, with 1.2 million acres, making them the fifth-largest private landholder in the United States and — together with over 2 million acres in Canada — the tenth largest on Earth, excluding monarchs like Queen Elizabeth, who notionally owns much of the United Kingdom and its former empire."

Indeed, the Irving forestry operations in Canada and the United States employ about the same number of people as all the information technology firms in New Brunswick — around 4,500 to 5,000 people (although thousands more IT professionals are employed by non-IT firms).

Consider that J.D. Irving Ltd. recently planted its one billionth tree since 1957, a national record for a private company. A 2018 press release pointed out that when the tree-planting program began in 1957 the company had two sawmills and a pulp mill. Today, "there are over 4,600 direct employees in Canada and the U.S., operating 10 sawmills and 1.5 million tonnes per year coming out of the pulp, paper and tissue mills. The company is one of a handful left in North America today that sustains a value chain from the seedling in the forest to the tissue products on the store shelf."

The other major Irving entity is Irving Oil, run by Arthur Irving, uncle of Jim Jr., and a nonagenarian force of nature. His biggest asset is the mega-refinery in Saint John, plus a petroleum distribution network that extends far down into New England. In addition, he commands a recently acquired refinery in Ireland.

His business is a creature of New England as much as New Brunswick. Eyebrows were raised when Dartmouth College, the Ivy

League school in New Hampshire, announced in 2017 the creation of the Arthur L. Irving Institute for Energy and Society, with a mandate to prepare future generations of energy leaders and "advance humanity's understanding of the field, driving change in the intelligent production, supply and use of energy."

The core funding of the institute came from gifts of $113 million U.S., of which $80 million was donated by the Arthur Irving family, including Arthur himself, his wife Sandra and their daughter Sarah, the current heir apparent in Arthur's tumultuous succession plan. Sarah is a graduate of the Rothesay Netherwood School, an elite boarding school, and holds an undergraduate degree and an MBA from Dartmouth.

Couldn't UNB have made great use of that $80 million U.S. donated by Arthur Irving and family? Or Dalhousie — or Acadia, the Irving brothers' traditional beneficiary in Nova Scotia? Yet Sarah, too, is surely entitled to support her alma mater, just as her father and uncles and cousins have. And consider the millions the Irvings have already poured into UNB over the years. Recently, a roundtable in advanced manufacturing at UNB, headed by economist Herb Emery, was seeded with a $2-million investment from J.D. Irving Ltd. When the pandemic threatened to swamp the province's health-care system, Arthur Irving was quick to step up with a $1-million donation to the Saint John hospital's Covid-19 emergency fund.

Bottom line: the Irvings just can't win in the public opinion arena, and they are often clumsy in how they deal with the conflicting images and messages. It is an Atlantic Canadian failing — great at operating things, bad at image-making.

With the McCains you feel another kind of tension, the global-local thing. There are always whispers they have abandoned New Brunswick. They still have extensive operations in the province, but the effective head office is in Toronto, and their large U.S. business is run out of Chicago. The company is headed by the Luxembourg-born Koeune.

McCain Foods has always been a globally active company but in the early days of brothers Harrison and Wallace in Florenceville, they could manage it all with two private planes in their backyard, swooping off to Chicago one day, Northern England the next. Now the size and complexity require a more globally distributed approach.

In the 1990s, the McCain family went through a period of dynastic strife, pitting the Wallace McCain branch against brother Harrison and a number of other relatives. If the old battles had one positive result, they heightened the resolve to let professional managers run the business while the family sorted out the divisions. The company actually flourished during the period of most agonizing dissension.

Those divisions seem to be in the past. Holding company chairman Allison McCain, who lives in New Brunswick, is seen as an able steward who mediates between the local roots and the global reach, working with cousins, such as Mark, the son of Harrison, and Scott, the son of Wallace.

Everyone seems to support the strategy around startups — "cases where we are teaming up to help them build a business," Max Koeune says. "Sometimes we invest, sometimes we don't." In the case of the equity stakes in TruLeaf and Resson, "what made us invest in them is they're very, very closely connected to agriculture. The others are more service providers." With the actual equity investments, it's a question of "how deeply connected are they with something that's at the root of who we are?"

He explains that McCain has also developed a relationship with a non-Maritime company that provides "back-end technology," a pre-revenue company with innovative ideas about plant-based proteins. He adds, "What we're trying to build is an ecosystem of technology companies around key areas of McCain, rather than a big startup incubator program."

Meanwhile, TruLeaf operates in the hot sector of vertical farming, which with its all-season model of intensive agriculture, is hailed as a way to stimulate local production in areas like the Canadian North. But to make it work, there has to be a kind of reverse piloting process — you need to do it big before you take it small. So TruLeaf's subsidiary GoodLeaf has built a vertical farm for green veggies in Guelph, Ontario, in the centre of the largest consumer market in the country.

There were reports that McCain Foods was instrumental in the removal of TruLeaf's founder-CEO and his replacement by a manager closer to the big company. Koeune acknowledges the founder did step aside, which is common in the early years of a startup. But he points out, "We are a minority stakeholder. We have two seats on the board. We have a voice and people tend to listen when we speak about what we know, but we don't run the show there."

The powerful East Coast families are the epitome of quiet money, which prefers to operate in the background. One exception is a rare collaboration among individual members of the Sobey and McCain families (separate from their family companies). Their private-equity company called SeaFort Capital makes long-term investments in smaller traditional businesses, ideally with some competitive market advantage.

For decades, McCain Foods and the Irving companies have served as two legs in a three-cornered stool that is the New Brunswick economy — the other leg being the provincial government. But in recent years, a fourth leg has been attached to the stool. Cooke Aquaculture has burst out of the little fishing town of Blacks Harbour in the province's southwest corner to become a behemoth in fish farming globally. Despite controversies swirling around aquaculture — the potential for fish disease, the environmental impact — the Cooke family has been steadily marching on a global acquisitions spree.

It has deep New Brunswick blue-collar roots, beginning with Gifford Cooke, a marine mechanic for the old Connors Bros. company, known widely for its sardines and based in Blacks Harbour. With his sons Glenn and Michael, he founded his own fishery business in 1985. Glenn, a high school graduate, emerged as the CEO and face of the company.

When I first interviewed Glenn in 2008, Cooke Aquaculture had sales of about $270 million a year. Just over a decade later, it has grown to ten times that level. In a 2019 speech to the Atlantic Provinces Economic Council, Glenn noted the company operates in ten countries — half of them in Latin America — with 25 processing facilities and over 9,000 employees. About 1,400 of those workers are in New Brunswick, where the company's activities have helped create another 1,000 jobs. It ships a billion pounds of seafood products to 67 countries, totalling $2.4 billion in revenues.

Glenn Cooke took pains to describe the local economic impact. The company works with almost 800 local partners and suppliers from New Brunswick and buys goods and services from 1,300 small and medium-sized businesses across Atlantic Canada.

It is in the midst of a multi-year capital expansion plan to spend $200 million in New Brunswick and $500 million across Atlantic Canada. It is an R&D player in its sector, having finished construction on a new genomics-based breeding station and gene bank library. Glenn Cooke nodded to the critical financial support they had received from Opportunities New Brunswick and ACOA.

He also pointed out the company's breadth of employment: tractor trailer drivers, IT and logistics staff, marine maintenance people, engineers, veterinarians, research scientists, vessel captains and deckhands, and fish farm managers and feed technicians. It is the very definition of an anchor company in an age-old maritime business, but fashioned to the demands of 2020. This seems to be worlds away from a tech startup, looking for a quick exit.

So the question becomes: Can you build a future through companies that explore new technology, that are venturesome and smart, and connected to the next new things — and yet behave like McCain, Irving and Cooke, firmly planted in the local soil or sea, with a commitment to jobs, value creation and keeping intellectual property in the region that begat them?

McCain's Max Koeune wants to put out a provocative thought. When there is talk about a company becoming "the next Radian6 or Q1 Labs," he questions whether that is the right yardstick. "I think the fact that these companies got bought out at these high valuations sets a great benchmark, a great validation for their success. But at the end of the day, they sold out."

When that happens, "the centre of power, sooner rather than later, gravitates somewhere else, and then depending on the goodwill of whoever the parent company is, you have an operation [in the original community] or you don't. And you have a brain drain or you don't." It really depends on the buyer, he says.

Instead, "I would look at the benchmark being more like, 'Who's the next Shopify?'" — referring to the Ottawa software company that has kept its local identity in the face of spectacular growth. If New Brunswick, or Canada, is to be successful in building thriving business ecosystems, that success will come from the ability to replicate the Irvings, the McCains and the Cookes, "which own the company and develop it for generations."

Instead, what he finds in many startup companies is the view that, "Okay, I'm starting this and then I'll sell out, and then I'll make money and that's it." For Koeune, there should be a bigger aspiration — of building something longer lasting in the community than, say, Q1 Labs or Radian6. (He is not talking about the companies in the McCain ecosystem, which are much earlier in their development.)

It takes an outsider, someone who has seen the world, to sum up the economic dilemma for New Brunswick. How can the province encourage the innovation of the tech hopefuls, and yet foster the deep roots that follow the tradition of the legacy firms? That is a challenge that vexes much of the North American hinterland, from Saint John to Boise.

17. Homebodies

The community of Grand-Barachois is strung along a gorgeous piece of coastline on the Northumberland Strait in southeast New Brunswick. To find Daniella DeGrace's place, you drive past a deep cove, turn down toward the shore, through a tangle of dirt roads. The scene opens to a vista of beach and marshes, with an extended Cape Cod house in classic weathered grey and a boardwalk reaching out to the sea.

The boardwalk and ocean dominate the scene from DeGrace's living room, her refuge from the tech frenzy she has navigated so expertly over the past three decades. She made some money from the series of startups she helped build and bought this piece of paradise, just a half hour away from Moncton and three hours away by car from where she grew up in the Bathurst region to the north.

DeGrace is one of the few veterans of all three seminal startups in the history of New Brunswick — iMagic, Q1 Labs, Radian6. (Others include Jeff White and of course Gerry Pond.) Her old colleagues call her one of the "double-dippers," because she was part of both the Q1 and Radian6 stories. She has travelled down the path of the region's emergence as a technology player. She was never a ground-floor founder, but she was the professional engineer and manager who could bring a level of experience and expertise to a frenetic startup. "Dani can do it," they would say, and she did. That has made her a formidable resource for another generation of young founders, and she loves that world and has never left it. She is addicted to startups.

She was born in Beresford, a community ten minutes out of Bathurst, to an Acadian family. Her mom worked for the government as an executive assistant, and her father owned a small contracting business. Daniella went to Université de Moncton, in a French-language program that focused on software development. After graduating, she went to Montreal, where she joined the Hydro-Québec utility and was responsible for implementing a new network system. There were almost no other women in tech back then. "I learned to exist in a very male environment. But it was never on my mind. I just loved the technology."

But surely managing males was a challenge? She found it was harder as a young woman among the Hydro-Québec engineers, but as she moved farther into the software side, it got easier. "I think they were kind of seeing me as just one of the guys."

She came back to New Brunswick for family reasons, and she landed at iMagic during its glory days under Marcel LeBrun. She had the nickname Dani, and she liked to hang out at car-racing tracks, even taking some driving spins around NASCAR and Formula One courses. She was passionate about photography, as were many of her male colleagues. When you share interests, it is easier to fit in. But she also collected hundreds of pairs of shoes, which to her are not just footwear but *objets d'art*. She travelled widely in her iMagic job, including spending six years in Paris, but she kept coming home.

After iMagic and those years in Paris, she worked for the company's new owner Alcatel for a while, but like most of the New Brunswickers still at Alcatel, the turmoil of a huge organization in transition wore on her. She was recruited by Q1 Labs, and when Q1 looked about to be sold to the industry giant IBM, she jumped to Radian6. She was instrumental in plugging the leak of Radian6 customers in the early days, before the fledgling company found its legs and roared toward its exit to Salesforce.

She worked at Salesforce for a while. She marvelled at the ability to replicate the small-company vibe in a massive organization. But she was a cog in a machine, and Dani DeGrace likes it best when she can see her impact on the company and its future.

Daniella DeGrace's interests include her love of NASCAR (as shown here at Charlotte Motor Speedway) and helping tech startups grow
(Courtesy of Daniella DeGrace)

She took some time off and invested a bit, serving as an adviser to a dozen or so small companies, but also poured her time into community-building pursuits. She is part of the efforts to transform Moncton into a technology hub with its own startup incubator, Venn Innovation, on downtown Main Street. Moncton has never been known as a tech centre, but there is a focus now on building something.

The city has a strong industrial core, built partly out of adversity — in 1988 Canadian National Railway closed its Moncton repair yard in a cost-cutting drive, cutting 2,000 jobs. It left a big hole in Moncton's industrial core, but it also sparked a renewed focus on attracting industry and on entrepreneurialism, building on the bilingual nature of the city.

Moncton is a magnet for young francophones, who swarm into the city for school and jobs from the little towns in the Northeast. It has done so well in conventional industry — from the new wave of call centres to its logistics companies — that it never felt compelled to become a technology startup powerhouse. And yet it did spawn Spielo, an early manufacturer of gaming equipment, whose founder Jon Manship has, since selling the company, forged a quiet but purposeful investment role in the city.

Moncton is the natural focus of a lot of DeGrace's activity, but her influence is broader. After taking some time post-Radian6, she got talking to the head of the New Brunswick Investment Foundation, a body that had provided seed money to Radian6 and others. He put her in touch with Saint John–based Innovatia and its two owners Roxanne Fairweather and David Grebenc. Innovatia is a descendant of the little cells that Gerry Pond built in NBTel. Its expertise lies in document services and knowledge management. After NBTel was merged into the other big three phone companies, Bell Aliant put Innovatia up for sale, and Fairweather and Grebenc stepped up to buy it.

The death of a huge client like Nortel could have sunk the company, but the two partners forged relationships with the new owners of the Nortel assets and diversified the client base. Part of a cluster of IT enterprises in Saint John's historic old downtown, it is now the quintessential Atlantic Canadian tech company, with a wide global presence. Some of its clients said that to retain their business, Innovatia had to be present in India, and so the two partners opened a unit in Bangalore.

Innovatia decided to launch a promising business offshoot, called ProcedureFlow, which services call centres and other customer contact points. ProcedureFlow — whose corporate name is Gemba — provides these companies with digital tools to help train employees and let them find information more quickly.

And who better to run it than Dani DeGrace? She now works in Saint John during the week, then heads back to Grand-Barachois for weekends. After travelling the world, she is now three hours from her roots.

Her story is typical of the people who came out of Radian6 and Q1. While earlier generations left, this cohort has stayed. "We've all asked ourselves the questions, 'Okay, what do we do now, where do we live, where do we go?'" DeGrace says. "We all had the opportunity to pack our bags and go live on an island. And none of us wanted to do that. None of us wanted to leave." There is this attachment to home — "It just gives me chills thinking about it." To find an explanation, she goes back to some of the associations with Gerry Pond, and how he taught the importance of community.

For her, entrepreneurship is a civic duty. "People ask me, 'Why are you doing a fourth [startup]?' And I will do a fifth one someday, God willing. And part of it is I want to give back to the community. What better way to do that than to train more of me, and more Marcel LeBruns and more of the others? It's like rabbits — we're multiplying."

She tries to put her finger on why she comes back. She has travelled the world and met a lot of people. "It is interesting how they recognize your culture as something so unique. Even when I was in Montreal, being French, in that environment they would always say the New Brunswick culture is just special. When I was in Paris, you're very colourful. And so even in other places in the world, you are New Brunswick, you feel New Brunswick. And so coming back home, it just feels right."

Maybe it is the blend of cultures, the bilingualism and recently the multiculturalism, the juxtaposition of forests and sea, of small towns and cities where everyone knows everyone else, and now the startups, which are easier to build in the connected world. It is possible to live and work and be successful in this environment, particularly with software as a service (SaaS) and the less formal tech culture.

"In the iMagic TV days, you needed the Gerry Ponds, you needed the heavy lifters to move anything. Now, the venture capitalists love seeing a young kid with a T-shirt that has no experience, because they love the image of it."

She is part of the generation that is saying, You can stay home. You don't need to build your career in Toronto or San Francisco and then, salmon-like, swim home to retire, or die. Once, there was a Canada-to-U.S. brain drain, and always an East-to-West brain drain. Both are now being slowed or even reversed. One way to do that is to build an even more livable community, which then becomes a magnet for people from all over the world.

That is the mission of people like Marcel LeBrun. After the sale of Radian6, he had reached the level of affluence and reputation where he could turn his attention to his life purpose. He was a man of faith, and he saw the chance to turn his Christian values into a concrete reality. The question was, how?

He had spent more than four years at Salesforce, and for a while, ran the software giant's key "marketing cloud" initiative out of Fredericton. He watched as the company built that business through organic growth and acquisitions, including the purchase of a larger operation in Indianapolis. Although Salesforce maintained a strong Maritimes presence, a number of functions concentrated in Indiana. LeBrun focused on the product, building his team to the level that he was not really needed and was able to leave the company on a positive note. Then, he says, "I spent an extended time figuring out what to spend my money on. I wanted to be wise with my new financial reality."

The young men and women who made some money from Q1 Labs and Radian6 grapple with where to make the most impact, both in their financial investments and their time and leadership in community-building. LeBrun threw himself into thinking about poverty and marginalization in New Brunswick and the world at large, and this opened up as a focus of his post-Radian6 career.

He decided he could not be effective with a simple transactional approach, in which he would just throw a lot of money at the problem. He would take a multi-faceted, holistic approach that merged his Christian values and strategic business sense. "When you get into looking at poverty, you confront how many of us take a material perspective — that it's just a lack of resources. But it is a much more complex situation — that is, social, material, mental, spiritual, all the dimensions."

Of course, he supports financial aid to mitigate poverty, but he recognizes that it is not enough. "There are all these entrenched narratives that box us in — about how we tackle this through relief efforts only, giving people food and goods and money." His conclusion: the disadvantaged need a sense of worth and belonging, and the tools and confidence to make their own way. The mechanism to create this transformation is social enterprise — using business approaches for social ends.

"I realized just pouring money into things could actually just do more harm than good. So what does good look like?"

In his search for "good," he travelled the world with a camera crew, exploring the dimensions of marginalization. The result is *12 Neighbors*, a film series produced with Hemmings House, a socially engaged Saint John media company. Available online, it takes the viewer into a number of communities, focusing on the powerful work being done by social entrepreneurs.

He met Del Seymour, a.k.a. the Mayor of the Tenderloin, in San Francisco, a former drug addict and dealer who once controlled the most notorious block in the rough underbelly of that affluent city but now tries to get homeless people back into the workforce. Seymour told LeBrun that what these people needed was not just food — they could often obtain enough food through various charities — but hope and dignity. What has to happen is that people "have to believe the narrative about themselves."

LeBrun saw the same equation in Los Angeles, in an organization that employs ex-gang members. They now have marketable skills, whereas once, despite their tough-guy bravado, they saw themselves as "a piece of crap." LeBrun says, "If you change their circumstances, but not change their narratives, they will go back to what they were before. Once they believe they are not who they are said to be, they will change."

LeBrun also took his mission closer to home, through a youth camp that had been sitting closed near Sussex, New Brunswick. He and his wife, Sheila, a trained occupational therapist experienced with children who have learning disabilities, bought and revived the camp, known as New Horizons. It is in part a standard camp for children, with a strong horse-riding component that reflects the LeBruns' — particularly Sheila's — equestrian interests. But the private camp helps underwrite their efforts to change the narrative for at-risk children in Saint John.

These non-fee-paying children potentially come for a weekend a month during the year, and engage in a number of activities. There is even an entrepreneurship program in which the children form their own companies in areas from carpentry to baking, with a *Dragons' Den*-like component where they make pitches for their businesses. But at first, the focus is on simple tasks, like learning how to clean their rooms. The LeBruns work with the Saint John Police Force and the local schools to identify potentially at-risk kids. A public health nurse helps build benchmarks to mark their progress.

The camp is now a self-sustaining enterprise: it offers year-round corporate retreats, which help to underwrite the youth camp. Marcel and Sheila believe that, if they can run it well, it will continue its work, using university students as camp instructors. The LeBrun Family Foundation is also active internationally, supporting, for example, a program in Ghana that provides a school on the streets for homeless children.

The LeBruns live in Fredericton, near the river just off Woodstock Road, with stables and animals on their 20 acres, all within city limits. The whole concept of rural life inside the city highlights why Fredericton remains such a magnet for the young startup founders of Q1 and Radian6. "We are eight minutes to downtown, and we have deer and eagles to look at every day," LeBrun says.

He has taken on angel investing around the province, as well as the role of venture partner with a Montreal venture capital firm, Real Ventures. As a venture capital adviser in New Brunswick, he knows the challenges. "You see a lot of deals and invest in very few." That is more efficiently done in places like Kitchener-Waterloo, where a venture capitalist could look at ten deals in a day — as opposed to the

Maritimes, where you might have to travel through three provinces to see that many opportunities, which you certainly couldn't do in one day. For Real Ventures, "My role is not to be the Maritime representative. It is bringing some execution knowledge. If I can help, I can help on the ground."

LeBrun is also active as a teacher in the technology, management and entrepreneurship program at UNB, including the master's program, where all the students have to form companies for their degrees. "Some will graduate and not look at these companies again; others will carry them forward."

As he approaches 50, he thinks about how he could have left the province and made a lot more money. In fact, Salesforce had toyed with the idea of making Newton and LeBrun executives at head office, until Benioff and his people concluded it was better to keep them with their team in Fredericton.

LeBrun asks, "What does a full life mean? I ask that in my films. It is not about toys or even experiences — it is about relationships. If we can be entangled with people here and do great things, it is a full life." He and Sheila are "rewired not retired." They are not looking too far ahead, taking the view that "this is a great day and this is what I am doing. What it will lead to tomorrow, we will see."

Another area of great interest is his involvement with the local multicultural association and with newcomers. He volunteered as a "First Fredericton Friend" in a program that has connected him to a Syrian refugee family. Through this counselling and support relationship he has come to understand the realities of jobs and life in the Maritimes. In the Syrian family, the oldest son works, but the father finds it hard to find employment at his more advanced age. His family were sheepherders, and there are no sheep here.

In Toronto, LeBrun notes, it is possible to go to work in your first language. That means New Brunswick has to work that much harder on immigration. "We will have a leak in the bucket — some people will leave for communities where they can enjoy a shared language and culture. Why some are staying is because their community is here. You have to have a community, but at some point, you also need a job." He wants to help with that dual challenge.

About an hour west of the New Horizons camp, in a Saint John suburban park beside a big bay in the river, David Alston is swinging from the trees. His new business, called TimberTop Adventures, is not social enterprise exactly, but it is creative, unconventional and teaches leadership, purpose and resilience.

He and his family have developed TimberTop as a treetop aerial adventure, situated on land leased from the city. You drive into the parking lot beside the bay, and within a few yards, you enter a crazy web of rope nets and zip lines, through which you can go wild for up to three hours as you explore as many as 11 different routes through the trees.

The always active mind of David Alston cannot rest very long, and TimberTop is the latest of his pursuits since coming out of iMagic 20 years ago. There was the marketing gig in Saint John; the full immersion into Radian6; the 2011 exit; and a role as busy director and mentor to startup companies, including five years with serial founder Jody Glidden's new venture, Introhive.

For two years he was a volunteer entrepreneur-in-residence for the provincial government, which involved advising startups and helping foster an enterprise mentality in the province — a calling he has never relinquished even as his formal appointment ended. Now his life is, literally, a series of ropes and pulleys.

He likes the feel of creating something new and doing it with his family. After Radian6, Alston had shifted from going deep with a single company to talking broadly to a lot of companies. Building TimberTop means that he and Mary-Gwen, his wife, are going deep again into a brand-new industry, learning as they go. Part of the fun is recruiting and training his young staff. "When we say on our website we're looking for leaders, we honestly mean we're looking for leaders."

Chris Ramsey was one of the
original six at Radian6 and
now strives to build Fredericton's
community spirit (Courtesy of
David Alston and Marcel LeBrun)

"I want to pay it forward," he says. "That's the New Brunswick way.
And Gerry literally set the tone for that. We all are trying to catch up
to Gerry, honestly."

An hour to the north, in Fredericton, Chris Ramsey is paying it
forward too, by taking on a big job in community-building. He is the
leader in a public initiative to build a new swimming pool for the city.
The old one will be closed in 2021, the decision of its owner, UNB, in
the face of conflicting budget needs. The pool served the entire city,
and Ramsey came forward as the leader of the replacement project.
He's becoming accustomed to a different kind of challenge: "It's so
incredibly political," he says.

This is his second adventure in preserving an institution in the
Fredericton area. The community has a small ski hill called Crabbe
Mountain, 35 or so miles away, with about 80 chalets built on the
hill, including one bought by Ramsey and his family after the Radian6
deal. But a few years ago, the owners, the Wilson family of Halifax
fuel-distribution fame, wanted to sell it and even raised the spectre
of closing it down.

Ramsey was part of a small consortium of chalet owners who stepped forward and bought the hill, and Crabbe Mountain never missed a season. "The thing with these little ski hills, if you miss a season, it's done." Even though it was a private transaction, it was not an investment, he says — more like an act of philanthropy that he does not expect to yield much, if any, financial return on his money.

This is a commitment to Fredericton, the community and province, and most of the Q1-Radian6 founders are going down that path. None of them feel the pressure to do another startup, and that is the joy — or the failing — of New Brunswick, depending on who you talk to. In Toronto or Kitchener-Waterloo, or Silicon Valley, they would feel the immediate pressure to go out and found new companies, make a lot of money and live a spectacularly ostentatious lifestyle. Not here. (The one exception is their love of nice cars.)

Some onlookers see this as the Maritime disease. There is no driving force, no hunger — they are too happy with being big frogs in a small pond. In Toronto — or Palo Alto — the atmosphere is contagious and compulsive. You need more money to live the good life, and you have to produce or die, or at least face dismissive comments like, "She's just not the kind to thrive in this challenging environment."

The argument goes that New Brunswick's knowledge elite, and Maritimers in general, are too comfortable, too insular, too unchallenged, to be successful serial founders and venture capitalists, and thus their tech communities are fated to be marginal and second-rate.

Some outsiders worry that the opportunities are not being exploited, because there is not enough "success culture." When success comes, as in the case of the two big exits, it is seen as a fluke, an anomaly, not a normal fact of life. You need constant success to breed more success. The worry is that in New Brunswick, people disengage from the chase more easily because they can retire on a lot less. You can be happy, you can do a bunch of things, and then you've reached the pinnacle of your community. Since you don't need as much, you are not as likely to strive as your colleagues in Central Canada. And that, they say, is bad for building a vibrant economy.

But what if we place greater value on building a healthy civil society, developing and supporting the human infrastructure, which goes hand-in-hand with creating the companies that bring wealth to the community? This work is just as crucial, and is highly valued in a place like New Brunswick. Ideally, companies here nurture a community where tech professionals — indeed any group in society — will want to live, raise families and in turn support the society and the economy. Where immigrants will want to come and can expect to find a welcoming home.

This is entrepreneurialism with purpose and impact. A lot of the fruits of successful startups are transported away — intellectual property flows to Toronto or skilled workers to Palo Alto. Profits go to venture capitalists in Boston or Sand Hill Road. But saving the pool or the ski hill, or teaching at a local university, or mentoring in an incubator, is work the results of which stay rooted in the community and become part of the competitive potential of a region far into the future.

David Alston concedes that in Atlantic Canada, "It's not this intense startup culture. It's more of a helping culture. And so honestly, we all try to do our best to guide and advise anyone who's willing to step up and try to do something new."

Nancy Mathis is a veteran of the entrepreneurial wars, having founded a company based on her PhD research in chemical engineering, working with her husband, Chris. But Mathis Instruments died, and she felt the road rash from scraping along the asphalt, her analogy for building, and losing, a tech company. But she and Chris have used that experience to be mentors and advisers.

After the end of her company, she was approached by several of the old guard in New Brunswick, including chocolate maker David Ganong, Moosehead's Derek Oland, Ed Barrett who co-founded the rural broadband company Xplornet and the ubiquitous Gerry Pond.

They wanted to recruit her to operate peer-based training and support programs for the region's businesspeople. With original funding from food magnate Wallace McCain and his wife, Margaret, the Wallace McCain Institute has helped hundreds of people, from leaders of family businesses to new entrepreneurs and senior executives. Now she is taking its peer approach across the Atlantic region.

She finds a lot of people in her network share her commitment to community, and are driven by the motivation to help others. In Atlantic Canada, "I don't find that the people I work with connect their purpose to financial value." It is a sharp contrast to the ethos of Toronto, where the primary focus is often on wealth. "In New Brunswick, I can't name one [business leader] whose purpose in business is wealth. It is the culture. They need to be comfortable but, down deep, it is to give back."

New Brunswickers are somewhat representative of what she finds in many Canadian communities outside Toronto. She laughs as she recalls a U.S. venture capitalist once saying to her, "Oh yeah, you Canadians, you go for the bronze." If that is the Canadian brand, so be it. Will it make for a better society? Maybe, even when faced with the challenges of dire poverty in Saint John and desperate rural towns, such as in Campbellton, where more than a third of the children struggle in poverty.

But surely, New Brunswick can only change its society, contain poverty and build a livable community if its businesspeople create wealth. Krista Jones spent a lot of her youth in the Miramichi and is now a senior officer at the MaRS Discovery District, the bustling innovation hub in downtown Toronto. She thinks successful New Brunswickers have to think bigger, to embrace the kind of city-building that Toronto and Waterloo has benefited from through their private-sector leaders.

"If you look at most innovation cities, they've been built on the backs of people who have been previously successful. They almost all have been. If you look at the Valley, success begets success. If you look at Waterloo, if you look at Toronto, if you look at Israel." She says the reason MaRS exists is that a group of private individuals got together and decided that they were going to devote their greatest effort, not just to volunteering on charitable boards — although they did a lot of that too — but to solving the economic problems of their community by creating high-value jobs and commercializing technology.

Jones's words resonate at this time in history, when already hard-pressed Atlantic provincial governments have become even more fiscally strapped than usual, as they deal with the devastating fallout from the pandemic. Private individuals, both through their gifts of time and money, have to step up more than ever before if the region is to move beyond the crisis. There need to be more Gerry Ponds or Marcel LeBruns, who fit the model of the private catalyst for public ends.

The good news, Jones says, is she sees some of that commitment. For example, UNB — her own alma mater — has been behind some innovative projects, but it needs to draw even more financial and volunteer support from the private sector and private wealth.

If you look at most innovation centres in the world, they're actually structured around a university, she says. University of Toronto provides an anchor for MaRS. Ryerson spun out the DMZ incubator. The highly successful Kitchener-Waterloo incubator Communitech has ties to local universities, including the University of Waterloo, which also spawned BlackBerry and other influential startups. You see the same roles in California with Stanford, or in Boston with MIT and Harvard.

By some scorecards, New Brunswick is doing well in innovation — in such rankings as "best startup city" or "best startup university." Yet it is often baffling to see the province alternately praised and derided for its record in fostering innovative businesses. It depends on what is being measured, and when.

One comparison in particular was devastating. The Conference Board of Canada, in its 2018 report on innovation worldwide, focused on the relative performance of Canada and the specific provinces. Its verdict: "New Brunswick ranks last among all provinces and international peers and holds the unfortunate distinction of being the only jurisdiction that fails to earn an A or B on any indicator." It went down the list: "In terms of innovation capacity, New Brunswick has mediocre public R&D (earning a C), has very few researchers engaged in R&D (earning a D–), and produces few scientific articles (earning a D). In the innovation activity category, New Brunswick scores C for [information and communications technology] investment, D for venture capital investment, and D– for business R&D."

The report added, "On a positive note, both the value and number of venture capital deals have grown in New Brunswick in recent years, indicating that investors see an increasing number of high-potential companies in the province." A nod to the legacy of Radian6 and Q1 Labs.

Unfortunately, a scorecard like this, which is read widely by investors and business people, does not have categories such as "most welcoming community," "nicest people" or "best small-city art gallery." As he discusses the report, David Alston is shaking his head. Sitting on a picnic table at his TimberTop Adventures site, he takes it as a personal insult. He wonders how the negative results are affected by New Brunswick's small population size. "If you talk to a lot of people that are in the startup space in New Brunswick, I think [they'd say] it punches above its weight."

The report is just a continuation of New Brunswick's traditionally underappreciated status. Even when it does something well — like create innovative companies — it fails to gain the recognition it craves, especially from Central Canada.

Meanwhile, the debate continues on how to change the long-term prospects of the region. You clearly need an appetite for wealth and success, but also a caring society that does not let anyone fall between the cracks. The Radian6-Q1 graduates continue to fight on both fronts.

18. In the Middle of the Atlantic

Gerry Pond is packing boxes again in his downtown Saint John office. It is mid-2019 and he will retire soon from Mariner Partners, though the date seems to be a moving target. One deadline passes, then another. Among the files and banker's boxes, he is a lot more measured than when he was interviewed in the aftermath of the Radian6-Q1 Labs exits in 2011. That was when he said, "I can assure you that there will be a third and a fourth [enterprise] of global scale." Nine years later, he is still waiting for the next big one.

He never expected to land a big deal every year; he knew he'd be lucky to get one every five years. Now it's approaching a decade, and he still has hopes. His goal is a company big enough to take to the stock markets in an initial public offering. "I'm 75 in a few weeks, and I want to be alive when we have a large enough one to IPO. Who owns it? I don't care, as long as it's got a headquarters in Atlantic Canada." It is, he admits, at the top of his bucket list.

He is tired of his region being pigeon-holed as a nice little breeding ground of nice little companies that sprout up and disappear. He hates that the attitude of outsiders is "make sure it's a cuddly size" for Atlantic Canada. He would like to see something less cuddly — more on the scale of BlackBerry, the Waterloo, Ontario, maker of smartphones, which in its heyday spun out a buzzing hive of economic activity. "We can do it as well as Waterloo, or as well as Montreal or Toronto or the Valley or Boston or Austin, once we get the right pieces together."

The next big one will probably take a different form than Radian6 or Q1 Labs. It may be run by a woman or a new Canadian, or by

someone who lives in the U.S. South. It might be in some entirely
new technology, electric cars or AI-powered agriculture or bottle-
line sensors for factories. And who knows where it will extend its
tentacles — from the rust-belt United States to Waterloo, Ontario, to
Bangalore?

Pond realizes luck plays a big role. "It's not something we get
allocated by the Supreme Being of Startups, whoever the hell that is.
It's not an allocation we get from the venture capital world. It's like
anything in innovation — it bubbles up everywhere, including in the
middle of the Atlantic Ocean."

Innovation is bubbling up as he speaks, and indeed, it's in the
Atlantic — on the island of Newfoundland, an even more remote part
of North America than New Brunswick. It is not part of Pond's stable
of startups, though it checks all the boxes — Canadian head office,
Canadian-controlled, with managers and employees constituting the
biggest ownership block. It is hiring Canadians at a ferocious clip,
building on the expertise of a Canadian university. In early 2020, its
value was estimated to be nudging a billion Canadian dollars. (Any
dollar estimates should, of course, be tempered by the impact of the
pandemic on asset values.)

The company, called Verafin, is just shy of two decades old,
founded about the same time as Radian6. Indeed, as Radian6 was
making a name for itself in social-media monitoring, Verafin's trio of
young entrepreneurs in St. John's were closely tracking the Fredericton
company's progress. "We knew of them, and the technology that
they were building was something that we were in the market for,"
remembers Brendan Brothers, who along with Jamie King and
Raymond Pretty built Verafin as a developer of anti–money laundering
and financial crime detection systems for financial institutions.

The Verafin founders had discovered that this company out in
New Brunswick was validating the kind of work they were doing
in St. John's. Maybe the Radian6 technology would be a good fit.

"Then, poof, they got acquired by Salesforce. It was like, 'Oh, my God,'" Brothers says.

The combination of Verafin and Radian6 would have made a formidable tech company in Atlantic Canada, the kind Gerry Pond could have taken public. In fact, Verafin would do pretty well on its own, even without the product complement from Radian6. In fall 2019 it announced a financing package that gave it the security of long-term funding with continued independence, the kind of deal that might have sustained Q1 Labs and Radian6 in their era.

The dollar value of the investment was $515 million, which according to the *Globe and Mail*'s technology writer Sean Silcoff, qualified it as the largest venture deal in Canadian history. In fact, the major investors were Verafin's existing equity backers, who, as their old investment funds closed, simply rolled over their Verafin shares into new funds.

It was a signal of their continued confidence in the company, its product and its strategy, and it was echoed by others. Given Verafin's advantage over competitors, "I would be shocked if this company does not reach unicorn status," says Mark Dobbin, the St. John's investor who backed the company in 2006, at a time of need, and now sits on its board. Indeed, this is a unicorn on the Rock, although that billion-dollar valuation can only be confirmed by some kind of public financing. And Verafin is in no hurry to do that.

Verafin is a template for how to build a significant Canadian tech company off the beaten path without selling out to foreign interests. It has managed to remain a Newfoundland company serving 3,000 far-flung banking customers, most of them in the United States. It has turned the so-called weaknesses of the region — remoteness, low population — into strengths. It combines a loyal workforce with a determination by its salespeople and managers to fly off the island regularly and spend insane hours on the road, making connections with customers.

In the small Newfoundland labour market, Verafin has been able to find and then retain a lot of the skilled technology professionals it needs. Most of its 500-plus employees work in the province, and Verafin has been hiring the bulk of Memorial University of Newfoundland's computer science graduates. According to the *Globe and Mail*, "Verafin, which also actively recruits employees from abroad, loses less than ten employees per year, an enviable turnover rate of under two percent in a sector rife with attrition challenges."

It all started as a solution to a mining problem. Jamie King had emerged from PhD studies at Memorial with the idea that he could bring artificial intelligence to the mines. Instead of having a bunch of men working underground, why not have semi-autonomous machines down deep, sending messages to one person on the surface in a safe environment? The system, in a scaled-up situation, would be able to manage requests for help and direction from the intelligent mining machines, with AI guidance on making the right decisions.

But the market in mining at that time wasn't perceived as big enough, so King, working now with his former grad school colleagues Brothers and Pretty, made the big shift to financial crime using the same basic AI model. "It's just a bunch of inputs and you're making decisions," Brothers explains. "Whether it's the customers' transactions, the way they interact with their mobile devices, or their online banking, you take all these different signals, put them together using intelligence and make a decision of whether or not it's suspicious."

There were some early lean years, and at one point they turned to Mark Dobbin and his investment company Killick Capital. Dobbin, son of the late Craig Dobbin, a legendary businessman who built a large helicopter services company, was a savvy investor in his own right. Mark had focused largely on the familiar sector of aerospace but was starting to diversify into new technology. He wrote a million-dollar cheque to Verafin.

Since then, Dobbin has kept backing local startups, but he is particularly admiring of Verafin's strategic discipline. Companies often say they employ a "playbook" of their goals, strategies, vision, but usually that is something stored informally in the back of their minds. Verafin actually has a physical playbook that defines how it operates. According to Brothers, that playbook includes "why we exist, what is it that we do, what's our three-year goal, what's the most important thing, all these kinds of concepts." The company is very disciplined in keeping to that game plan.

There is broad involvement in writing the playbook, an exercise that draws people in from across the company. Everybody knows his or her role in the business' success. The founders are former academics, and they read broadly on starting and growing companies. They comb through books for ideas — a favourite is the Geoffrey Moore classic, *Crossing the Chasm*.

A fundamental pillar of their playbook is people. "One of the strategic anchors that we think we have here is employees for life," Brothers says. That is an alien concept in the fast-moving technology sector, but not in Newfoundland. "The reason that we think we have employees for life is because we're basically living on an island with a moat around it out here in the North Atlantic." Verafin's approach would not work "if we were to try to do this in Boston or Silicon Valley or Toronto, with just the sheer number of opportunities that would be in front of people, the mobility that people have — there's not that sense of mobility here."

The result is that Verafin can rely on a deep reservoir of intellectual capital. It employs people who have been building anti–money laundering and fraud analytics for over ten years. "Our customers don't have that. So being here is by far one of the greater advantages I think we have," Brothers says. According to Mark Dobbin, Verafin is the first tech company to proclaim that it can "achieve success not in spite of being in St. John's, but because they are in St. John's."

What's more, Verafin shares what it has learned with the community in Newfoundland and Labrador. The founders help a lot of companies emerging from the highly fertile ground of the Genesis Centre at Memorial University, and from other resources at the university and local college. "We bring companies in, show them our strategy playbook," Brothers says. One of the stars of the local startup universe is CoLab Software, which works to develop engineering management systems — and was a recent graduate of the elite Y Combinator accelerator program in California. For a time, Verafin let the company use its offices when it needed a home.

The province of Newfoundland and Labrador faces a challenging economic outlook, only exacerbated by the 2020 pandemic crisis — tumbling revenues from its offshore oil industry, an albatross of a hydro-electricity mega-project, a critical public-debt crisis, high structural unemployment — the list goes on. Like New Brunswick, it seems to be heading toward an economic train wreck.

Yet even amid this negative climate, ideas and people can offer hope. The success of Verafin, and smaller companies that have sprung out of the Genesis Centre, has created a new narrative for St. John's as a startup hub. Although the numbers may be relatively small, the quality of companies outpaces that of other Atlantic Canadian cities, says Patrick Hankinson, at 31 already a veteran tech founder who runs Concrete Ventures out of Halifax, investing in very early, often pre-revenue enterprises throughout Atlantic Canada.

He credits a tight community in the capital of Newfoundland and Labrador, where there is good access to local mentors and support systems, with much of it flowing out of the Genesis Centre and Memorial. "Verafin is the shining star," he says, in an Atlantic Canada startup world that he estimates created 1,500 net new jobs in 2019 alone and added 240 new companies.

He also notes that the province has one city, St. John's, which is a clear focus for startup activity (although innovation happens everywhere). It is the same with Nova Scotia, where Halifax is the definitive epicentre for the province. He feels New Brunswick may be hampered by the fragmented nature of its efforts, with three cities vying for attention from venture capitalists, angel and government funding and other links in the chain.

Indeed, the success of another economic cluster — the biotech industry in Prince Edward Island — may partly stem from the compactness of that island community, barely over 150,000 people with one university and one city of any size. Charlottetown accounts for about a quarter of the island's people.

Over the past two decades, the fertile soil of PEI has yielded a biotechnology hub, the PEI BioAlliance, a private-sector coalition of more than 60 companies that helps startups incubate and grow, works on industry issues and aids in developing a stream of talent. The mandate is to enable "a bioscience-based cluster to develop and thrive in a place where bio-businesses are not supposed to develop and thrive," says Rory Francis, the alliance's executive director.

The province's biotech industry employs about 2,000 people, but finding talented people with the necessary training poses a big challenge in a small province, where the constraints on the labour force have sometimes led to poaching among the fast-growing firms. The alliance is working with universities and a local college to widen the people pipeline. One boon to the province has been the role of "comebackers," islanders who have left and returned with a dash of big-time business experience. One of them, Alex MacBeath, headed the accounting firm Grant Thornton in Canada and worked internationally; today, he runs the island's biggest venture capital investor and has served as chair of the Wallace McCain Institute.

Despite the people challenges, biotech has emerged as the second largest PEI industry in economic impact, behind agriculture/food processing but ahead of fishing and tourism — even Anne of Green Gables is taking a back seat to biotech. PEI has no Verafin yet — a large Canadian-owned player — but there are hopefuls, and a core of substantial internationally owned firms has invested in the sector.

One externally owned firm, BioVectra, is the successor to Diagnostic Chemicals, a local pioneer in the sector, founded in 1970 by Regis Duffy, ex-priest, scientist and the first dean of science at the new University of Prince Edward Island in 1969. Regarded as the godfather of the industry, Duffy founded Diagnostic as a contract producer of complex chemicals. Now 87, he is amused by his "godfather" status. It's not hard to claim this title, he says, since no one else was paying much attention to this potential in the 1960s. Now owned by a global private-equity group, BioVectra carries on that work, serving mostly the biotech and pharmaceutical industries.

Maybe there is something special about being on an island that makes you resourceful — even for PEI, which is now connected to the mainland by a bridge. Mark Dobbin feels that Newfoundlanders have an advantage in their relative distance from major centres. "Innovation is a bit like evolution," Dobbin says. "It takes place on the fringes, in harsh environments — like the tidal pool where the water's rough.

"We've always been innovative in Newfoundland and Labrador, not necessarily in a tech way. But when you are on the very end of a supply line that doesn't function in the winter time, or when your boat needs fixing or your house needs repairs, you figure out how it's done. That is in our DNA."

The role of government is always a source of fierce debate in Atlantic Canada. Jevon MacDonald, the former Prince Edward Islander who now lives in Halifax, is outspoken in his criticism of the immense effort required to navigate bureaucracy and get funding under government programs. Others question the value of top-down economic development of the kind now being embodied in the Oceans Supercluster. And yet public agencies can supply early non-dilutive funding through grants and other aids that carry small firms through their growing pains. The answer is balance: don't let the grant-chasing distract you from the core business.

Verafin has been very lucky in its timing, as it grew during a period when there was so much private-equity money swishing around the world. It wasn't always so easy. Verafin had gone after financing in the past, an exercise that became a huge distraction when the founders were trying to run a fast-growing business. So, in the latest round, they welcomed that their primary investors, Toronto venture capital firm Information Venture Partners (IVP) and American growth-capital firm Spectrum Equity, were interested in rolling over their Verafin holdings into new funds. The financing includes banking support for employees to buy more shares.

But, as Gerry Pond puts it, will they ever go public? It might happen, but not right now. Besides, the IPO event is no longer as much the Holy Grail for high-growth startup firms. Jamie King, the CEO, commented to the *Globe* in early 2020, "The private equity world has become more attractive for companies like ours." Verafin could go public, he said — but not until 2024 or 2025. And extreme market volatility could always extend that timeline even further.

His partner Brendan Brothers says that an IPO could wait. "I think we used this [recent financing] as an opportunity to say 'Okay, we want to have some more runway just to keep going with this.' There's no exit ramp in front of us right now. Let's keep going for a little bit and see what we can do with this. Those lights on the exit are always there."

19. Whale Hunting on the New York Thruway

Writing in the *New Yorker* magazine, Nathan Heller tells the story of 19th-century whale hunters who would set out on the Atlantic Ocean in search of the big mammals, a potential source of huge wealth derived largely from their precious oil. Most would return empty handed, if they returned at all, from their confrontation with the seas and the whales. But the captains and mates who sailed back with harpooned whales would be well compensated.

Heller draws on a recent book about venture capital, *VC: An American History*, by Harvard professor of business administration Tom Nicholas, who sees whale hunting as akin to backing today's startups. The biggest potential returns went not to the sailors, but to players in the financial industry that developed around whaling. Agents would assemble financings for these trips, linking private investors to venturesome captains. They all knew it would be a high-risk proposition, but a lucky trip could yield $150,000 worth of whale products, "a fortune several times the outlay, and for many investors this was enough to justify the risk." Venture capitalism is the modern whale hunt, and venture investors are latter-day Ishmaels in search of an elusive prize.

So I set out on my own personal whale hunt, searching not for huge financial returns but for insights into what drives the current generation of startup founders who may produce the next big payoff for Atlantic Canada. That trip took me to places and people who lie outside the predictable narrative for an East Coast startup.

The Road to Buffalo

When I was a kid, my dairy farmer father would instruct me, as I approached one of our black-and-white Holstein cows, to squirt some milk onto my hand before attaching the milking machine to her bulging udder. Sometimes I would squeeze, and out would ooze congealed milk. It was a signal the cow had contracted mastitis, an all-too-common infection that rendered her milk undrinkable and knocked her out of the milking rotation while she underwent medication.

In our small herd of 20 to 25 cows, it was a grievous blow to lose the production of just one cow, even for a short interval. Mastitis was the scourge of our little Ontario farm, triggering a dread that stays with me to this day. Indeed, it is the scourge of dairy farms everywhere, as the industry has moved from small family outfits to vast industrial farms, many with tens of thousands of cows. Estimates are it costs North American farmers $2 billion U.S. a year, a sure pain point for any tech problem solver.

My late father would be delighted to learn about the efforts to produce an early warning detection system for mastitis. One of the most promising is being developed by a Canadian company. But he would be bewildered by its wildly roundabout genesis. Headed by a young Indo-German-French-Canadian woman, the daughter of a basement scientist in Guelph, Ontario, it has its headquarters in Fredericton but maintains a development team in Buffalo, New York — and it is funded by a strange amalgam that includes the Dairy Farmers of America and the New Brunswick Investment Foundation. Further, it is a beneficiary of New York governor Andrew Cuomo's plan to spend more than a billion U.S. dollars to rejuvenate Buffalo, the state's once vigorous industrial hub, now reduced to a shadow of its old glory.

Such is innovation in the modern economy, amid the insatiable appetites of jurisdictions and politicians to find a unicorn in their midst, a big hit that could recharge an economy and change the narrative, in the same way that Radian6 and Q1 Labs have changed the conversation in New Brunswick.

In search of this next big "whale," I am driving along the New York Thruway, the green corn fields and tall barn silos flitting past my car window, a reminder of agriculture's role in the upstate economy. I am on my way to visit Bethany Deshpande and her team at SomaDetect, in an incubator centre in downtown Buffalo.

I head into an office building in the medical quarter of Buffalo where Governor Cuomo's Buffalo Billion project has sunk hundreds of millions of dollars in creating an island of gleaming offices floating in a sea of parking lots. It is a block away from a pub called the Big Ditch, the old nickname for the Erie Canal, the 1820s mega-project that connected Buffalo to New York City and signalled its rise as a commercial centre — a status it would lose after the Second World War.

I head up in the elevator and step out to be greeted by a sign: New York UP, with one arm of the U pointing up into an optimistically raised arrow. Glass doors open into a large room with young people and computer terminals, the kind of thing you might find at MaRS, Hatch or other outposts of the New Economy. Off to one side, a smaller glass enclosure houses the development team of SomaDetect, where Bethany Deshpande holds court.

She is the daughter of Satish Deshpande, a PhD in biophysics from the University of Guelph, who moonlighted from his regular jobs by doing his own research, including work on medical diagnostic tests. In 2012, Satish discovered that he could measure fat content and somatic cells in milk using his light-scattering sensor technology.

According to SomaDetect, somatic cells are formed in the cow as predominantly white blood cells. During mastitis infections, the number of somatic cells present in the udder increases to help the cow fight the infection. So if you can track the somatic cells, you can get an early warning of the disease.

Satish Deshpande was the kind of scientist who was happy inventing and making things — he had less interest in developing trials. Bethany loves her father and admires his perseverance in the face of hard knocks. "I thought it was cool — Dad makes these things and gets so excited about them." But his daughter worried that Satish was missing out by not talking to dairy farmers about his innovation. She became the perfect ambassador for him — a devoted daughter, very social, who could visit a farmer at 6:00 a.m. to collect milk samples or sway a jury at a business-plan contest.

Bethany earned her PhD in biology from Université Laval in Quebec City and, after her education, stayed there to work for a youth entrepreneurship program called Shad Valley. Her husband, Nicholas Clermont, was also working there. After a decade in Quebec, they wanted a change. Barry Bisson, the Maritimer who ran Shad at the time, suggested the University of New Brunswick and Fredericton as a good working environment for the couple. (Small world: Bisson is now CEO of Propel, the Atlantic Canada virtual accelerator.)

Nick got a job with the Pond-Deshpande Centre, a business incubator with a social enterprise thrust, the co-creation of Gerry Pond and U.S. serial entrepreneur Desh Deshpande — who is no relation to Bethany. The couple took in the rich broth of ideas and people in Fredericton in the wake of the big tech exits.

Bethany dusted off her dad's patents and started talking to people, and received plenty of encouragement. A big supporter was Karina LeBlanc, director of the Pond-Deshpande Centre, which provided both accelerator training and early seed money. In July 2016, Nick and Bethany decided to start a company, almost as a lark; it was all about detecting somatic cells — hence, SomaDetect.

They had a bit of their own money, and were able to find funding from ACOA and the National Research Council's Industrial Research Assistance Program (NRC-IRAP). They drew on the experience of the Radian6 group. They discussed the sensors' potential with Marcel LeBrun. David Alston, who grew up on a hobby farm in rural Sussex,

Bethany Deshpande built a
company around her father's
design of a milk-quality sensor
(Courtesy of SomaDetect)

took them around to meet dairy farmers, and one of them would become an early angel investor.

In Fredericton, the two founders were introduced to the Mathis family, which had lots of experience in the trenches. Chris Mathis worked on technology-transfer with academia and the private sector. He would help as an adviser and then become the chief technology officer at SomaDetect.

The founders also managed to find Bharath Sudarsan, working in northern New Brunswick and a graduate of Macdonald College, the agriculture school at McGill University. His master's research was in machine-vision sensor development. "Very quickly we discovered that compared with traditional statistics, AI-based computer vision can take the technology much further, much quicker," Sudarsan says.

The team started winning business-plan competitions. They had a message to impart, the idea of being commercially important and socially good. Bethany focused on "better farmers, better data, better milk for consumers, better lives for cows." They started getting interest from south of the border, and the large Kansas-based co-operative Dairy Farmers of America lent its help in venture money and advice.

The big moment came when they entered 43North, a startup contest that is part of Governor Cuomo's Buffalo Billion project. Its grand prize was a million dollars. One catch was that the winner had to spend a year in Buffalo. They won, and they moved to Buffalo, setting up a wholly owned subsidiary.

The 43North contest is controversial because some winners, after the required year in Buffalo, skip town. The organizers knew this was a risk, but it was worth taking if some promising enterprises stuck around to generate activity. SomaDetect's founders did not leave. They liked this foothold in the United States, which provided access to a much larger base of dairy farms. New Brunswick has fewer than 200 dairy farms, and although New York's farming industry is in crisis, it still has 4,000 milk supply farms. Bethany estimates New Brunswick has 20,000 dairy cows, and New York State has about a million, and nearby Vermont and southwestern Ontario are other data-rich sources for SomaDetect's analytics.

My father would be impressed with the technology — a sensor at each milking station, alongside each cow, measuring not just the onset of mastitis, but a cow's reproductive status, the proportion of butter fat and other milk-quality indices and general bovine health. But he would still be bewildered by SomaDetect's organization: a couple dozen people in total, with a team in Buffalo and the rest scattered among a head office in Fredericton, an Ontario branch (just across the border from Buffalo in Thorold), and some working remotely in other Ontario locations.

Bethany Deshpande likes the current balance, at a time in history when U.S. immigration policy, and the messaging around it, make it so much harder to hire an immigrant in Buffalo than, say, in Fredericton. She believes that openness to outsiders is one of Canada's great gifts. "My dad came here speaking no English," 32-year-old Bethany says of her Indian-born father, now 61.

As a young boy, Satish took a while to learn the new language, she explains, but some of his teachers helped him cope with schoolwork.

"As long as he could talk them through it, and explain what he had done, they would accept his work. That is a really lovely accommodation — that a teacher would do this for a little brown boy from India who can barely figure out how to ask to go the washroom, never mind multiplication and all that."

He went to university and got a great education, and he started developing technology, which his daughter is now taking to the world. It is the classic Canadian story, and yet its next chapter might be written in Buffalo, the Midwest or California, where SomaDetect's new partner, a large dairy management software company, is based. My father would be scratching his head.

From Miramichi to Miami

The next Atlantic Canada technology breakthrough might be the product of a serial company founder from the Miramichi, who is on his fourth startup, this one based in Fredericton, although he chooses to live in Miami, Florida.

At 46, Jody Glidden has made a career of bucking the norms, of working outside the mainstream. Glidden is a cocky maverick, with a bit of a swagger, someone who stands out in the unassuming East Coast business world. He actually declares he may have the next big winner, and he has, at various times, recruited the likes of Radian6's David Alston, Rich McInnis and Jerry Carr to help him out.

The child of two Miramichi entrepreneurs, Glidden was always obsessed with technology, starting with science fairs in grades 4 and 5, when he wrote software that won the top prize both years. In Grade 10, just for fun, he made a form of video lottery terminal and gave them away to fellow students. While his schoolmate Chris Newton was quietly exploring technology from his bedroom, Glidden was a full-fledged kid entrepreneur.

He went to UNB but flunked out because he felt the first-year course couldn't teach him anything he didn't know. "I just about fell asleep in the class, because it was just introductory programming." He went to work for a local technology company, founded by Ben Watson, then a star of the nascent Fredericton startup scene. Glidden took on a lot of responsibilities in Watson's internet learning company, Scholars.com, before it was acquired by an Irish firm. After a transition, Glidden started his own training-related business, IC Global, which he sold just before the dot-com crash in 2001.

Amid the carnage of the crash, he decided that he might as well go back and get his degree. "I always felt a little bit self-conscious being in management meetings, and people would say, 'Who's this 24- 25- 26-year-old that seems to have no qualifications for the job he's in?'"

By accelerating his course work, he finished his UNB business degree in two years. Then, as he went back to work, he took on a master's program at Harvard in information systems management, a blend of computer science and MBA courses.

Having participated as a builder or founder in two exits, he joined another young company, Chalk Media, the developer of the Mobile Chalkboard, which delivered media content to the BlackBerry smartphone. He became a partner in Chalk, teaming up with its president, Stewart Walchli. Glidden was then based in the Washington, D.C., area, with access to U.S. government markets. In 2008, the two partners sold Chalk to the BlackBerry company, Research in Motion (RIM), for about $23 million.

As part of the deal, Glidden joined RIM, and he moved from Washington to Florida because, he says, he liked the lifestyle and the lack of state income taxes. "BlackBerry didn't care where I was going to be." As a self-confessed workaholic, Glidden had been clocking 12- to 14-hour days. "I thought maybe moving to a place that's a little bit more relaxed would give me a little bit more work-life balance." That didn't exactly work out.

At RIM he got a chance to see inside a lot of big companies. One of their biggest technology investments is a program called "customer relationship management," or CRM, a type of software aimed at managing the company's vast interactions with customers. The idea is to provide tools to retain present customers, close sales with new clients and drive growth. It has been a tremendously profitable business for a number of companies, including Salesforce, which bought Radian6 to strengthen its CRM offerings.

Glidden observed that companies weren't really using CRM to its full potential. He would log on to a company's CRM platform and most of the valuable relationship data would be missing. "You couldn't really get good information on who the salespeople were on certain accounts." Glidden thought that there had to be a way to sift through the billion messages on the mail server and in the calendar invites. "It could tell you who actually knows people in those companies best, because you could see by the frequency of communication."

Glidden, who can't abide working long periods in a big company, was ready to leave RIM. He figured he could use machine learning and AI techniques to figure out what was missing from the CRM programs, and put that information into the system without burdening the salespeople. "We would end up fixing the CRM problem, one of the biggest problems you could possibly imagine in business technology right now."

That was the idea behind the company, Introhive, that he and Walchli founded in Fredericton. It turned out to be much more difficult than he anticipated. "It took us about three years of work before we ever even made our first sale."

Over the nine years the firm has laboured away, people would often say, "Oh, that Introhive company, didn't they go out of business?" Glidden echoes Mark Twain: "The reports of my death are greatly exaggerated." The business finally hit its stride in the years leading up to 2020, doubling or tripling revenues annually. "It's just been off the charts. And it took a long time."

As Introhive attracted investors — Salesforce among them — one of them told Glidden he should look at the old Radian6 team as a source of directors and managers. So Glidden hired some of Radian6's leading lights. Because the product took time to gel, some of the prize hires drifted away to other companies. Even so, Glidden employs a contingent of old Radian6 hands, who provide the core of his expertise.

Radian6's well-regarded engineer Jerry Carr is now Introhive's chief technology officer, and he says Glidden reminds him of Chris Newton — and both are from the Miramichi. "He's a real product strategist, a big picture guy. He sees the patterns, decides what to invest in next and stays close to customers."

Always the maverick, Glidden is unrestrained in explaining what's wrong about Atlantic Canada. There is a dire shortage of skilled tech people, and he blames universities and colleges for not turning out nearly enough talent to accommodate how fast the companies need to grow.

He remembers going to a premier's event to discuss the skill sets the province should be building, and the participants settled on the area of cybersecurity. "But if you look at what the world wants, and what people are investing in, cybersecurity is just one area, as are artificial intelligence and machine learning. Those areas are even more talent-starved in New Brunswick.

"I feel like I've been complaining about this people shortage issue for like 15 years now," he says. He advocates, for one thing, subsidizing tuition for students who want to take degrees in areas of dire talent shortages. That way, they would quickly generate the $100,000-plus incomes that would provide taxes the fiscal managers so badly need.

Glidden was never great at playing office politics, and he was always eager to escape the cocoon of an established company. "When I started Introhive, I quit a job where I was making a quarter-million a year at BlackBerry, and I went and made zero for a couple years and just hoped for the best. I was burning all the money in my savings, but I always just had this belief that it's all going to work itself out."

Glidden is confident Introhive is finally working out, and so are a lot of people around New Brunswick. Of course, its success will always be measured against the two earlier big exits. Even in the midst of the

Jerry Carr went from head of engineering for Radian6, as shown here, to chief technology officer at Jody Glidden's startup Introhive (Courtesy of David Alston and Marcel LeBrun)

pandemic, Glidden felt a public offering with a billion-dollar valuation was entirely possible in the future. And that would make it bigger than Radian6 or Q1 Labs.

The Reality Man

Ryan Groom has a big ugly wound on his arm, the product of an encounter with a concealed tree stump on one of his jaunts by all-terrain vehicle near his home outside Fredericton. He's popped an Advil or two and is coping with the pain. "I probably did three or four somersaults," he says with pride.

It's nothing new for Groom, for whom life is a seamless melding of serious fun and very serious games, all the while sending out his little Fredericton company Kognitiv Spark as an explorer in the technology of augmented and virtual reality.

Kognitiv Spark deploys Microsoft-developed smartglasses, combined with artificial intelligence and other technologies, to help remote workers — say, military personnel or oilfield mechanics — who face tough technical challenges they don't know how to fix. They can don the glasses and, using Kognitiv's platform, send a video feedback to an expert, who can walk them through the problem visually.

"It is not to replace people, but to enhance people on the ground," Groom says, explaining that the product is called "remote worker support." It relies on mixed reality, often defined as virtual objects integrated into a physical view. Using very low bandwidth and enjoying ultra-tight security, the product has gained a following in military forces, as well as in companies that have far-flung operations.

Groom is a native of St. Stephen, New Brunswick, in the far southwest of the province. He grew up as a kid who loved the woods, and was devoted to his bow and arrow and his Commodore 64 computer. His bruises come not just from ATV trekking, but from being involved in startups. One company where he was a manager failed; another he founded and sold, probably before he should have, he admits. "I was young — and what an experience! I built something somebody wants."

He is also into filmmaking, an avocation that blends his creative and technical sides. He and his business partner, Duncan McSporran, an ex-British army officer, bonded on an RV trip around Scotland, while Groom shot a documentary. Between takes, they developed the idea for Kognitiv Spark. Later, they brought on a seasoned manager, Yan Simard, as CEO.

For Groom, 48, who is Kognitiv's chief technology officer, the Radian6 and Q1 deals mean "you can never say, 'Oh, we can't do it from Fredericton.'" If you do make that admission, "it means you're just not working hard enough." And it does take work. "The resources aren't here, we have only a talent pool of a certain size, but you play the cards you're dealt. Don't complain about it — those are the cards."

In playing their cards, Groom and partners are not afraid of tackling distant markets. Little Kognitiv Spark has an office in Britain. Yet some of the best business development tools reside in the local environment. When foreign customers or partners come calling, he might take them lobster fishing or for a trek on the wild Fundy Trail in the south of the province. (Larger New Brunswick companies that want to impress outsiders make use of the salmon-fishing camps on the Miramichi River.)

He expects Kognitiv Spark might someday be acquired, as the technology improves and its product continues to penetrate world markets. If it happens, he will have time to pick up a camera and film the documentary he always yearned to do, the story of his grandfather, Lorne Groom, who lost both legs on Christmas Day in 1943, at the Battle of Ortona in the Canadian Forces' bloody Italian campaign. The man Ryan knew as "Gramps" went on to be an optometrist and mayor of St. Stephen, a father of five and a local political figure.

Ryan Groom says this film, like his startup company, is important to the narrative of this often beaten-down province. Sometimes, New Brunswickers get down on themselves and miss the bigger picture. "I really want to tell the story of the heroes we're cut from."

20. Twenty Years Ago Today, and the Band Still Plays

Frank McKenna never really stopped being premier of New Brunswick, in spirit if not in office. In 1997, he quit formal politics and went on to a stint in corporate law, a period as Canada's ambassador to Washington and a brief flirtation with the federal Liberal leadership. For the last 14 years he has been deputy chair of Toronto-Dominion Bank, which, among his other duties, allows him to shake his dense tree of contacts and relationships to enhance the economy of his province and the region as a whole.

He hovers over the East Coast like a protective parent, running his summertime get-together of movers and shakers, serving as an advocate for an east-west pipeline or holding sessions in his offices at Toronto's TD Centre to introduce small Atlantic Canadian companies to the financial community.

The glow of the McKenna Miracle has faded since the 1990s, as the demographic and fiscal challenges of managing a small province with limited financial resources have overwhelmed successive governments. McKenna would look back fondly on the time — his time — when New Brunswick was the magnet for global policy-makers who wanted to learn how a small economy can flourish through innovation.

Today, that role is often played by little Estonia in Eastern Europe, the epitome of a digitally connected society, the home of Skype and a vibrant startup community that defies its small scale and plight as a post-Perestroika survivor of the Soviet empire. "We were Estonia at one time, and now Estonia is us," McKenna says. "Everybody goes to Estonia to see what they're doing. That was us, and we should never have let it slip away."

For McKenna, the mission never ends — to create good jobs in the short term and a sustainable technologically adept economy in the long run. He is happy to point out that his own bank recently moved a thousand back-office jobs to Moncton, a McKenna-era type of economic transfusion.

If New Brunswick is to regain its role as a leader among striving regions, it must build on the hard work and dreams of the middle-aged men and women who once, as kids in Miramichi, Bathurst and Chipman, were turned on to technology through Frank McKenna's digital transformation of the province. They went on to become university and college students, and then company builders, with startups under their belt; they are now in their 40s and 50s, and they have to step up again.

They are people like Sandy Bird, the first of the young founders of Q1 Labs and Radian6 to plunge again into the "valley of death," that excruciating, exhilarating process of building a new company from scratch. And Dwight Spencer was right with him, the indispensable customer support ace, the Watson to his Holmes.

Almost 20 years after the founding of Q1 Labs, Bird launched Sonrai Security, his new company, with $18.5 million in venture capital funding from U.S. investors. (Sonrai means data in Irish.) Finally, the great promise of the Q1-Radian6 dual exits was bearing tangible fruit — even though the impact of the two companies had already pervaded the Atlantic Canadian scene in many more subtle ways.

Sonrai helped open a bigger window of possibility for the fledgling cybersecurity ecosystem and the entire region. All eyes are on Bird — the pressure to succeed is enormous. No small startup has ever been so exalted, so discussed, by a tech community.

Sonrai follows the Q1 formula that worked so well: Delaware corporation, development team in Fredericton and U.S. backers, including one of Q1's cast of investors — Polaris of Waltham, Massachusetts — plus TenEleven, a venture firm with a foot on both coasts, Boston and Silicon Valley. The big difference with Q1, Brian

Flood observes, is that "in the old days, it took 64 tries. Sandy did it in one try." For experienced players, "the next deal is always easier."

Even the new company's market sector was the same — cybersecurity, although this time fashioned for the age of the cloud. The CEO, and Bird's partner, was familiar too: Brendan Hannigan, whose strategic insights took Q1 over the final hurdle in product development, and then built IBM's commanding role in cybersecurity.

What was different was the reputation of Sandy Bird, who had grown a lot in a decade. He took the big job at IBM, was head of development for QRadar and was a key agent in growing that cybersecurity business to billions in revenue a year. He became an IBM Fellow, which put him among the innovation leaders in the global IBM constellation. He lived in Fredericton, but he travelled the world for Big Blue.

Bird is in his mid-40s and still youthful looking, with that intense squint and "little cockeyed grin," as Brian Flood calls it. He always knew he would step out with another startup. He was tired of the wear and tear from travel and being away from his family. He yearned to get back to the excitement of the blank slate.

"I stayed at IBM for five years, but I wanted to get back to ten people and a white board," Bird says. "At IBM I had 42 different products under me," as compared with Q1 Labs, where he had been able to demonstrate any part of QRadar to a client. It was the same with Spencer, who gained a lot of breadth at IBM but was yearning to play with one technology at a time.

Brendan Hannigan had left IBM in 2015 and had parked himself at Polaris Partners. More than a year later, as Bird was planning to leave too, he and Hannigan agreed to do a startup together. They just didn't know what. All Bird knew is he wanted New York–based Hannigan to be CEO, while he would focus on the technology in Fredericton.

The two met up in Halifax, renting an Airbnb near the harbour for a few days of intense brainstorming. What would it be? Blockchain? Virtual reality? Health-care systems? They landed back on their cybersecurity turf, but this time, they would build a product for the cloud. They saw companies in desperate need of systems to protect them in this new climate.

Dwight Spencer, who had been working post-IBM for a sports data company, came on board as "customer success" officer. All of them were thrilled to be reliving the Q1 experience at Sonrai, though Bird was almost as excited about his cars. His cherished possession is a Datsun 510 station wagon from 1972. Always a gearhead.

The rise of Sonrai also rekindled memories for Brian Flood, who is looking back on a career of big dramatic wins and a hard knock or two. When he was leaving Q1 Labs, he wondered what he would do — he had already got out of the restaurant business during the Q1 years. He spotted a promising Moncton startup with an experienced and respected CEO. The company was working on a product called TrustMe, a program that provided instant, secure email document delivery — a solution that appealed to Flood's cybersecurity instincts.

He dove into TrustMe, with the idea of selling this service to the big express companies. He sent the program to FedEx, and they were interested. Then came the crucial demo and there was a technical failure. He went to another express company, DHL, which couldn't get the thing to work. That effectively ended TrustMe.

Flood had beaten the bushes for angel financing and, given his experience with Q1, came up with 250 investors, most of whom put in $10,000 to $15,000. There were many unhappy investors in New Brunswick when TrustMe shut down, but Flood took the biggest hit. "It cost me over a million bucks, cash. But I'm all right with that. It just didn't work." He always turns to a baseball analogy: "I was out there to hit a colossal home run. It worked with Q1. With TrustMe, I was out there to knock it even further, and it was a giant swing and a miss. But my God, we were close."

TrustMe was Brian Flood's last tech fling. Carolyn did not want to do another one, with the stress and uncertainty. Then Brian was diagnosed with prostate cancer. In 2019, he was undergoing treatment, reading voraciously, telling great stories and making connections with people and ideas. He was still swinging for the fences.

His Rothesay neighbour Gerry Pond was very hopeful about Sonrai, but he worried that the startup scene was otherwise far too quiet. He had some quality candidates in his stable of East Valley Ventures — Resson, Eigen, Smart Skin, among others. There had been some decent exits, but no big one — yet.

So who will be the next Gerry Pond, angel investor and Atlantic Canada advocate? It likely won't be a single person, but a combination of dynamos such as Marcel LeBrun, Dhirendra Shukla and Nancy Mathis. There is no replacing Gerry, unless it is by Gerry himself. Retirement might mean simply stepping back into a pure investment role, maybe the occasional directorship, with no day-to-day management duties. He owns stakes in 29 companies, he says. "It's hard to give up having fun."

Pond does not get philosophical very often, but he sometimes wonders what is the final verdict of his life work in technology: "What is the net-net of all this shit?" He is disappointed that "there are not a lot of people in the region who give a damn and care enough to go the extra mile — or the extra dollar." For him, the investing and mentoring are visceral, but he doesn't see that fire in others. Yet he tells young people they can make a difference by giving Atlantic Canada a try, and do it by staying in the region.

Up in Fredericton, Chris Newton is giving it a try — again. We meet early in 2020 at a Tim Hortons on Woodstock Road, and he is clearly pumped, having taken an interest, both financial and managerial, in a new company. This is more than eight years after the Radian6 sale and the diagnosis of cancer that had stopped his career in its tracks. He is listed on the website of this new company, Potential Motors, as "chief scientist." Marcel LeBrun is the chair.

During Newton's eight-year hiatus, he dealt with the cancer and watched his two kids grow into teenagers. He built a house along the river with his schoolteacher wife, Tracey, that had all the bells and whistles — indoor pool, indoor gym big enough for basketball and the latest in energy efficiency. He poured himself into every aspect of its design.

And he read voluminously. "It is what consumes most of my time, and it explains my creativity." What does Chris Newton read about? Everything, it seems. He rhymes off some of his current interests: cameras, architecture, electric cars, drones, the future of energy, smart homes, raspberry pie and the maker movement — this global refocus on making things with your hands.

It was Marcel LeBrun who discovered Potential Motors — more precisely, he found three graduating students at the University of New Brunswick who were doing the TME program for startup founders. The graduates' thinking was they would develop kits for converting fleets of conventional internal-combustion vehicles into electric propulsion.

LeBrun enlisted Newton, who had been pondering the future of software in automotive control. The two "greybeards" urged the fresh-faced founders to do a pivot. The conversion business would inevitably end as all cars became converted. But a brighter future lay in artificial intelligence systems to control and steer electric cars, functioning under difficult weather conditions. Where better than New Brunswick to develop and test this technology?

Newton knows this may not be a colossal hit — it might not even make first base, in Brian Flood's baseball lingo. But Chris is back. It is cars, it is technology, it is with Marcel and, most of all, it is in New Brunswick.

The concept of the unicorn — a young company with a billion-dollar U.S. valuation — has lost a bit of its lustre, in part because of the precipitous rise and crash of WeWork in 2019. The global workspace provider's charismatic founder Adam Neumann became the embodiment of spectacular hubris. In Atlantic Canada, the dream still burns brightly of building a unicorn-scale success, maybe even a half-unicorn — in the woods, on the islands or along the sea.

Q1 Labs and Radian6 forever redefined Atlantic Canada's status in the country — in the world — as a breeding ground for innovation and technological prowess. That prowess is even more valued in the post-pandemic environment, when technology will shape our global capacity to recover and adapt. But the great project of building a resilient knowledge economy on the East Coast is incomplete. It needs another chapter in the narrative, a startup that will grow and stay and become something much bigger.

Could it be formed, in whole or part, from Jody Glidden's corporate relationship software, Bethany Deshpande's milk cow sensors or Sandy Bird's new cybersecurity entry? It may be propelled by the already exceptional Verafin in Newfoundland, or something not yet formed, the dream of a young boy or girl in Edmundston, Summerside or Glace Bay. One thing is clear: the world holds many more possibilities for the kids from the sticks than when Chris met Brian at UNB two decades ago.

Index

(Photographs indicated by bolded page numbers)